TRAINING & RETRAINING
HORSES
THE TELLINGTON WAY

*Starting Right or Starting Over
with Enlightened Methods and
Hands-On Techniques*

——————

Linda Tellington-Jones

with Mandy Pretty

Editorial Assistance Provided by Andrea Pabel

T$
TRAFALGAR SQUARE
North Pomfret, Vermont

First published in 2019 by
Trafalgar Square Books
North Pomfret, Vermont 05053

Trafalgar Square Books encourages the use of approved safety helmets in all equestrian sports
and activities.

Library of Congress Cataloging-in-Publication Data
Names: Tellington-Jones, Linda, author.
Title: Training & retraining horses the Tellington way : starting right or
  starting over with enlightened methods and hands-on techniques / Linda
  Tellington-Jones with Mandy Pretty.
Other titles: Training and retraining horses the Tellington way
Description: North Pomfret, Vermont : Trafalgar Square Books, 2019. |
  Identifiers: LCCN 2018052329 (print) | LCCN 2018053077 (ebook) | ISBN
  9781570769504 () | ISBN 9781570769375
Subjects: LCSH: Horses--Training.
Classification: LCC SF287 (ebook) | LCC SF287 .T425 2019 (print) | DDC
  636.1/0835--dc23
LC record available at https://lccn.loc.gov/2018052329

All photographs by Lynne Glazer *except:* pp. v, 2–3, 52–3, 57, 59, 63, 65–7, 76–7, 81, 83, 87–8, 90–1,
93–5, 100, 106–8, 110, 115–7, 119–25, 127–8, 134 (Jessica O'Donoghue); p. 4 (Caroline Larrouilh);
pp. 8, 10,12 (courtesy of Linda Tellington-Jones); pp. 14, 18, 98, 104 (Gabriele Boiselle); pp. 16–17,
132, 234–8, 292–3 (Eugenia Mola di Larissa); pp. 25, 38–9, 41, 71, 97, 102, 111 top, 182, 194–5
(Gabriele Metz); pp. 26, 33, 37, 48–9, 51, 146, 198, 214, 247, 271 (Mandy Pretty); pp. 32, 40,
45 *bottom*, 58, 129, 199 (Barbara Owens); p. 45 *top* (Brigitte Heyer); pp. 46–7, 105, 133, 145, 170,
176, 193, 210, 273 (Indra McMorran); p. 50 *top* (Rebecca Booth); pp. 72–5 (DareVets); pp. 61
bottom, 207 (Horst Streitferdt); pp. 130–1, 276 (AnnaLena Kuhn); p. 147 (Rebecca Booth); p. 159,
186 (Robyn Hood); p. 173 (Daniela van der Berg); pp. 224, 278, 279, 280 (Andrea Pabel)

Illustrations by Cornelia Koller
Book design by Lauryl Eddlemon
Cover design by RM Didier
Index by Andrea M. Jones (www.jonesliteraryservices.com)
Typeface: Berkley Oldstyle

Printed in China

10 9 8 7 6 5 4 3 2 1

I dedicate this book to two of my closest friends, who have inspired me for more than 30 years:

Kate Riordan, who, since our initial meeting on the Great American Horse Race in 1976, has been a confidante, collaborator, and dear friend, helping to spread TTouch around the world,

and

Gabriele Boiselle, whose courage and dazzling creativity continue to encourage me to share my rarely seen, emotional side.

Contents

Foreword

By Magali Delgado and Frédéric Pignon

We met Linda Tellington-Jones for the first time at a trade show in Germany. She came to our booth and introduced herself. Magali and I were excited as we had admired her work for many years but had not yet had a chance to connect with her.

It was love at first sight! We felt an immediate connection. We told Linda about our stallion Fasto, who was going to perform in our show that night in front of a large audience. We were concerned because he had been nervous and overly excited in the practice sessions. Linda asked if she could work with him; without hesitation, we agreed.

Fasto never really liked having his ears touched, but Linda's gentle Ear TTouches (p. 115) relaxed him visibly. That night, in his premier performance, Fasto shone, and we knew then that Linda's methods were going to become very valuable to us.

We will always remember Linda's first visit to our home in France. She noticed our stallion Gracil right away. He was fearful and insecure, and Linda wanted to work with him. We were impressed by how she was able to understand Gracil so quickly—it deepened our trust in her.

Paulus, one of our young Friesian stallions, had a lot of trouble with the Spanish walk when we first started working with him. He would not respond to the signals we were giving. Linda explained that the nervous system of the young horse is not yet fully developed. She recommended small lifts on Paulus' legs, and with these, we were able to make huge strides in improving his body awareness.

We have learned so much from Linda over the years and now use her *TTouches* on every new horse we get. We often use *Ear TTouch,* in particular, with our young horses, because it is such a useful preparation for bridling. The horse learns to lower his head right away. We think that it is really important to know what feels good to each horse. Linda adjusts what she does to each individual. Even after a short, 15-minute *TTouch* session, you see results. With *TTouch* we can enrich the beginning and end of each training session. Linda's techniques help us with a tense or tired horse. Her groundwork and using her *Playground for Higher Learning* (p. 175) gives young horses a sense of security and builds trust. With this preparation the young horses follow us all by themselves.

Most importantly, Linda's methods help us find an even deeper connection with our horses.

Linda is one of the best horsewomen we have ever known. She knows what is going on with each horse. She feels what the horse needs. She accepts each horse as a teacher. She always sees the good in a horse. And… she loves them.

It is a wonderful and very special experience to be able to watch Linda work. We highly recommend seeing her live, in action. And of course you need to read this book—it is a treasure for all riders and trainers who want a partnership with horses and want to train horses with respect and feeling.

We wish you much joy reading this book, and the best of luck with your horses.

Magali Delgado and Frédéric Pignon

Publisher's Note:
In this book, when referring to horses in a general sense we have used masculine pronouns, and when referring to people in a general sense, we have used feminine pronouns. This is not to show preference for either gender but to ensure clarity.

PART I

Starting Points

CHAPTER 1

Introduction

W hy another book about starting young horses or retraining older ones?

My step-by-step method of starting young horses and retraining older horses peacefully and safely has been used by thousands of horse owners on five continents for more than four decades. And yet this is the first book to explain the Tellington Method with training and retraining specifically in mind.

You will find examples in this book of green horses who began the process of under-saddle training in just five days, completely without stress and with only a growing trust in their human partners. And you will read about other horses—some with years of training already behind them—who were out of balance physically, mentally, and emotionally, but were transformed in an amazingly short time. Here is why:

1.1 Whenever I work with a horse, I focus on looking at his "perfection" rather than his "problems."

➤ The Tellington Method offers a new perspective to the world of training and retraining horses. It's a harmonious, reliable method that results in mutual trust and takes horses *beyond* the instinct of flight or fight and teaches them to think (fig. 1.1).

➤ The goal of the Tellington Method is to *develop the intelligence of the horse,* referring to the definition of *intelligence* as "the ability to adapt to new situations."

➤ A basic priority is the desire that horses will enjoy being with humans as much as we humans enjoy being with them. This is a must for the safety of both horse and rider in our modern world.

➤ Respect is one of the key words of my method—in this case, the rider/handler's *respect for the horse.* Respect comes from the base word "inspect" or "to see." I invite you to see the personality and individuality of each horse.

In the pages ahead I will introduce you to my TTouch bodywork. The second "T" in the name "TTouch" represents "trust." TTouch bodywork uses a basic one-and-a-quarter circular movement that has been proven to develop a deep trust between horse and handler. Many people have reported a feeling and a sense of "oneness" and connection with their horses when using it.

In this book you will find a culmination of proven results gained while starting and restarting hundreds of horses who benefited from my Tellington Method techniques. It combines well-researched and refined training procedures that any person can safely use.

And So It Began

My first riding teacher, Mrs. Alice Metheral, owned Briarcrest Stables, located on the outskirts of Edmonton, Alberta, Canada. A prominent rider herself, she stabled more than 80 horses, many of them Thoroughbreds. She had a string of 20 school horses that she used for students and weekend trail riders, but her primary business was boarding and training hunters, jumpers, and hunter hacks.

When I was nine years old, my dad moved our family to a farm on the west side of Edmonton, just a mile down the road from Mrs. Metheral's bustling barn. For three years, I'd been riding my own horse back and forth to school every day, but I'd never had any riding lessons, so I was excited to learn from Mrs. Metheral. She quickly recognized my natural rapport with horses and moved me from the gentle school horses onto the young ones that she was "breaking."

Under pressure or when they are spooked, a common reaction for young horses is to buck. Typical of the day, Mrs. Metheral used the standard practice of "bucking horses out" when she started them: She put every horse under saddle in a small round pen and let him buck until he settled. Then she dallied the lead rope around the horn of her big Western saddle and ponied the youngster beside her at the walk, trot, and canter until he learned the aids for turning and stopping.

Usually, I was then the first rider on the horse's back. The painful belief of that era was that a rider wasn't considered "skilled" until he or she had fallen off a horse 99 times! I often joke that I'm shorter than my sister, Robyn Hood, because I landed on my head so many times when I got bucked off at Mrs. Metheral's. Today, safety is a number one priority and is maximized with the Tellington Method, where "getting the bucks out" is not a step in the training process.

By age 14, I was showing sales horses for Mrs. Metheral at the Edmonton Spring Horse Show. I also picked up "catch rides," which meant riding in classes for owners or boarders who wanted a competent rider to show their horses for them. I would have 10 or 15 minutes to get acquainted with the horse before entering the arena for the class. I attribute my success as a catch rider to my ability to quickly establish a connection with every horse I rode. My priority wasn't winning but to make sure that each horse was enjoying the experience with me as much as I enjoyed being with him. Additionally, my mother always stood by the edge of the arena, watching me ride, and each time I passed, she would quietly say, "Smile, dear," and I did. Those words are still inspirational for me today. Studies have proven that smiling activates the "feel-good" hormone serotonin in the body. When a rider enjoys the riding and training experience and embraces a happy attitude, it affects the horse. The mindset of creating happy horses who enjoy being with their people is a cornerstone of the Tellington Method and the techniques I share in this book.

Developing My Own Method

Even though "bucking out" horses was common practice, and the only method I'd been exposed to at the time, it didn't feel right to me. Then one day, I was blessed by a kind gesture from a veteran horseman, which directly contributed to the foundation of the Tellington Method.

I was riding home to our farm from Briercrest Stables when an elderly man with a noticeable limp walked the long distance of his driveway and stood waiting for me at the road, resting on his cane. When I approached him, he told me that he had a clear view of Mrs. Metheral's round pen from his house and had been watching me ride her young stock. He'd also noticed me regularly ride past his home, even in the harshest of Canadian weather conditions. Perhaps he thought it was time to offer a young girl a gift because she quite possibly could have a bright future with horses. I don't know.

The man explained that he had been a member of the Canadian Cavalry Brigade while fighting in Spain in the 1930s and reached out his hand, offering me a book he no longer needed but wanted to pass along. He said the book was written by a U.S. Cavalry officer and contained information about starting young horses...*without* "bucking them out." It was a simple method: how to teach a horse to stop, turn, and stand quietly before ever being mounted, just by ground driving first.

I appreciatively thanked him.

I am forever grateful for that pivotal moment in my life because it gave me new possibilities for starting young horses. It combined with my instincts to establish relationships with horses based on mutual trust and respect to become the true beginnings of my own training methods.

In the year 1949, lucky for me, my dad brought in a few horses to board on our farm. One was a three-year-old, 16-hand Thoroughbred mare. I chose her as my first training "test subject" because, although she had never been saddled before, she was friendly and easy to catch and lead. She was the perfect partner for me. I carefully followed the detailed instructions in the book the old man had given me, and within a few weeks, the mare stood still when I mounted her. Soon she was quietly walking and trotting under saddle. A month later, she calmly cantered for me, exhibiting no issues whatsoever. I was convinced from that day forward that I had found the correct way to start young horses (fig. 1.2).

1.2 Here I am *Ground Driving* a horse in the 1960s. *Ground Driving* is an excellent exercise to build communication and confidence. Today we *Ground Drive* from the halter and run the lines higher up so there is less weight on the horse's head.

It wasn't until 1958 when I had opportunity to repeat this method on my special endurance mare, Bint Gulida. She was a well-bred and highly sensitive Arabian who became instrumental in teaching me how to control my own emotions while working with horses. She reacted to my every feeling when I was near her, reflecting my emotions right back to me! A few words of wisdom from my grandfather, Will Caywood, came in handy in my moments of frustration: "If you start to lose your patience, put your horse away, sit under a tree, and cool off." His advice still rings true in the Tellington Method today, where I advocate innovative techniques to maintain calmness and something called "heart coherence" (explained in detail on p. 21), which directly influences our own behavior and that of our horses.

Another significant milestone in the development of the Tellington Method for starting and restarting horses was the introduction of bodywork, which was brought to me by my grandfather, as well. He had been a successful racehorse trainer in Russia, and in his eighties, he started to share enthralling stories from his days in Moscow. He'd developed a friendship with his Romani translator, Orlo, a towering figure of a man and a formidable character around the racetrack. Orlo took my jockey-sized grandfather under his wing, teaching him not only the local horsemanship customs but also traditions from his own Roma culture. One particularly useful gem was how to massage horses.

My grandfather avidly used this "gypsy massage," which was considered secret information at the time, on his racehorses to enhance their performances. He attributed his success to the fact that every horse in his stable was "rubbed" for 30 minutes a day, using a special Romani massage technique. In addition, my grandfather said he never entered a horse in a race unless the horse "told him it was feeling fit enough to win." In 1905, my grandfather won the coveted Czar Nicholas II Trainer of the Year Award.

It was these stories from Moscow that inspired me to use bodywork with horses and listen to what their bodies were telling me—the seeds had been planted for the Tellington TTouch.

Several years later, when my then husband Wentworth Tellington and I had the Pacific Coast Equestrian Research Farm and School of Horsemanship, in Badger, California, I continued honing my methods with both young horses and those who needed a fresh start (figs. 1.3 A & B). In order to graduate from our nine-month residential Riding Instructors Program, our students learned to start young horses with this method. (You can find the details in a book about my early life and school entitled *Strike a Long Trot: Legendary Horsewoman Linda Tellington-Jones* written by PCERF graduate Shannon Yewell Weil.) A vital lesson that I learned from Wentworth was the desire and willingness to share what many horsemen consider their "secrets." This dedication to sharing techniques and knowledge is a practice that I carry forward today.

1.3 A & B In the 1960s, I and my then-husband Wentworth Tellington started the first residential instructors program in North America, The Pacific Coast Equestrian Research Farm and School of Horsemanship (PSERF) in California (A). PSERF required students to ride a variety of disciplines on many different horses, based on classical cavalry principles (B).

Seeing with New Eyes: The Feldenkrais Influence

In March of 1975 I presented at Equitana, the world's largest equine expo, held every two years in Essen, Germany. I introduced Europeans to the idea of riding a horse without a bit or hackamore or even halter for control—with only a ring around his neck. It caused a sensation and every major horse magazine wrote about it. As a result, I was asked to teach weekend and 10-day clinics in Germany, Switzerland, and Austria.

July of that year marked a completely new era of training horses for me. I had been applying my grandfather's equine bodywork with our endurance and eventing horses for more than a decade. Related to that, Wentworth and I produced our first book in the English language, entitled *Physical Therapy for the Athletic Horse*. I had been successfully starting young horses and retraining others as a professional for over 15 years, but suddenly, I began to see horses with new eyes. The shift was as significant as my original move from "bucking out" horses to starting them with *Ground Driving* techniques in a more peaceful way. The catalyst was the Feldenkrais Method®.

I had enrolled in the four-year, 12-week professional training at the Humanistic Psychology Institute in San Francisco, thinking I would use the method to help my riding students become better athletes. It never crossed my mind that I would personally benefit by developing a life-long physical flexibility beyond measure. And I had no thought at that time that I would apply the principles to horses in a way that would eventually spread around the world.

On the second day of my training in San Francisco, Dr. Moshe Feldenkrais made a statement that caught my full attention: He explained that human potential for learning could be enhanced by gentle non-habitual movement of the body that would activate unused neural pathways to the brain, resulting in new brain cells. That very day I began exploring gentle movements on the horse's body that the horse could not do himself (fig. 1.4). The results were immediately successful. During the ensuing summers I worked with horses to further explore this new potential for learning, and in the winters I returned to Europe to continue teaching weekend and 10-day trainings that focused on problem horses and developing a method that any amateur could use successfully to give a horse a fresh start.

1.4 Introducing my integration of Feldenkrais philosophy with horses to Moshe Feldenkrais and a group of students in the mid-1970s.

Breakthroughs in Retraining Horses

A major milestone in the area of retraining was conceived of and organized by Ursula Bruns, publisher of the popular German horse magazine *Freizeit Im Sattel*. She was fascinated in the changes she saw in horse behavior and performance as I found ways to move horses in exercises on the ground using techniques that differed from classical methods of lungeing or Western-style, round-pen trainings. She suggested I should provide a guide that would teach amateur horse owners my methods and proposed we make a book together. Ursula organized a five-week study program at her Reken

Test Center in Germany. I took 20 horses of varying breeds with a wide range of behavior issues, including shying, bolting, balking, and horses who could not be rated or lunged. Ursula chose four amateur riders who were to follow my instructions as we worked with the horses. The result was *An Introduction to the Tellington-Jones Equine Awareness Method,* which taught a safe, peaceful method that anyone could use when dealing with behavior and training issues. It was in this book that I introduced the *Playground for Higher Learning* principles and techniques, with specially chosen *Elements* developed to teach horse and rider to trust each other (see p. 175).

In 1978 in Germany I taught my first "Start Your Own Young Horse in Ten Days Training." I took the ground driving principles I had been using and modified them, realizing that having a person at the horse's head, for example, made the horse more confident and kept the handler safer. I built on that concept by adding a secondary person on the opposite side of the horse's head and named the movement *The Homing Pigeon,* as I had begun to use "animal names" to identify various techniques, much like the movements are named in Tai Chi (see more about this on p. 84). I began driving off a flat leather halter instead of a bridle and bit, and I used lightweight, 9 mm climbing rope instead of heavy, leather reins to further protect the horse's mouth. Even now, my techniques are always evolving like this: I am continually searching for ways to keep horse and rider safe while developing a mutually enjoyable relationship.

The Birth of the TTouch® Circle

In 1983 at the Delaware Equine Veterinary Center, my path took another turn. After many years using my grandfather's massage techniques and eight years of very successful clinics teaching the Feldenkrais Method® to hundreds of humans and horses, I discovered the basic one-and-a-quarter circle that is at the heart of the TTouch bodywork I teach in the Tellington Method.

Tellington TTouch was birthed on a warm July day, during a weekend training at a veterinary center. I was asked to work with a very reactive Thoroughbred mare who objected fiercely to being groomed or saddled by pinning her ears, flashing her teeth, and often threatening to kick. It was hoped there would be a way to help this mare with the Feldenkrais Method. When I placed my hands on her shoulder and began the gentle movements

1.5 Working in small groups at the Starting Young Horse Clinic at the Bitterroot Ranch develops trusting, safe horses for the ranch guest string.

of Functional Integration, the mare became very quiet and showed no signs of her usual aggressive behavior. Her owner was amazed at how her normally reactive horse showed no signs of fear or resistance.

She asked me in a surprised voice, "What are you doing to affect my horse in this way? Are you using energy? What is your secret?"

Without thinking, I responded with the prophetic words, "Don't worry about what I'm doing, just place your hand lightly on her shoulder, and move the skin in a circle."

I had never before thought about "moving the skin in a circle"; however, I trusted my instincts because many years before I received an astrological chart for my thirtieth birthday. It foretold that in my lifetime I would develop a form of communication that would spread around the world, and stated that in order to do so, I must learn to trust my intuition.

I watched quietly as the mare's owner followed my minimal instructions. To my surprise, the mare became as quiet and accepting of the light circles on her shoulder as she had been for my Feldenkrais movements. I had an intuitive feeling of the importance of these light circles. It takes years to become proficient with the brilliant Feldenkrais Method, but anyone can learn to move the skin in a circle. I began to explore the mystery of these simple circles, and the Tellington TTouch was born.

Three Decades of Young Horse Training in Wyoming

I have now held a "Starting Young Horses Clinic" at the Bitterroot Ranch in Wyoming every year for almost three decades, where participants incorporate all the techniques I've developed over the years for training and retraining horses, and which I outline in this book. We have accumulated an outstanding record of success stories from this ranch alone. The group usually ranges from 16 to 20 people, and many attendees have never started a young horse before. Using the Tellington Method, they can all produce excellent results by the week's end. It is my hope this book provides you the tools for the same training success.

Also By Linda Tellington-Jones

BOOKS

The Ultimate Horse Behavior and
    Training Book
Dressage with Mind, Body, and Soul
Getting in TTouch with Your Horse
The Tellington TTouch
Getting in TTouch with Your Dog
Getting in TTouch with Your Cat
Getting in TTouch with Your Puppy
TTouch for Healthcare

VIDEOs

TTouch for Dressage
Hit It Off with Your Horse!
Unleash Your Dog's Potential
Solving Riding Problems from the Ground
Solving Riding Problems from the Saddle
Starting a Young Horse
Haltering Your Foal without Trauma
The TTEAM Approach to
    Handling Stallions and Mares
Riding with Awareness
TTouch of Magic for Horses

CHAPTER 2

The Heart *of the* Tellington TTouch Method

The Cornerstone

The Tellington Method provides you an incredible training system, but it is so much more than a collection of exercises and techniques. The mindset in which you approach the training of your horse—whether he's young and green or older with a need for a fresh education—makes all the difference and is a cornerstone in everything you do (fig. 2.1). Honoring the mind, body, and spirit of the horse through your language, actions, and intention creates some truly amazing results in our horses.

The Tellington Method trains horses with patience, understanding, respect, and compassion. It is important to release any old beliefs that horses are trying to "win," dominate," or "trick" you when they are not cooperative or seem to be "resistant." It is my experience that when a horse is not cooperative it is usually an issue of balance, discomfort, fear of discomfort, or simply a lack of understanding. Horses that are unbalanced physically—this can be displayed in rushing, balking, and reactivity, to name a few symptoms— generally also display emotional or mental imbalance, and tend to seem more difficult.

From Instinct to Intelligence: Self-Carriage, Self-Confidence, Self-Control

A key tenet of the Tellington Method is the connection between physical posture and behavior (fig. 2.2). When horses are in "flight mode" their sympathetic nervous system takes over and they leave their "thinking" state. A horse in this mode is usually high-headed, tense through the back, disconnected from his legs, and rapid or shallow in breath. In this posture, a horse is ready to react and flee or freeze in a stressful situation. He is not well-balanced, and is ready to work on reflex rather than with any finesse or control. His mental or emotional state is as disconnected and reactive as his physical.

When a horse is shown a way to be in a healthy, released posture, we have found that he comes out of this state of reactivity and into more of a thinking state. A balanced posture allows the horse to be in better control of his body and actions, and feel safer because he knows where his feet are and how to move in a coordinated way. As a horse learns to be in self-carriage,

2.1 Trust and understanding without ego is an integral part of the Tellington Method.

he feels more confident and is able to *think and act* instead of *react*. When a horse can act he develops self-control, which helps him override instinct and be capable of making choices in a variety of scenarios.

By taking a horse through the Tellington Method, he learns to think and becomes less driven by instinct. This means that a horse can adapt to new situations with self-confidence so that he does not reflexively default to the instinctual habit of flight.

The connection between physical, mental, and emotional balance is intrinsic, and it is why we find the saying, "Change the posture, and you can change the behavior," to be true. When tension and imbalance are alleviated, behavior and performance improves dramatically. It is an imperative part of starting or restarting a horse in a healthy way.

Reducing Stress

The goal of the Tellington Method is to train the horse with minimal stress. While some stress is required when any being is learning something new, excessive stress releases the hormone ACTH, which triggers the production of cortisol in the body. Horses cannot think clearly, or learn, when they are under excessive stress or fearful. Maintaining low-stress sessions will result in learning without excessive repetition and engage your horse in a cooperative, curious way.

2.2 Over the past few decades we have discovered what an integral part posture plays in affecting behavior. As we change a horse's habitual posture, we can positively affect how adaptable and cooperative an animal can be.

The exercises in this book will teach your horse how to be more physically balanced, which will lead to a more mentally and emotionally balanced state. When your horse is in physical balance or in self-carriage, he feels safer and is able to exercise self-control and act in an appropriate manner. A horse that can exercise self-control is typically a willing and cooperative partner.

Learning to Act Instead of React

Another important part of the Tellington Training philosophy is to not take a horse's undesirable behavior personally but rather assume that he is doing the best he can in that moment, and is simply reacting to some kind of perceived stimuli. This understanding helps you (like the horse) to *act*, rather than *react,* and be a more proactive guide for your horse. This is what is important to me: With this attitude, you will not just turn your horse into a safe partner, but you will also cultivate and improve your own self-control and flexibility. These abilities create a foundation on which you can build a lifelong partnership and two-way connection with your horse. It is my wish and desire that your horse will have as much fun being started or restarted under saddle as you will have working toward that goal with him.

Our world has become very small in the twenty-first century, and we are becoming more aware of how we are all connected. Research has made great strides toward knowledge about cell function and heart coherence, which shows that our thoughts and actions don't just affect our own lives but those of people and all life on the planet around us (see sidebar).

This philosophy behind Tellington Training has inspired many students to search for a new way to live in a harmonious connection with their animals. The Tellington Method is used and taught successfully in 30 countries and more and more people are opening their hearts to a new way of dealing with horses and themselves.

Chunking It Down

An important way to help horses young and old learn to think instead of simply "training" specific behaviors is by "chunking down" exercises. Any one of the techniques and exercises outlined in this book can be broken

A horse that can exercise self-control is typically a willing and cooperative partner.

....

Heart Coherence

In my book *Dressage with Mind, Body & Soul,* I explain the concept of heart coherence as follows:

Coherence is defined as a logical, orderly, and aesthetically consistent relationship of parts. Understanding how the mental and emotional energy emanated and controlled by your heart can become coherent, and learning to manage this energy can be a powerful force in your work with horses. It's called "heart rhythm coherence." As I'm sure you can guess by now, positive emotional states produce coherence within human systems, and this in turn can drastically improve your effectiveness when addressing tasks, large and small.

Most of us have experienced this on more than one occasion: perhaps your child gives you a hug and a kiss before he or she goes off to school, or your significant other reminds you how much he or she loves you before you hop in the car to go to the barn. Your positive emotional state, in this case the result of an exposure to love and caring, makes the mundane magical and the difficult a little easier. You may find yourself humming while you warm up your horse, perhaps with more patience than usual, and the movements you've struggled to grasp until now suddenly seem to come more easily.

According to the Institute of HeartMath, research has shown that "sustained positive emotions lead to a highly efficient and regenerative functional mode associated with increased coherence in heart rhythm patterns and greater harmony among physiological systems." In other words, when you handle your horse or ride him with positive emotions weighting the scale, your body will react to his movement and the demands of your schooling figure or test more smoothly, cohesively, and in a more skilled manner than it will when you are anxious or angry, for example.

And, even better, research has also shown that human beings can regulate their own heart rhythm coherence by actively generating positive feelings and intentions. You can achieve a higher performance state by "thinking good thoughts."

down into smaller, easier, and more achievable steps, should an individual horse find something difficult.

Taking the extra time at the beginning means that a horse really learns to understand and think through a situation rather than simply be pressured through it with skillful timing. When a horse realizes that he is not going to be forced through a difficult situation, he becomes less reactive and trusts his human partner to listen to his concerns.

Virtually any exercise—not just those in my method—can be chunked down. For instance, when a horse is anxious or resistant about being touched around the mouth, the exercise could be chunked down by using the back of the hand, a sheepskin mitt, or warm washcloth to change how it feels. In some cases you might have to start at a place where the horse is comfortable other than the mouth, and slowly work your way closer and closer to the muzzle area, pausing and slowing down if the horse becomes anxious. Chunking down an exercise requires you to be observant and sometimes think creatively to come up with ways to alter an exercise so it is less threatening to the horse. When stress is kept at a low level, learning can take place. When stress gets too high, learning is blocked and instinct takes over. Taking the time to keep stress levels low and investing in extra

"Change Your Mind, Change Your Horse"

Like "Change the posture and you can change the behavior," which I mentioned earlier, this too is a fundamental Tellington Method principle. But what does it mean?

Words are important. How common is it to place a label based on an animal's specific behavior? "Oh, she's stubborn." "He is dominant." Once a label is placed, it can be hard to shake. How fair is it to label someone's general personality based on a particular behavior in a specific context? If you were to label my general personality based on one context—say, my reaction to rush hour traffic or my lack of self-control around chocolate after a particularly stressful day—it would be very different from my tendencies in different situations. *Behavior* is separate from *personality*.

Changing the way you see and talk about your horse can greatly influence how you react to his behavior and your ability steps will actually save you time in the long run and provide your horse with learning and confidence.

Keys to Success

The Tellington Training Method consists of five components each designed to work with one another in the process of educating, re-educating, and simply handling your horse (fig. 2.3). Each piece works with the others to comprise a complete and holistic system that honors the body, mind, and spirit of your horse.

The basic components are:

➤ *State of Mind:* Intention, "change your mind, change your horse" (see sidebar), setting yourself up for success.

➤ *TTouch:* My method of bodywork, which includes *Circular TTouches, Slide* and *Lift TTouches,* and *Extremity TTouches,* releasing tension in the horse's body.

When stress is kept at a low level, learning can take place.
....

to diffuse and redirect it. Once a label is assigned, it can be very difficult to remove.

Seeing the "perfection" in every horse you work with, without preconceived opinions, gives you the ability to *act* rather than *react,* setting yourself, and the horse, up for success. Visualize that your goals have already been achieved. Feel the emotions you would be feeling if you had that "perfect" horse. Experience the joy and elation *now* that you know will be yours when your horse has grown or improved in desired ways.

Your horse's behavior is strongly influenced by these five parts of your being:

➤ Your expectations.
➤ Your posture.
➤ Your breathing.
➤ Your intention.
➤ Your clarity of communication.

Hold the picture of your "perfect" horse in your heart and your thoughts. It opens up the opportunity for the horse to change and become the way you wish.

➤ *Dance Steps: Leading Exercises* and *Ground Driving* to support a healthy posture in motion.

➤ *Playground for Higher Learning:* Leading over *Elements* that help enhance confidence and trust.

➤ *Riding:* Preparation, signals, confidence, and cooperation.

This overview of the basic components can help give you an idea of which lessons you and your horse have mastered and which ones you still need to learn. Start with the basics and expand on them as you and your horse are comfortable with them. Do not fret if you are not able to perfect an exercise before moving on to another one. Sometimes by going on to other techniques and then coming back to an area where you had trouble, you will find that you and your horse can suddenly do it with more ease and proficiency.

This system was conceived intuitively through many years of experience and countless equine teachers who allowed for the dynamic development and progression of the exercises and techniques. Nothing that is outlined in this book is set in stone. We should always allow for innovation and problem solving when working with our equine friends. If something isn't working the way you would like, change how you are asking, make the lesson easier, or simply pause and take a moment to do something else before attempting it again. Ideally, training or working with a horse should be a slow, methodical, and uneventful process that takes as long as it takes, not an adrenaline-fueled spectator sport (fig. 2.4). It is not about "winning" any battles but about building a trusting and cooperative partnership.

As you are going through the pages ahead, remember these keys to success:

A "Problem" Is a Gift
I am always excited when a horse has a so-called "problem." I think, "Great! This horse and I can learn something." Overcoming a "problem" in a non-threatening way builds trust and confidence.

Be Open
Visualize how you want a situation with your horse to turn out—only then

2.3 The Tellington TTouch Method is comprised of five major components that all work together to enhance balance, trust, cooperation, and overall well-being.

can it change. For example, if you keep thinking, "Oh, my horse will never go into the trailer," it will be much more difficult to be successful with loading. Instead, imagine your horse enjoying a ride in the trailer. Horses try very hard to follow your "pictures," so be mindful to make them positive.

Give Clear Directions
Horses will do what you ask as long as you give them clear directions.

2.4 At the Bitterroot Ranch in Dubois, Wyoming, participants at the Annual Starting Young Horse Clinic use Tellington Training principles to quietly start lightly handled four-year-olds.

Only an intelligent question or request can be answered with an intelligent response. When a horse seems "uncooperative," check to see if you could be any clearer in your request or if you are inadvertently giving mixed signals.

Tomorrow Is Another Day

There are days when nothing goes right. For example, maybe you were going to work your horse over a plastic tarp, but he gets more and more upset, and you are losing your patience. In a situation like this, just stop for the day. It is not true that you have to finish an exercise no matter what. That will only cause a fight and subsequent stress. Tomorrow, when you and the horse are fresh, the exercise may be much easier, and you may have more success in chunking it down into smaller pieces.

It Is Not About Winning or Losing

Training a horse should not be a competition. It is a process that you are lucky enough to partake in with an equine partner. Each challenge should not be seen as a new scenario that you, as the person, must "win," but as a

A New Level of Trust

Many years ago, I bought a six-year-old Arabian mare who did not have a lot of contact with people. Her owner had tried to start her under saddle but found her too difficult and let her run with the broodmares. I was interested in the mare because her bloodlines had produced some excellent endurance horses. I worked with the mare and she slowly started to trust me. One time as I was brushing her I ran the brush just a little bit too quickly over her neck. She squealed, turned her head, and bit me in the stomach! Immediately, she jumped back in surprise. Even though I had never punished her for anything, she was obviously afraid that I would hit her.

I counted to 30 very slowly, took a few deep breaths, and calmly laid my hand on her neck. I let her know that I had forgiven her and that I understood that her reaction was just a reflex.

That was the beginning of a wonderful friendship that was based on a new level of trust and understanding. I am telling you about this experience to prove that the attitude you have toward your horse plays such an important role in your relationship. Change your attitude and you will be surprised how much your horse will change!

Like anyone, we want horses to listen to our requests and comply. However, compliance can come at a price. I want a partner who can think and interact with the world, not simply go through it with blind obedience. It is important to maintain the joy in your horse. Your interest is that the horse enjoys being with you as much as you enjoy being with him. The enjoyment in the interaction should be mutual.

situation you and your horse can figure out and succeed in together. Your ego has no place in a training session. Remember that you are doing the best you can in that moment, and so is the horse.

Be Your Horse's Advocate

It is an honor to work with a horse. It is really a testament to the kind and giving nature of the horse that you are able to ride and influence him so readily. Having a horse in your care means that you are the only one who is going to advocate for him, and that can be extremely difficult, especially when you are considered a "layperson" or "amateur," and an "expert" is telling you what to do. This does not mean that expert advice is not potentially invaluable. However, you know your horse best, and you know how you want to treat your horse.

Attitude Is Most Important

The Tellington TTouch Method for starting and re-educating horses can be an excellent tool for all levels of horse owner to help prepare a horse for a more rigorous education under saddle, or help a horse that has been started under saddle but is missing some layers. As you read on, remember that the most important part of this method is not every single detail and exercise but the attitude in which you approach working with your horse. Give your horse a chance. Assume that he is trying his best and that he is not starting with the intent of "testing you" or "getting away with something." From a logical point of view, it has never been in a horse's best interest to act "stubborn," "resistant," or "dominant." His behavior is simply a kind of communication and the only way he can convey that something does not make sense, is physically difficult, or scares him.

At the risk of anthropomorphizing, it is worth putting yourself in the horse's shoes when trying new exercises. If you are not particularly gifted or trained as a dancer, attempting to learn any choreography, even seemingly simple steps, is next to impossible when attempted in one large piece. Just like us, horses learn more deeply, with less stress, and longer-lasting results when the exercise is chunked down into small, easy pieces. Humans have flourished thanks to our cognitive prowess yet when working with horses we can still default to attempting the use of force, pressure, and coercion. Approach training your horse with the goal that you want to work with a few pounds of brain rather than a thousand pounds of muscle.

Taking the time to have your horse really learn an exercise in a low-stress way is safer for everyone involved. Letting go of preconceived ideas about how quickly a horse should master an exercise is incredibly important and helps foster long-term success, thus building a deeper relationship with your horse.

PART II

Sensible Steps

CHAPTER 3

Start Where You Can

Plan to Be Flexible

The Tellington Training Method outlines a wide variety of exercises and techniques, many serving similar purposes but different enough to support the fact that no two horses are exactly the same. Sometimes the process is not totally linear, and there are countless options and modifications to allow a lesson to become accessible for virtually any horse. This flexibility is certainly a strength and helps in the overall effectiveness of the Tellington Method; however, it can also serve as a difficulty for those hoping for a linear recipe "from A to Z."

The reality is that not every horse will respond to a situation the same way the last horse did, or even the same way he did a week ago! As you go

3.1 When using the Tellington Method, the process may not be linear. The key is to start where you can.

through this book, you will see many different lessons outlined, and some have clear, progressive steps—like mounting for the first time, for example—while others, like the *TTouches* and *Leading Exercises*, are offered as optional exercises to explore and practice at any time, as you see fit (fig. 3.1).

The key is, *start where you can*. A very shut-down or nervous horse may feel most comfortable starting with a session of *Body Exploration* (p. 56) or *Lowering the Head* (p. 65) followed by a selection of *TTouch* bodywork (p. 78), before starting any of the *Leading Exercises* (p. 132). The young, impatient, anxious, or high-strung horse may do best starting in motion with a variety of the *Leading Exercises* on through to the *Playground of Higher Learning* (p. 175). Let the horse guide you to a starting point, and work your way from there. (At the beginning of each section I do outline some basic guidelines for what to use and how, depending on the age and experience level of your horse, which I explain in more detail just ahead.)

As my sister Robyn Hood says, "Let your plans be set in sand rather than stone." Sometimes a session will not go in the direction that you planned; that's okay! It is invaluable to be flexible and know you do not have to perfect something before moving on to another exercise. As mentioned in Part I, leaving an "imperfect" exercise as is until tomorrow can find it miraculously improved overnight without extra repetition or pressure. As you take a young horse along—or are reeducating an older horse—approach the process as a type of experiential learning. You do not necessarily have to repeat every exercise multiple times. Some will be ones you go back to time and time again as a reminder; others may only be done once or twice to give the horse a non-habitual experience that can result in a massive transformation that lasts. Many of the bodywork *TTouches* will get easier and more "enjoyable" to the horse the more you do other, seemingly non-related exercises. Some of the *Leading Exercises* will click as your horse becomes engaged with the *Elements* of the *Playground of Higher Learning* (fig. 3.2).

One good rule of thumb: For horses that have not yet been started, you will want to be at least somewhat comfortable with the *Observation and*

3.2 When working with a young horse that has not been started, it will make sense to progress through the *TTouch* bodywork, *Leading Exercises,* and *Playground for Higher Learning* before mounting for the first time.

The Five Fs

As horse people we have it drilled into us that horses are prey animals that tend to favor their "flight" instinct when faced with a scary situation. The reality is that domesticated horses have a variety of ways to cope with situations they may otherwise choose to avoid. I have observed five coping mechanisms or displacement behaviors that horses may default to in times of fear or stress.

Flight: This is when a horse's reaction is to leave an unfavorable situation. This horse may be outwardly fearful or simply spin and pull away from his handler to find safety.

Fight: The animal may seem to become defensive or aggressive in a stressful situation. This horse may threaten to kick, strike, or bite. He will often be mistakenly labeled as "dominant" or "alpha" even though he is just as stressed or lacking in confidence as a horse that defaults to flight mode.

Freeze: This coping mechanism is one that is often unobserved but can result later in sudden explosive behavior—a horse that tends to freeze in stressful situations is ignored until he reaches his "breaking point." A horse in "freeze" will often take short, shallow breaths and be "too still." It is important to recognize the difference between a horse shutting down in freeze and one that is standing quietly because he is genuinely relaxed.

Fidget or "Fool Around": This displacement behavior is almost always misunderstood and rarely recognized. A perfect example of a horse that uses "fool around" to cope with stress is the horse that paws when the saddle comes toward him. This horse would typically be labeled as "bored" or impatient; however, when the saddle goes away, he suddenly stops pawing. Pawing, nibbling on the lead rope, scratching, or rubbing whenever he is touched in a certain place or asked to do a certain thing is often a signal that he is slightly anxious or stressed.

Faint: This is the least commonly exhibited coping mechanism but is generally seen in times of extreme stress. In these cases, the animal will simply lie down and shut down. Faint is most often seen in trailer loading or saddling, and in young horses having their feet trimmed and restrained without any preparation.

By acknowledging and understanding the variety of coping mechanisms, you can begin to recognize the smallest signs of anxiety and stress in your horse before they escalate into such extreme behaviors.

Trust Exercises (p. 53), *TTouch* bodywork (p. 78), *Leading Exercises* (p. 132) through to the *Playground for Higher Learning* (p. 175) before going on to *Ground Driving* (p. 209), and exercises under saddle (p. 269).

Remember: You Have Choices

At the beginning of each section is a guide as to how to apply the techniques and exercises to three different age ranges of horses:

➤ The foal or weanling.

➤ The not-yet-started three- or four-year-old (though it could apply to an unstarted horse of any age).

➤ The mature horse that needs to be re-educated.

Most horses, no matter what their level of experience or training, can benefit from any of the techniques described in the book. By doing things in a methodical, incremental way that is non-habitual, you will see long-lasting transformations from exercises not obviously related to the changes.

As I've said, the *TTouch* bodywork and *Leading Exercises* can be incorporated into your sessions at virtually every stage. The *TTouches* can be easily done during other lessons as well as part of their own dedicated bodywork sessions. Familiarize yourself with your options so you have choices if your horse is not responding as planned. Having choices means that you can *act* instead of *react* and will help you stay calm and relaxed in even potentially stressful situations.

When taking your horse through to the *Playground for Higher Learning*, you will find that some of the *Leading Exercises* are easier for you and your horse than others. That is okay. As you both become more balanced—physically and mentally—and you, the handler, become more precise, you will probably find that previously challenging lessons become easier. There are no rules about *what* you have to do *when* as far as this book is concerned (fig. 3.3). The only rule is that you listen to your horse and are prepared to chunk techniques and exercises down into smaller pieces and easier, incremental steps.

3.3 With the Tellington Method, there aren't set rules for how you progress with your horse through the exercises and levels. What *is* important is that you listen to your horse.

Keep a Record

Use the checklist found at the end of this book (p. 285) to help guide you through the process of using the Tellington Method to educate a horse and prepare him, or improve him, as a riding horse. Do not feel as though you have to master every step before going on to another one, but keeping a record helps you remember which techniques and exercises you may want to revisit and which were straightforward and easily learned for both you and your horse. Each time you do an exercise from this book, use a scale of 1–5 to indicate the horse's level of acceptance of the activity on that date.

1 = No acceptance.

5 = Optimum acceptance.

Always use 3 to indicate average acceptance the first time you try something. It can be helpful to make descriptive notes when there are surprising, unusual, or extreme reactions to a particular lesson.

And it is so important that I'll say it again: Remember that horse training should not be a timed event! Enjoy the process and the privilege of having a horse in your life (fig. 3.4).

3.4 Working with a young horse or restarting an older one should be a process that both you and your horse enjoy. One of the most effective ways to gain trust and deepen your relationship with your horse is to use the warmth of your hand and the *Abalone TTouch* (p. 92) on his face.

CHAPTER 4

Groundwork Equipment

Tools for Trust and Clarity

When practicing the Tellington Training Method there are several pieces of equipment to make the techniques and exercises easier and clearer for your horse. Every tool is specifically used to make a positive connection and help him function in a healthy posture.

4.1 I prefer to use flat nylon or leather halters for groundwork.

Correctly Fitted Flat Halter

You will need a well-fitted, solid, *flat nylon or leather halter*. A halter with an adjustable noseband is ideal.

I like to use flat halters instead of rope halters so I can give precise signals from the side of the halter rather than underneath the chin, which is where the lead is typically attached (figs. 4.1 & 4.2). Giving a signal from the side of the halter helps prevent tilting or tipping of the horse's head and allows for a more correct bend when asking for a right or left turn. Horses that are tight in the poll area will also find it easier to lower their head and release tension when the signal comes from the side rather than underneath.

Note that the knots on a rope halter are strategically placed on sensitive points of the horse's head, which can be painful when pressure is applied. For this reason it is difficult to know if your horse is responding to discomfort rather than understanding when using a rope halter.

Tellington Lead

For young, sensitive horses we generally use a soft *Zephyr lead* that can be threaded over the nose or up the side of the halter (fig. 4.3 and see p. 42). These leads are very lightweight and can easily be folded safely in the handler's hand.

Most young horses are started at the time when they are experiencing natural changes in their teeth. For this reason, we often attach the

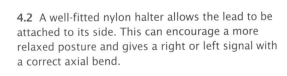

4.2 A well-fitted nylon halter allows the lead to be attached to its side. This can encourage a more relaxed posture and gives a right or left signal with a correct axial bend.

Zephyr lead to the side of the halter, rather than over the nose as you would with an older horse (figs. 4.4 A–C). Most young horses have caps coming off their teeth, which can make pressure across the nose uncomfortable.

Horses that have difficulty slowing down or coming to a halt may find it easier to understand the *Zephyr* lead over the noseband.

If you do not have access to a *Zephyr* lead, you can use a *regular lead rope* attached up to the cheek piece of the halter (fig. 4.5). This will not have the same specificity in signals as the *Zephyr* lead, but it can get you started with the Leading Exercises.

4.3 A well-fitted flat halter and Tellington *Zephyr* lead are key pieces of equipment for teaching a horse to lead in a healthy, relaxed posture.

4.4 A–C There are three ways to attach the *Zephyr* lead. Over the nose (A) is often used with older horses. Most young horses do best with the lead attached on the side ring (B). Higher-headed horses may find it easier to respond when the lead threads up the side (C). See *Taming the Tiger*, p. 71, for step-by-step instructions on attaching the lead to the side hardware of the halter.

4.5 If you do not have a *Zephyr* lead you can try using a regular lead rope fastened up the side of the halter. Any lead will be more effective in releasing the head and neck when attached to the halter's side hardware, as opposed to under the chin.

4.6 A & B These two chain lead configurations can be useful for horses that are extremely high-headed, or those that fall through the shoulder or forward.

In some cases, a *chain lead* may be better suited if the horse is very heavy on the forehand or extremely crooked, because the weight of the chain provides a clearer signal without added pressure. The chain is never used directly against the horse or as a shank, but it can work well attached to the side of the halter (figs. 4.6 A & B).

Know that you have options. When one configuration does not seem totally successful, try one of the other ways of attaching the lead. The Tellington Method is constantly evolving and developing as we meet four-legged teachers that show us there is more than one way to do something. Having many possibilities and "tools in the toolbox" is a sure way to be more successful and confident in whatever situation you find yourself in.

Tellington Wand

The *Tellington Wand* is a 4-foot-long, white, stiff, dressage whip (fig. 4.7). This specific dressage whip is perfectly balanced and has enough rigidity to give precise signals, but is not so stiff that it does not easily bend with a little pressure. I call it a *Wand* because it can work like magic when you use it as an extension of your arm to give the horse a clear sense of his body and to provide clear, gentle cues (fig. 4.8). The name also changes how you see this piece of equipment. When we say or think "whip" we instantly think about pain or punishment, even if we have never used a whip in this fashion. Changing our words can go a long way in how we perceive and even use an item.

4.7 I use a 4-foot. white dressage whip called the *Tellington Wand* as an extension of my arm.

4.8 When working with the *Wand* it should be used as a tool of awareness, not one of punishment. Even horses that have been fearful of "whip-like" objects in the past quickly learn that the Wand is a source of relaxation and grounding.

Body Wrap

A *Body Wrap* can have an amazing effect on a horse's balance, focus, confidence, posture, proprioception, and body awareness. It is made of several 4-inch tensor bandages that are tied or fastened together with Velcro (fig. 4.9). The wrap can be applied in many different configurations, depending on the desired result. It is lightly attached and provides feedback rather than support. (For more detailed information on *Body Wraps*, see the book *All Wrapped Up: For Horses* by Robyn Hood and Mandy Pretty, available through my website www.ttouch.com).

Body Wraps are simple but effective tools that can be extremely beneficial when starting or re-starting horses. They are very useful when beginning any of the *Leading Exercises* (p. 132) or exploring the *Playground of Higher Learning* (p. 175). They are not a necessity but can be incredibly effective in supporting a horse's self-confidence and body awareness (fig. 4.10). Additionally, they are a great step in familiarizing a horse with

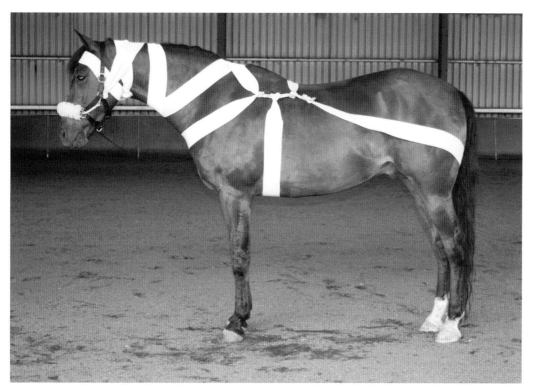

4.9 The *Body Wrap* can be applied in a variety of configurations to tailor-fit each horse's needs. It is not at all tight and does not restrict movement in any way. The bandages enhance body awareness and proprioception.

4.10 *Body Wraps* can help horses feel more secure and confident.

Sourcing Body Wrap Bandages

Tellington TTouch *Body Wraps* can be used in a variety of configurations, depending on what is suitable for the individual horse. The most challenging thing about using *Body Wraps* can be finding good quality bandages. Elastic bandages differ from brand to brand. Each type has varying stretch, length, and longevity. I have had good success with ACE™ and Mueller® brand bandages. The ideal elastic bandage is stretchy without losing its elasticity or being too firm and tight. Once you find a great bandage it is useful to have them in a variety of lengths and widths identified by different colors, which you can apply using fabric dye.

having tack or equipment put on, as well as being comfortable with new experiences.

When introducing the *Body Wrap* it is important to always put safety first. Choose a calm, wind-free day, or start in a stall or small space. If you are unsure about actually handling the wraps with ease, it can be a good idea to practice with an older, quiet horse first.

It is a good rule of thumb to treat *Body Wraps* as you would a rug or blanket. When applying a *Body Wrap* always start at the front and move to the back, and when removing, go from the back to the front. Keep the bandages gathered rather than letting them flap around, and be mindful of your horse's response as you apply any of the *Body Wrap* configurations.

I describe a few of the *Body Wrap* configurations helpful when starting and restarting horses, and their common applications, on the pages that follow. None of the *Body Wrap* configurations are meant to be used all the time. They are an excellent tool providing the horse's nervous system with valuable information and, as mentioned, can help change postural habits and increase self-awareness. Often horses need only wear one a few times to have long-lasting results.

Head Wrap

Using a 3-inch-wide bandage, this configuration makes a figure eight across the horse's forehead and TMJ, around the jowl, and across the poll (fig. 4.11). Avoid tightening the bandage too much. It should simply sit flat on the horse with plenty of stretch left.

If your horse is not comfortable having you work around his head, try wrapping the *Head Wrap* twice

4.11 The *Head Wrap* is an excellent choice for horses that have difficulty concentrating, hold tension in the poll, toss their heads, or rear.

around the neck as far behind the ears as necessary, and then taking one part of the bandage forward over the ears, placing it onto the forehead.

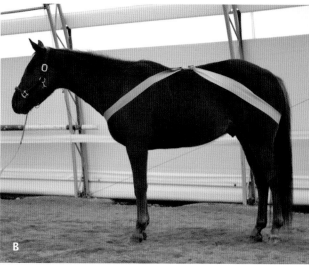

4.12 A & B The *Link Body Wrap* configuration can be easily chunked down into safe, quiet steps for horses that are not familiar with things around their hindquarters.

When to Use It

The *Head Wrap* is a great tool for high-headed, fractious, unfocused, or rushing horses. It can act like a "thinking cap," and often has immediate results. But if your horse is on the slow side, this may not be an ideal choice as it could make him "too relaxed."

When practicing *TTouches* (see p. 78), a *Head Wrap* is a great addition for horses that are concerned about having their ears handled or those that are tight in the poll.

Link Wrap

This configuration requires 2-, 3-, or 4-inch bandages, depending on how big your horse is. The *Link Wrap* affects the entire body but can easily be put on in two parts, which allows you to chunk down the process and make sure that your horse is really comfortable wearing the wraps.

The *Link Wrap* initially goes around the base of the horse's neck, just behind the withers and above the point of the shoulders. This, in itself, will often encourage a horse to lower his head and release the base of the neck. Once you have allowed your horse to feel this, and he seems comfortable, you can attach the second part of the *Link Wrap* around the hindquarters (figs. 4.12 A & B). Make a second loop with one or two bandages, linking it through the first link at the withers. Secure the loop with a quick-release knot (see p. 71 for how-to) and calmly slide the back link over the hindquarters, adjusting so that it sits halfway between the point of the buttocks and the gaskins.

When to Use It

The *Link Wrap* is a great configuration to use if your horse seems disconnected from back to front, is nervous about movement behind him, does not like going through narrow spaces, or seems overly sensitive to touch on his sides or hindquarters. It is an excellent choice when lungeing or ground driving.

First Contact—Educating Foals

The first time a foal is haltered will set him up for many expectations about human interactions for the rest of his life. Raising a foal with the Tellington Training Method will develop a trusting, willing partner. Treat your foal with the same respect you expect from him. Make contact all over his body with *TTouches* (I teach you these in chapter 6, p. 77), including around his mouth, ears, tail, and chin. You want to create positive postural habits and reduce tension patterns to help the foal grow up to be more cooperative as a willing partner, without fear or pain.

Many foals are taught to lead through force and pressure on a single point of contact, which often causes them to resemble a "fish on the end of a line" until they learn that they have no choice. When you first introduce the halter with the Tellington Method, the initial step does not include the halter at all! Your first step is to use a figure-eight *Body Rope* (see p. 50) to teach the foal about containment rather than restraint, and begin to teach stop-and-go cues without pressure

on the head or neck (figs. 4.13 A & B). Once a foal is comfortable with being gently influenced by the handler, the halter and lead are slowly introduced, never using steady pressure but instead using a "combing" or "milking" of the lead so that a bracing response is not engrained and the foal first learns to *release with relaxation*

Promise Wrap

The *Promise Wrap* got its name because it offers the "promise of engagement." This configuration is used while under saddle and is a great tool for horses that are newly under saddle or when reeducating older ones (fig. 4.14).

The *Promise Wrap* uses a 4-inch bandage that sits around the horse's hindquarters between the point of the buttocks and the gaskins, and attaches on either side to the saddle's girth billets or D-rings (fig. 4.15). It is a good idea to try the *Link Wrap* (p. 47) before using the *Promise Wrap* so you can check in and make sure your horse is comfortable with it.

and come forward, rather than *brace* first and *then* come forward. This, too, is done with the figure-eight *Body Rope* to support good posture and show the foal how to use his body in a functional way when being handled.

4.13 A & B Handling a foal should be low-stress and enhance the foal's trust in humans rather than creating an adversarial relationship. Too often foals have things "done to them" because they are smaller, not because they are really comfortable with the process and understand it.

4.14 The *Promise Wrap* is a great tool for horses that are nervous about things around their hindquarters or seem disconnected under saddle.

When to Use It

The *Promise Wrap* is a great tool to use for horses that seem disconnected to their hindquarters under saddle or do not engage. It is also very helpful for horses that are nervous about others being ridden near them or those that are overly sensitive to the leg or a grooming brush touching their sides.

Body Rope

The *Body Rope* is a 21-foot nylon rope that is attached to the horse in a figure eight (fig. 4.16). The *Body Rope* differs from the *Body Wrap* in that it sits loosely around the horse and moves slightly with the horse's movement. This characteristic makes it a very useful tool for horses that are sluggish under saddle, dull to the leg, fearful of other horses coming up from behind, or horses that do not engage their hindquarters, to name a few.

The *Body Rope* can be used with groundwork as well as when the horse is ridden.

4.15 A few sessions with the *Promise Wrap* can greatly improve a horse's way of going and posture. It is simple to attach to the girth billets or stirrup billet keeper.

4.16 The *Body Rope* can be used in a variety of configurations to help horses develop body awareness, release tension, and become comfortable with contact around their bodies. It is not tight and provides a light contact rather than any kind of constraint.

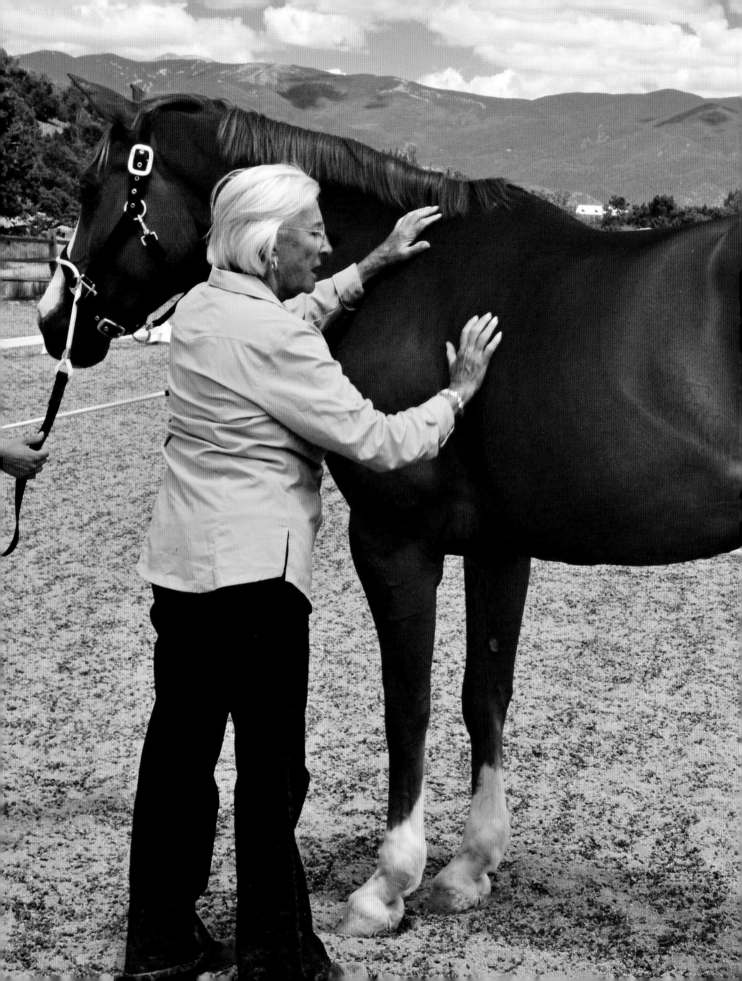

CHAPTER 5

Observation *and* Trust Exercises

Be Your Own Detective!

No matter the age of the horse or the level of his training, the simple *Observation and Trust Exercises* in this chapter will go a long way in providing you with invaluable information about his physical tendencies while creating new, more functional postural habits. Where you begin depends on your horse's stage of training:

FOAL OR WEANLING

1 The very young horse (a foal) should be introduced to being stroked by the *Wand* first (p. 62). Doing this in a contained space is ideal—small enough to maintain proximity, but not so small that he cannot walk away if he is concerned. A stall-like space works well. If he seems nervous about it, you may want use the "button end" of the *Wand* initially, so it does not look so long. Stick to very short sessions; you should resist the temptation to do "just a little more" when the foal seems comfortable. Stopping before the foal tells you that it is too much is the way to go.

2 Once your foal is happy being touched all over with the *Wand*, then you can do *Body Exploration* with the back of your hand (p. 56). You may not be able to do the whole body in one session at first.

3 Gently teaching a foal to *Lower the Head* (p. 65) can be a great way to start good postural habits early. Quietly stroking the line to encourage relaxation is very useful; however, be sure that the foal can be comfortably touched around the ears and poll before you ask him to do this exercise.

4 Unless you are planning on tying your foal, wait to introduce *Taming the Tiger* (p. 68) until you have taught him some of the *Leading Exercises* in chapter 7 (p. 132). There is a lot to be said for letting foals be foals and only doing enough handling so they are comfortable with basic haltering, leading, hoof care, and grooming.

UNSTARTED THREE- OR FOUR-YEAR-OLD

1 All of the exercises in this chapter are invaluable for the horse that is just beginning his education for work under saddle. A horse that can happily be touched all over his body with your hand (p. 56) or the *Wand*

(p. 62), as well as lowering his head in a relaxed way (p. 65), will be better prepared to navigate through the whole process up to and including being backed. Work successively through them, although as with the young foal, you can reorder as necessary, depending on the horse and his comfort zone.

2 Most young horses have an easier time with *Taming the Tiger* (p. 68) once they are comfortable with the Dance Steps in chapter 7 (p. 131).

REEDUCATING THE MATURE HORSE

1 For a horse that is going through the retraining process—for any number of issues or concerns—all the exercises in this chapter are appropriate and potentially transformational. Ensuring that your horse is comfortable with contact all over the body with your hand (p. 56) and with the *Wand* (p. 62) can create a huge change in behavior in itself.

2 The above is also true for the horse learning to calmly *Lower the Head* and release through the topline from the ground (p. 65).

3 *Taming the Tiger* (p. 68) is an excellent exercise for the older horse that has a history of pulling back, rearing, or just lacking patience. Be sure that you use a contained area, so there are clear spatial parameters.

A Good Place to Come Back To

As you progress with your horse's training or retraining in this book, you may find yourself occasionally coming back to a certain exercise in this chapter, such as *Body Exploration* (p. 56), as it provides a reference to see what has changed—your Checklist scores and notes will come in handy as baselines to measure against (see p. 285). Other exercises, such as *Lowering the Head* (p. 65) and *Introducing the Wand* (p. 62), are useful should your horse default to old patterns in times of stress.

We wish to prepare a horse so that he is easy to catch, lead, tie, and groom. He should be comfortable picking up all four feet and being touched all over his body while standing quietly. If any of these are difficult, you can use the following exercises, along with *TTouch* bodywork (see p. 78), to prepare him for a smooth start or restart.

As you progress with your horse's training or retraining, you may find yourself occasionally coming back to a certain exercise.

Body Exploration

Before starting any exercise, take the time to connect and listen to your horse with your hands. You can easily do this by mindfully running your hands all over your horse's body (fig. 5.1). This simple *Body Exploration* exercise will provide you with valuable information regarding your horse's state of body and mind as well as his level of trust in you as a handler. A horse that is very comfortable being touched all over his body will be better prepared for any experience under saddle than one that is defensive, ticklish, or tense.

Having a horse that is truly happy and comfortable about being touched is incredibly important. Not only does this signify relaxation and physical well-being, it also tells you a lot about how much he trusts you. This is also very significant for horses that are already trained but may be having specific issues under saddle. Going back to the basics and helping your horse become comfortable about being touched everywhere will often help seemingly unrelated training issues (fig. 5.2). For instance, if your horse has a tight, clamped tail, you will often find that this same horse may be nervous about noises or movement behind him.

How to Use It

Begin by checking the horse's body with your flat hand. It is helpful to have someone holding your horse, or you can work freely in a stall-sized area, rather than having him tied up, so you can observe his reactions. Stroke the horse on the shoulder before beginning your *Body Exploration* to prepare him so he does not respond just because he was surprised. For some very sensitive horses the flat of the hand may be too much. If this seems to be the case, try using the back of your hand.

Starting at the poll, right behind the ears, let your hands slide over the strong neck muscle, paying close attention along the way. Your hands are feeling for slight irregularities: swellings, change in temperature, quality of the tissue, hard muscles, twitching, knots, change in the hair, scars, or areas where the horse is uncomfortable being touched. It is best to start with a number 3 pressure (I explain my pressure scale in the next chapter—see p. 85), which you can adjust if the sensitivity or reaction of the horse requires you to do so. Sometimes horses are surprised by the touch of the fingertips; therefore, it is important to check if it was a startle reflex, or the

5.1 This is like a detective exercise. Quietly run your flat hand over your horse's entire body to discover areas where he does not trust contact. Once you have found the areas, use the *Abalone TTouch* (p. 92) and *Tarantula Pulling the Plow* (p. 99) to help release fear and come to a new level of trust.

5.2 Paying attention to how accepting your horse is about being touched all over his body will give you valuable information about his tension patterns and trust in you.

horse reacting because he is tight. A healthy horse that is not tense will usu-ally show a light response to a number 3 pressure. When going over the poll and neck this horse will lower his neck, while a horse that is tight will raise his head and possibly show pain or fear (fig. 5.3).

Horses express themselves with their body language by holding their breath, pinning their ears, raising their heads, chewing on things, pawing, or moving away from the touch. Pay close attention to small signals. Horses are very different from one another and some breeds are more expressive than others. For example, an Arabian or Thoroughbred will respond quite differently from a Quarter Horse or draft horse whose responses may be barely noticeable. This is where it is incredibly important to move slowly and watch for subtle reactions. If you have a helper, ask her to tell you any-time she notices a shift in the horse's posture or body language. A more stoic horse may demonstrate his concern or anxiety with rapid respiration or a tightening of the eye or nostril. Take the time to pause and then go back to the place where you found these subtle responses to see if it was a fluke or if it happens every time you touch the area. Becoming an observant detective to these subtle cues will make you a better "horse listener" and improve the way you understand your horse.

As you move on to exploring the horse's back remember to check about 4 inches to each side of the spine along the *longissimus dorsi* mus-cle. It is also very useful to check the muscles along the croup and down

5.3 This mare is displaying a typical response to tension in the neck. She has raised and tightened her neck while tens-ing through the back and pec-toral muscles. It is also worth noting the expression around her muzzle and nostril area.

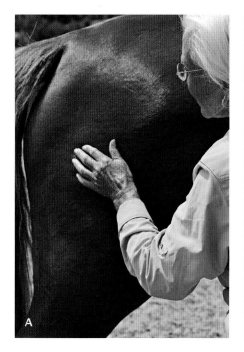
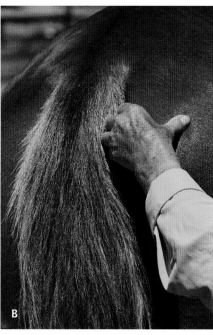

5.4 A & B You do not need a lot of pressure to check for tension in the body. Simply curve your fingers inward to press as you slowly move your hand along.

the hindquarters along the hamstrings (figs. 5.4 A & B). Horses that react strongly here are often nervous of sounds or movement behind them or when going through narrow spaces.

Recognize and Respond

Learning to recognize the signals that your horse is providing you is so important. Respond to these signals appropriately by noting the sensitive areas and coming back to them later with a more gentle touch. When a horse "does not like something" simply change how you're doing it by using a different speed, pressure, part of the hand, or add a sheepskin mitt or soft cloth to diffuse the contact.

The more you can show your horse that you are listening to his whispers and adjust your actions accordingly, the less often your horse will feel that he has to "shout" at you with big behaviors (fig. 5.5). My sister, Robyn Hood, has this wonderful saying that with the Tellington Method we are not horse whisperers, we listen to the horse's whispers.

Explore the horse's entire body with your flat hand. Don't miss any areas and remember to note your horse's response on your Checklist (fig. 5.6). You may want to get in the habit of doing this whenever you groom your horse.

"Checking In"

When doing *Body Exploration,* or any exercise, it is important to "check in" with your horse's level of acceptance while you do it. As you move your hand over the different areas of the body, do you see a "Fear" or "Trust" Response? Being mindful of noticing these small responses will give you clear information about how your horse is feeling about the situation—whether he is uncomfortable or comfortable, whether he is anxious or relaxed.

The Fear and Trust Responses can be displayed in any training or handling scenario, so it is important to become aware of them.

Fear Responses

Head tossing

Avoidance

Pulling away

Change of respiration
   (accelerated breathing or
   holding the breath)

Ears pinned

Tail swishing

Stepping from side to side

Pawing

Biting or chewing/grabbing the
   rope or hitching rail

Dropping the back

Dropping the hindquarters
   (tipping the pelvis)

Hardened eye

Nostrils pulled up

Trust Responses

Lowering the head and neck

Soft, partially closed eyes

Licking and chewing (although this is context
   specific and can be a response to a prior stressor)

Calm and deep breathing

Standing relaxed

5.5 This photo shows the look of relaxation I'm looking for in a young horse. Standing on the mounting block and doing *Lying Leopard TTouches* (p. 91) along the crest of the neck teaches the horse to stand quietly and keep the neck level in preparation for mounting. Trust is developed from mutual appreciation and a feeling of confidence in one another. You achieve trust by letting the horse know you're listening to his concerns. Taking the time to build a relationship with any horse goes a long way in making the training process more enjoyable.

5.6. The dotted lines indicate the areas of the body where you will want to pay the most attention during *Body Exploration*. It is also worth checking around the temporomandibular joint (TMJ) and the ears.

This "mindful grooming" will give you information about how your horse and his body are feeling each day and will allow you to reduce any developing tension patterns before they turn into unwanted behaviors or increased pain.

Introducing the *Wand*

While it may look like just another dressage whip, the *Wand* is an incredibly powerful tool that can have a huge impact on your horse. By stroking his entire body with the *Wand,* the horse's body awareness increases, and he learns to accept being touched all over his body. You can calm and ground the horse by stroking along the underside of the neck, over the chest, and down the front of the legs. The *Wand* helps to increase the horse's concentration during *Leading Exercises* {p. 132) and shows him the direction we want him to take. Precise signals from the *Wand* can slow the horse or create more energy.

How to Use It

Introducing the *Wand* to your horse is a very important step before starting any leading work. Ideally you will be able to stroke your horse everywhere with the *Wand* while the horse stands quietly in a relaxed state of mind.

It is important to use the *Wand* in a mindful way. Notice your own posture; release your joints, stand balanced over the middle of your feet, breathe evenly, and use enough pressure so that the *Wand* makes a positive contact with the horse rather than being ticklish.

In most cases, I introduce the *Wand* by stroking from the base of the horse's neck down the front legs to the hooves (figs. 5.7 A & B). This in itself can be an excellent way to help an unsettled horse ground himself and settle. Remembering this tool with the farrier or vet can go a long way in calmly helping a horse stand quietly.

Once the horse knows what the *Wand* feels like, mindfully explore the rest of his body (figs. 5.7 C & D). Stroking the hind legs and belly with the *Wand* is a great way to safely check in with the horse's level of touch acceptance in these potentially sensitive areas. Always make sure to stand in a safe place where you are not in reach of a leg should he kick out reflexively.

When working with a fearful horse, start the stroking on an area where the horse shows the least amount of fear—usually the chest and the base of

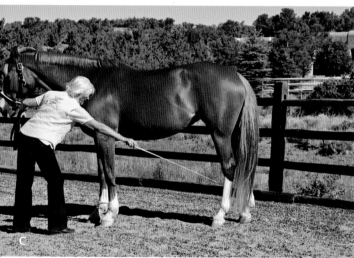

5.7 A–D *The Wand* is an invaluable tool that really does help connect a horse to his body and provide clear signals that support a relaxed, healthy posture. At no point is the *Wand* used to increase pressure or cause pain.

the neck—without going all the way down the legs. Initially, only do one or two strokes before pausing and letting your horse know that it is not a non-stop exercise. This will also give you a chance to check in with how your horse is responding to the *Wand* and will allow his nervous system a moment to integrate the information.

Whether your horse seems concerned or not, it is important to remember all the subtle signals of anxiety or acceptance that you looked for when doing *Body Exploration* with your hands (see p. 56). You want the horse to see the *Wand* as an extension of your hands and a tool of positive communication rather than a form of punishment.

For horses that are extremely fearful of the *Wand*, you may have to use your creativity to chunk down the exercise. Besides making the *Wand* smaller or using it on a less threatening part of the body, you can wrap its end with a tensor bandage to change the feel and look of it.

Whenever you make any contact with the *Wand*, be sure to take breaths yourself and remember to pause every once in a while so the stroking does not become incessant and mindless. Pausing every now and then allows the horse's nervous system to integrate the experience.

Incorporating TTouch

During *Body Exploration,* remember to make note on your Checklist of the areas where the horse shows sensitivity. When you start using my *TTouch* bodywork (see p. 78), you will want to begin in places where the horse seemed comfortable—not in areas where he was sensitive. This ensures that the horse does not become defensive but relaxes and starts to build trust in you. You can then gradually move to more difficult areas, adjusting the level of pressure, part of your hand, and speed you use to find ways to contact your horse that are acceptable to him. Try the different *TTouches* I provide in chapter 6 to see which ones are most preferable to your horse.

Let's say your *Body Exploration* finds that your horse has no problem areas. Great! Will he still benefit from *TTouch* bodywork? Definitely! *TTouches* are designed to release tension and ease tightness, but also heighten the horse's ability to learn. Instead of responding instinctively, the horse learns to think. *TTouches* encourage the optimal function of the cells, improve coordination, balance, self-confidence, and self-control. Horses become more sensible with *TTouch,* and those that are oversensitive learn to react more appropriately.

Whether you are starting a young horse or retraining a problem horse, he needs these basics in order to be able to accept your guidance. The *TTouches* build trust and a good foundation for the partnership you are looking for. A horse that is comfortable being touched everywhere on the body, has no pain, and has a clear body awareness is best prepared to become a safe, reliable riding horse.

Lowering the Head

The ability to *Lower the Head* in a relaxed manner is one of the most important basic training cornerstones your horse should know before you attempt other exercises (fig. 5.8). How readily a horse will lower his head can give you valuable insight into how comfortable he is around people and in his own body. A high-headed horse cannot think and control his movements but will react instinctively with the flight reflex (see sidebar, p. 34). Therefore, it is very important to teach the horse to lower his head.

As soon as the horse lowers his head, the flight instinct is eliminated.

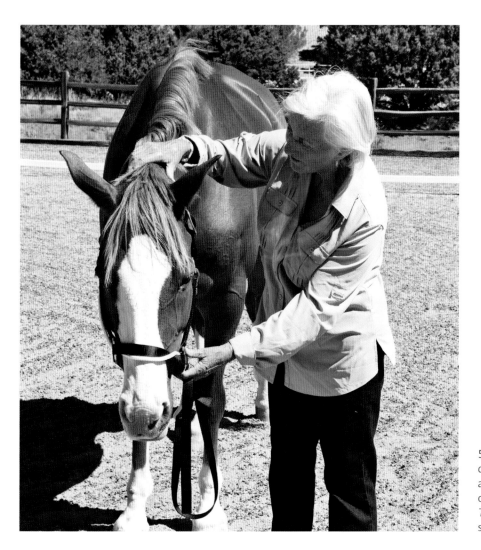

Integrating the Wand with Other Exercises

Once your horse seems accepting of the *Wand*, stroke and talk to him while at the same time *Lowering the Head* to override the flight reflex (see p. 34). You can also use the "button end" of the *Wand* to make small TTouch circles, or you can combine *Wand* stroking with *TTouches* done with your other hand (see p. 77 for more on *TTouches*).

5.8 *Lower the Head* with a light downward contact on the halter, as shown here, and the other hand on the crest of the neck applying *TTouch* circles (p. 89), also with a slight downward request.

The horse can breathe, relax, become aware of you, and follow your cues. *Lowering the Head* builds and strengthens the connection between you both. It is also an incredibly practical exercise to instill: haltering, bridling, administering medication, and general handling are made much easier with a horse that comfortably and willingly lowers his head when asked (especially a very tall horse!)

The head should not be so low that the nose is almost touching the ground, but about 10 inches below the withers—about level with the chest. When the head is too low, the horse will often tune you out. Needless to say, tying the head into this position is counterproductive; the horse needs to find and maintain the relaxed position from your cues. Likewise, a horse that has only learned to *Lower the Head* as a way of avoiding pressure is not necessarily really relaxed and comfortable in that posture.

Start by teaching the horse to *Lower the Head* in a quiet, relaxed situation. Once learned, you can remind the horse to bring the head down whenever he gets frightened and throws his head up. In addition, becoming comfortable with the body language, lead, and *Wand* cues for *Lowering the Head* will be important as you progress with your horse through the Dance Steps (*Leading Exercises,* p. 132) and the *Playground for Higher Learning* (p. 175).

5.9 Asking for the horse's head to lower while walking forward is often easier than doing it at a standstill, at first. Gently stroke ("milk") the lead downward with one hand while drawing the horse's attention down with the *Wand* to help encourage a lower head carriage.

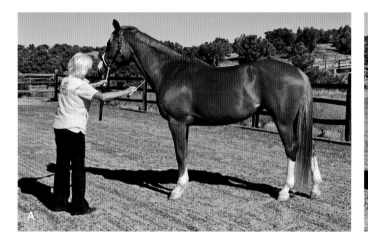
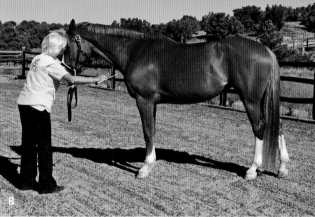

5.10 A & B Using the stroking ("milking") motion on the lead while stroking downward on the underside of the horse's neck to the chest with the *Wand* is another gentle, easy way to *Lower the Head*.

How to Use It

There are three different ways you can ask a horse to lower his head. You need a well-fitted halter, a *Zephyr* lead, and a *Wand*.

In Motion

Introduce the idea of *Lowering the Head* while in motion, at the walk (fig. 5.9). Attach the lead line to the side of the halter (see p. 71). Fold your body forward slightly and slide your hand down the lead while asking the horse to *Lower the Head*. Use the *Wand* to gently stroke the horse's nostrils, holding it so it points forward and downward. The horse will follow the *Wand*. For many horses, encouraging this posture while in movement is easier than when standing still, initially.

Stationary

While standing still, stroke the underside of the horse's neck, his chest, and all the way down his front legs to the ground with the *Wand* while gently stroking ("milking") the lead downward (figs. 5.10 A & B). The motion of the *Wand* grounds the horse and brings his awareness down while the stroking of the line invites the horse to lower his head from a signal on the halter.

Using TTouch

Another possibility for *Lowering the Head* is to place one hand on the nosepiece of the halter and the other on the crest of the horse's neck, just behind the poll. With light pressure on the halter and *Clouded Leopard TTouches* on the neck (see p. 90 in chapter 6 for instructions as to how to do them), you can ask the horse to lower his head. You can also ask him to lower his head while you are in the saddle. Simply reach forward and use *Clouded Leopard TTouches* (p. 90) on the crest of the neck, just behind the poll.

It is important to note that this exercise is not about the horse lowering his head to pressure. Ideally, your horse will lower his head as he releases and relaxes through the poll and neck, reducing tension through the entire topline. There are some horses that are so locked through the poll that they cannot relax when there is even a *hint* of pressure on the head. This can be especially true for a horse being reeducated. In this case, you might have to "think outside the box" and begin with *TTouch* bodywork (p. 78) to start to release the horse's body before coming back to this exercise and showing him that it is possible to *Lower the Head* and let go.

Taming the Tiger

Too often, horses are not really taught how to tie or be patient in a thoughtful way that does not just leave them to "figure it out." The *Taming the Tiger*

Pressure vs. Release— Recognizing the Opposition Reflex

Teaching a horse to lower his head to a signal is not new, nor is it unique; however, *how* you do it with the Tellington Method is quite different from the norm. While most methods teach that the horse must yield to a steady pressure before it is released, the Tellington Method acknowledges that most beings instinctually react with the *opposition reflex* (push against a push, pull against a pull). Instead of holding a pressure and waiting for the horse to release out of discomfort, we know that horses will generally "give" at the release of pressure. It is for this reason that we use a stroking of the lead to encourage *Lowering the Head* rather than steady pressure.

Horses will certainly learn that the only way to avoid pressure is to yield; however, it does not necessarily mean that they are relaxed during the process. When asking a horse to do anything, whether bringing the head down, picking up a foot, or moving over, using the idea of "Ask, release, then pause," will generally result in the horse responding quietly and calmly without the need to increase pressure.

5.11 *Taming the Tiger* is a logical, quiet way to teach horses about containment without causing panic or anxiety.

exercise teaches the horse self-control, patience, and how to stand quietly, and prepares the horse for being tied (fig. 5.11). These skills are important for mounting and to ensure cooperation under saddle. This exercise also provides the handler with a good idea of where the horse is in terms of his development. As you and your horse go through more of the Tellington Method exercises, *Taming the Tiger* becomes easier, reflecting his increased level of self-control.

Acting as a "sliding cross-tie," *Taming the Tiger* is a very useful exercise for retraining difficult horses as it teaches them to accept boundaries without panicking and to actively participate in their surroundings because they can still move their head—for example, during a grooming session or when being tacked up (fig. 5.12).

Taming the Tiger requires a *Wand*, a *Zephyr* lead, a 15-foot-long rope (a long line or driving rein works well for this), a ring or carabiner, and a safe place to tie the horse with a corner and solid wall behind the horse. It is ideal to have a space that is not too small, so you have room to give the horse distance, but not so big that there are not parameters around him. The horse should not be able to back up more than 6 feet.

5.12 *Taming the Tiger* has one "fixed lead" and one "sliding lead," allowing you to set clear parameters of containment for your horse. It is a great exercise for teaching the horse how to safely tie, stand in cross-ties, and practice patience and boundaries.

How to Use It

Attach the *Zephyr* lead (or the chain lead) to the side of the halter closest to you and place the horse parallel to the fence or wall, next to a stable ring or carabiner (figs. 5.13 A–C).

Now take a 15-foot-long rope and thread it through the halter ring under the horse's chin, through the ring or carabiner attached to the fence or wall, and tie it to the opposite side ring of the halter with a safety or "quick-release" knot (figs. 5.14 A–C). Tie the knot to the top back corner of the halter hardware, so when there is pressure, the hardware does not push into the horse's face. Note: If you are dealing with a horse that is claustrophobic, don't take the rope through the ring under the chin—just slide it under the jowl piece of the halter. If your halter does not have a vertical ring for chin hardware, you can use a carabiner as a handy modification. It is very important that the rope can slide easily through the halter and ring or carabiner, and does not get caught up.

You now have the rope as well as the lead line in your hand. (When you are first learning to use this exercise, it can be helpful to have a rope and lead of different colors.) Mentally note that the lead will bring the horse toward you, and the rope will take the horse toward the wall.

You can separate the rope and the lead line with your index finger when holding both in one hand so you can use the other hand to stroke the horse with the *Wand*, add *TTouches* (see p. 78), or bring him back into position if he has moved. The *Wand* is a very important tool in this exercise and can be used to stroke the legs, ground the horse, and give signals. Note: If the horse pulls back, immediately release the pressure. (It can be helpful to use the *Dingo* leading position, which I teach you on p. 148, to ask him to step forward again, and sometimes it is easier to hold the rope and the lead line in separate hands to make it simpler to take or release one or the other when you need to turn the horse's head.)

Use *Taming the Tiger* to ask your horse to move forward a step or two, halt and stand, or back one or two steps at a time, quietly. You can keep yourself at a safe distance and allow the horse to move as asked while being *contained* rather than *restrained*. It is important not to keep the horse too close to the wall or fence, or crowd the horse yourself. Some of the most important lessons in *Taming the Tiger* are in the moments you allow the horse to just stand quietly.

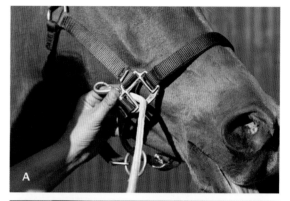

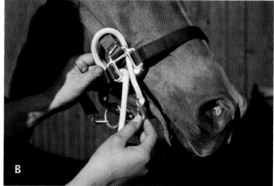

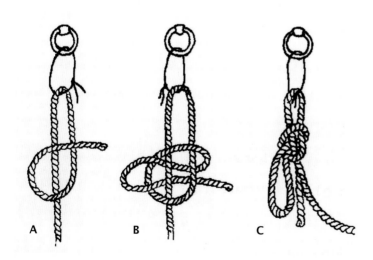

5.14 A–C Knowing how to tie an effective quick release knot is an invaluable tool for any horse person. It is the safest way to tie a horse or attach long lines or leads to him, and it allows for a quick release should the lines get tangled or the horse spooks.

5.13 A–C How to attach the lead: Take the *Zephyr* lead through the side hardware on the halter, from the outside in, and point it up (A). Loop the *Zephyr* lead around the front of the cheek piece of the halter and back through the hardware, this time coming from the inside out (B). Twist the lead so there is no coil the horse could accidentally step into if he should drop his head, and connect the lead clip to the loop on the *Zephyr* lead.

The Story of Parytet

I met the 13-year old Arabian stallion Parytet in Italy. He was part of the Italian endurance team and had competed at the World Championships in Kentucky in 2010. Nobody could touch his ears or poll to bridle him—the headstall had to be taken apart every time. The snaffle was set very low in his mouth and kept sliding around, which in my opinion added to the horse's high head carriage (figs. 5.15 A & B).

Besides having to take the bridle apart each time the stallion was bridled there were two other issues.

1 Parytet could not be rated at the trot. He had one speed and that was extremely fast. However, there were times in competition when it would have been useful to be able to adjust his speed—in rough terrain, for example, or to give his rider a break.

2 Because the stallion was head shy, he did not trot well in-hand for the veterinarians and judges at the end of an endurance race. How the horse trots out in-hand can make a significant difference in the impression given to the judges.

So I had three goals for the horse in a three-day clinic: deal with his head shyness, find a way to rate his speed at the trot, and develop a better way of going in-hand. In order to achieve these, I worked with Parytet and

5.15 A–O In just three days, with the combination of *TTouch, Chest Line Driving, Homing Pigeon,* and riding with the *Lindell Sidepull* and *Balance Rein* over *Ground Poles,* Parytet was transformed.

his team through many of the exercises on the Checklist (p. 285), which is the standard for starting young horses with the Tellington Method. The results were spectacular.

On Day One, we treated his whole body to *TTouches* (p. 78) because he was very tight. I freed up his tail in order to activate the cranial sacral fluid and give the horse a better sense of his body (fig. 5.15 C). Parytet's hind leg movements were very limited due to his tight muscles, but five minutes of gentle *Hind Leg Circles* (p. 109) began to release the tightness and gain the horse's trust (fig. 5.15 D). I was able to raise his back, which further released tight muscles and allowed the stallion to lower and lengthen his neck (fig. 5.15 E).

On Day Two, we concentrated on *Lowering the Head* (p. 65) to free up the very tight underside of his neck. Increased trust allowed me

to use *TTouches* along his crest and behind his ears where he had previously resisted contact. Parytet also allowed me to do *Mane Slides* (p. 117) on his forelock, and I was able to slip the *Lindell Sidepull* (p. 275) over his ears, both of which would have been impossible when he first arrived at the clinic (figs. 5.15 F–I).

Then we did *Chest Line Driving* (p. 213) with a heart monitor around his girth, which was a huge learning experience for Parytet. I stroked his hindquarter with the *Wand* in my right hand while I moved the rope up and down, asking him to stand still until given the signal, "And waaaallllk," paired with a light flip of the driving line against his side. At first we used two handlers at his head in *Homing Pigeon* (p. 143) to give him boundaries and confidence (fig. 5.15 J). We went forward with the two lines crossed over the horse's back at first, so he had more chance to get used to my movement behind and the feeling of the ropes sliding on his hind end (fig. 5.15 K). The person driving should always walk to one side so the horse can easily see you and you can see what the horses is thinking as you begin

to expect him to listen to your directions rather than those of the handlers. *Chest Line Driving* gives a horse confidence and connection through the whole body without restricting his head. This increases balance and trust dramatically (fig. 5.15 L).

On the third day we tried the *Lindell Sidepull* (p. 275) and the *Balance Rein* (p. 275) with work in the saddle. They helped Parytet relax his neck and lower his head when ridden. When using the *Balance Rein*, I prefer to hold the sidepull or bridle reins in each hand, hooking the middle finger of my outside hand through the *Balance Rein* to use when needed to slow the horse (fig. 5.15 M). The stallion went beautifully as I reached back behind the saddle with one hand to do light *TTouches* to bring awareness to his hindquarters. *Ground Poles* (p. 187) encouraged him to lower his head further and focus, which helped develop his balance (fig. 5.15 N).

We adjusted his rider's seat, and much to the elated 65-year-old's surprise, he was now able to regulate the stallion's trot and canter with the help of the *Balance Rein*, which he had never been able to do before. Parytet was supple and connected through the body—no more ewe-neck—with a free-swinging gait (fig. 5.15 O). The stallion was also completely comfortable having his head TTouched and bridled by Sunday and confident trotting beside his rider on a long lead.

Parytet's rider had just brought his horse to the clinic hoping to solve the bridling problem. He had given up on solving the problems under saddle—so his surprise was immense! Thanks to the various components of the Tellington Method used on him, addressing Parytet's reluctance to have his ears touched started a series of physical changes that led to a vast improvement in his overall behavior—and his comfort, too.

CHAPTER 6

The Tellington TTouches

Bodywork—Releasing Tension and Building Trust

The Tellington *TTouches* are a versatile, effective tool to incorporate at any point in your horse's education—and beyond. By bringing awareness and relaxation to his body, you help develop his trust in you as the handler. The *TTouches* also encourage him to be able to think, move, and remain in balance.

The *TTouches* listed in this chapter do not need to be used all at once, every time, or in a particular order. Ideally, a horse will work to become completely accepting and happy about all of them, but be assured that not mastering one does not mean you cannot continue progressing with others. Tellington *TTouch bodywork* can be incorporated as you move on with *Leading Exercises* and work under saddle in the chapters ahead (pp. 132 and 241), or it can complement the exercises you began with in the last chapter (p. 65), when you go back and check in on your horse's progress. In addition, you'll find that each *TTouch* has certain listed "effects"—for example, the *Clouded Leopard TTouch* helps relieve a sore back and tight muscles. Your *Body Exploration* from chapter 5 and your growing understanding of your horse's progress in training, or lack thereof, should help you determine which *TTouch* effects will be the most helpful, and when.

Here are a few specific recommendations, depending on your horse's stage of training:

FOAL OR WEANLING

1 With young foals, you will probably find that they are most receptive to any of the *Sliding TTouches* initially (p. 95).

2 The *Zebra* (p. 96) and *Troika* (p. 97) are wonderful ways to make mindful contact with foals, especially when they are shedding their baby coats.

3 Once your foal enjoys contact, introduce *Tarantula Pulling the Plow* (p. 99) and *Lick of the Cow's Tongue* (p. 95).

4 From there, move on to very short sessions of *Circular TTouches* (p. 89)—only one or two—before you pause and give him a moment. Always plan to stop before he "tells" you to stop.

5 *Ear TTouches* (p. 115) and *Mane Slides*, working from the withers to the ears (p. 117) are an excellent way to help encourage a relaxed poll and familiarize the foal with being handled around potentially sensitive areas.

6 *Mouth Work* (p. 126) should be done very mindfully in short sessions. It can, somewhat counter-intuitively, be very helpful for foals that are "mouthy" or nip.

7 Very short sessions of *Tail Slides* (p. 120) and *Leg Circles* (p. 106) can also be introduced. Work up to them and only ask for moments—as opposed to minutes. *Leg Circles* are a great way to help prepare your foal for a low-stress trimming experience. With smaller legs you may find it easier to only use one hand to support the leg rather than both hands.

8 If your foal seems very sensitive down his legs, go back to stroking with the *Wand* (p. 62) and introduce *Python Lifts* (p. 101) to reduce "snatching up" of the legs and encourage a sense of groundedness and body awareness.

UNSTARTED THREE- OR FOUR-YEAR-OLD

1 Depending on his previous level of handling, a youngster may or may not be comfortable standing for an extended period of bodywork. The *Zebra* (p. 96), *Troika* (p. 97), and *Tarantula Pulling the Plow* (p. 99) are great starting points. Do not plan to do all of these at once. Pick and choose a couple to do each session, and gauge which are most appealing to the individual horse. Taking a few minutes to do some of these *Sliding TTouches* are a nice way to begin a training session and give your horse a sense of his body.

2 While your young horse may not be able to stand for a complete *TTouch bodywork* session at first (patience is a learned skill after all), you should be able to add each *TTouch* into your other lessons when there are quiet moments before, during, and after. Ideally, your horse will learn to enjoy all of the *TTouches*, even though not necessarily in one session, before you ever sit on his back. Keep track of his progress with your Checklist (p. 285).

By bringing awareness and relaxation to the horse's body, you help develop his trust in you as the handler.

3 *Ear, Nostril,* and *Mouth TTouches* (pp. 115, 125, 126), as well as *Mane Slides* (p. 117), are very helpful to prepare your horse for being bridled—with and without a bit—and can encourage relaxation in the poll and jaw.

4 The variety of *Tail TTouches* (p. 120) and *Leg Circles* (p. 106) are invaluable to the young horse for balance, proprioception (awareness of the position and movement of his body), and overall acceptance and ease of handling. These are important to practice regularly so your horse is familiar and comfortable with them.

5 *Belly* and *Back Lifts* (pp. 111 and 112) are very important for a horse to experience before he wears a saddle and carries the weight of a rider. Ideally, your horse will be completely comfortable with both exercises before you introduce a surcingle or girth.

REEDUCATING THE MATURE HORSE

1 A more mature horse, depending on his reasons for being restarted, may or may not enjoy longer sessions of bodywork. As with a younger horse, the *Sliding TTouches,* such as *Zebra* (p. 96) and *Troika* (p. 97), are often good places to start.

2 As your horse becomes more relaxed with what you are doing, incorporate any number of the *Circular TTouches* (p. 89) and other *Lifts* and *Slides* (p. 117), noting which ones seem to encourage the most relaxation and perceived enjoyment.

3 Many older horses with "issues" have deeply engrained tension patterns that can be direct causes of complex or unwanted behavior. Any of the *TTouches* will help alleviate these tensions patterns, but *Extremity TTouches* (p. 105), such as *Ear, Nostril, Mouth, Hair, Tail,* and *Legs* will be especially effective in encouraging relaxation throughout the body.

4 When a horse is very tight in the body, consider using the *Jellyfish Jiggle* (p. 101) on large areas of muscle, as well as *Lick of the Cow's Tongue* (p. 95). Then introduce *Belly* and *Back Lifts* to bring awareness to the topline and begin to release postural habits (pp. 111 and 112).

5 As with any age horse, do not feel obligated to do as many different techniques as possible in one session. Simply add in *TTouches* as you can, using your horse's favorites to help support relaxation during new lessons on the ground and under saddle.

With the Horse, Not *to* Him

As the handler and guide, it is useful to practice these techniques on a number of horses so you are comfortable with their technical aspects. Young horses may only have the patience to stand still for a few moments at first, so do what you can—as your horse is able. Pay attention to which specific *TTouches* your horse seems to enjoy the most and start there the next time. Which Tellington *TTouch* creates the most relaxation? Remember, you are doing this *with* the horse, not just *to* him.

The Collection of TTouches

TTouch is a form of bodywork, but it is *not* massage (fig. 6.1). *TTouch* seeks to work with the horse's entire nervous system and fasciae at the cellular level rather than directly influencing the muscles. The non-invasive, gentle nature of *TTouch* means that it can be used in even the most sensitive of areas without creating more bracing or defensiveness and has the effect of promoting an overall level of trust.

There are dozens of different *TTouches*, depending on the way your hand is used and how the movement is applied. These *TTouches* are organized into three different groups, each with their own unique characteristics and applications (fig. 6.2). Note: If you wish for even more detail on the *TTouches* and how to use them, see my book *The Ultimate Horse Behavior and Training Book*.

Circular TTouches

The gentle *Circular TTouches* consisting of 1¼ circles reduce stress and fear, promote relaxation, and elevate trust, self-assurance, and the ability to learn. Your fingers or hand do not slide across the tissue but gently move the tissue itself.

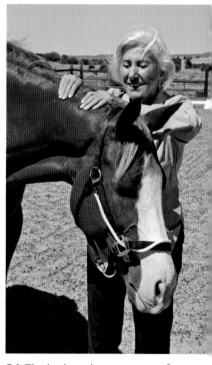

6.1 The bodywork component of the Tellington Method is widely known as *TTouch*. These gentle, mindful, and varied techniques each have their own purpose and influence various parts of the body in different ways.

CIRCULAR TTOUCHES (p. 89)	SLIDE AND LIFT TOUCHES (p. 95)	EXTREMITY TTOUCHES (p. 105)
Clouded Leopard TTouch (p. 90) Lying Leopard TTouch (p. 91) Abalone TTouch (p. 92) Raccoon TTouch (p. 94)	Lick of the Cow's Tongue TTouch (p. 95) Zebra TTouch (p. 96) Troika TTouch (p. 97) Tarantula Pulling the Plow TTouch (p. 99) Jellyfish Jiggle TTouch (p. 101) Python Lift TTouch (p. 101) Coiled Python TTouch (p. 105)	Front Leg Circles (p. 106) Hind Leg Circles (p. 109) Belly Lift (p. 111) Back Lift (p. 112) Ear TTouch (p. 115) Mane Slides (p. 117) Tail TTouches (p. 118) Pelvic Tilt (p. 124)

6.2 The collection of *TTouches.*

Pieces of the Puzzle

At the heart of the Tellington *TTouch* is the recognition of *cellular intelligence.* In my quest to understand the remarkable effects of *TTouch bodywork,* I have explored the fields of quantum science and spirituality. Four books have provided keys to my understanding:

Man on His Nature by Nobel Laureate Sir Charles Sherrington (Cambridge University Press, 1951) was my first introduction to cellular intelligence with the premise that "every cell in the body knows its function in the body."

Spontaneous Evolution by Bruce Lipton and Steve Bhaerman (Hay House, 2010) discusses the brilliant and cooperative nature of cells and their process of communication.

The Code of Authentic Living: Cellular Wisdom by Joan C. King (Word Keepers, 2009) opens with the premise that "every cell is a genius."

The Book of Ho'oponopono by Luc Bodin, MD, Nathalie Bodin Lamboy, and Jean Graciet (Destiny Books, 2016) explains the science behind the Hawaiian "prayer of forgiveness." In this book, the use of the phrase the "Divine Spark" gave me a major piece of the puzzle that would help explain my success with TTouch. There is "Source Energy" that we can impact in every cell!

Recognizing the "Divine Spark" in every horse (and rider/handler) connects us to cellular intelligence and to the creative Source Energies at work throughout the universe.

6.3 There are three groups of *TTouches*. Here I demonstrate an *Extremity TTouch*.

Slide and Lift TTouches

These *TTouches* activate circulation, release tension, and increase the horse's body awareness. Your hands slide across the tissue or gently lift and release the tissue in specific ways.

Extremity TTouches

The names of these *TTouches* refer to the different parts of the body that you mindfully work to enhance trust, performance, and well-being (fig. 6.3).

The Nine Components of TTouch

The nine components of *TTouch* are ways in which you can influence how each *TTouch* feels to the horse and how effective it is (fig. 6.4). When your horse does not seem to respond to the *TTouches*, check in to see if you can adjust any of these components. In most cases, a change in pressure, use of the hand, or speed will greatly affect how much a horse seems to enjoy a *TTouch*. One of the most beautiful things about these techniques is that they allow for flexibility and recognition of the different needs and preferences of individual horses and help handlers become better at reading their horses.

1. The Basic TTouch Circle

As already noted, the shape in which you make the *Circular TTouches*

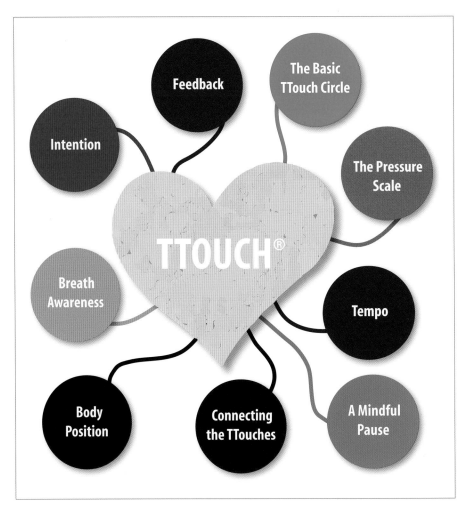

6.4 The nine components of *TTouch* in the form of a mind map.

(p. 89) is important. Imagine the face of a clock on your skin. Start with your fingertips at six o'clock, wherever the lowest point of gravity is; move the skin clockwise, passing six o'clock again and continuing to nine o'clock. This adds up to a full circle-and-a-quarter, and it creates a lifting sensation at the start and the end of the *TTouch* (fig. 6.4). Try this on your own arm and notice how it feels compared to ending or starting without a lift. Most people find that the latter feels harder and perhaps less complete.

The *Circular TTouches* are generally done clockwise. When your horse does not seem to enjoy a *Circular TTouch*, try going counterclockwise, adjust the pressure or speed, or simply change to a different *TTouch*.

2. The Pressure Scale

The pressure of the *TTouches* is measured on a scale of numbers 1 through 5. Which pressure you use depends on what part of the horse's body you are working on, how sensitive the horse is, what his muscle tone is like, and whether you are in an area of tension or soreness. Try different pressures until you find the right one. For most horses I would use Pressure 3 on most of the body. Numbers 2 and 3 pressures are suitable to build trust and strengthen physical, mental, and emotional balance. In the case of pain or inflammation, a lighter *TTouch* is best, and on the opposite end of the spectrum, a number 5 pressure may be used on extremely muscled horses or in areas where the skin is very taut and more pressure is required to avoid sliding across the tissue.

6.5 The basic *TTouch* 1¼ circle, as visualized on the face of a clock.

If you are wondering how such light pressure as 1 through 3 can be effective, remember that you are influencing the cells, not the muscles directly (see sidebar, p. 82). By using a light pressure you actually encourage the nervous system to pay more attention than you might with really deep tissue work.

To get an idea of what the pressures feel like, try it on yourself, using a number 1 pressure, the lightest contact, where you apply just enough pressure to move the skin without your fingers sliding over the skin, and a number 3 pressure, which I recommend for most horses:

Pressure 1: Supporting your right elbow with your left hand, anchor your right thumb on your right cheek, and using the middle finger of your right hand, move the delicate skin just below your eye as lightly as possible in a 1¼ circle. Don't let your fingers slide over the skin; move the skin underneath your fingertip. You will feel as though you have to support the weight of your fingers as you make the circle rather than like you are allowing them to rest. Try a few circles using the same pressure on your arm and notice how much of an indentation you can see. You will notice that the size of the circle with a Pressure 1 is quite small and that the tissue does not move as much as it will with a higher pressure.

When to use Pressure 1: Pressure 1 would typically be used around very sensitive parts of the horse's body. Horses that are very tight in the poll or sensitive about their ears may appreciate a Pressure 1 *TTouch*. This is also a very good pressure to use around an injury site to help increase circulation and promote healing.

Pressure 3: You can experience the number 3 pressure by going back to the same place under your eye and making a circle with just enough pressure so you can feel your cheekbone, but light enough so it feels comfortable and safe—essentially the weight of your fingers. Once again, anchor your thumb on your cheek for support, and allow your fingers to be curved. On your arm, apply a number 1 pressure again, and then number 3 pressure, and compare the two. Note the difference. A number 2 pressure is right in the middle, and numbers 4 and 5 intensify what you can see and feel with 3.

When to use Pressure 3: Pressure 3 is typically used on larger parts of the horse's body, along large muscle masses, or when using a flat-hand *TTouch*, such as the *Abalone TTouch* (p. 92), where the pressure is diffused slightly.

3. Tempo

The tempo of the *TTouch* circle varies between one and three seconds. To activate and energize the horse's body, use faster circles; to relax and calm, slow down the circles. When using *TTouch* on acute injuries, one-second *TTouches* can be very effective to prevent swelling and reduce pain.

4. A Mindful Pause

A few *TTouches* are always followed by a mindful pause that allows the horse's body to integrate the information. The original intention of this component was P.A.W.S. (Pause Allows Wondrous Stillness) and an easy way to

> **Allowing for a moment without any input makes the information more powerful.**

TTouch Success Secret

Touch supports the horse's self-confidence by helping him feel more comfortable in his body. When a horse is not holding excessive tension through the body, he is usually in better balance and feels safer. This helps override his flight instinct in unusual situations. Once you are able to eliminate one of your horse's fears, his fear in other situations will be reduced dramatically. This enhanced confidence tends to allow a horse to act and think instead of reflexively reacting to new situations. There are a lot of different definitions for intelligence, but my favorite in connection with horses states that intelligence is the ability to adapt to new situations.

6.6 Ensuring that you are in a comfortable position while doing *TTouches* will enhance effectiveness and make the experience more enjoyable for you.

understand it is to think about music. Unless there are pauses between the notes, music is just noise. Allowing for a moment without any input makes the information more powerful.

5. Connecting the TTouches

The *Circular TTouches* are typically done in connected lines along the horse's body. After each circle-and-a-quarter, slide your hand along to the next spot of the body and repeat. This assures that you are covering the whole horse, giving the animal a sense of connection and body awareness. Note that in the cases of injury or pain, *TTouches* are not connected and are done in a more random pattern with your hand coming off the horse's body in between each point of contact.

6. Body Position

If you hold tension in one joint in your body, it will affect the rest of your joints. This means it is very important to find a position that is comfortable for you and allows you to use the *TTouches* in a relaxed manner (fig. 6.6). Adjust the angle of your hand or body so that you make contact with your horse in a way that does not cause you to feel awkward or create holding

6.7 Standing quietly with a lowered head, soft eye, and relaxed ears are clear indicators that a horse is enjoying himself.

patterns. Checking that you can allow your wrist to be straight is very important.

If your horse is comfortable with human contact, have both hands on him when applying *TTouches*: One hand applies the *TTouches* while the other hand supports the sensation of connection and improves your balance. Allow all the joints of your fingers to take part in the circular movement. Notice that your back is released and that you are not locked in your leg joints or jaw. Stay in your own balance by keeping your feet about hip-width apart. Make sure your knees stay soft and keep your weight over the balls of your feet. This also allows you to quickly move into any direction, should the need arise.

7. Breath Awareness

Aware breathing helps to keep you focused and calm. It also relaxes your entire body. By placing awareness into your breath, the horse and handler stay in sync. Consciously exhaling when working with a nervous or "frozen" horse can encourage him to take a breath and help him relax.

Inhale through your nose and slowly exhale through your mouth as if you are blowing out a candle. Don't make noise while exhaling and don't blow. Notice if you can allow the breath to expand through your entire torso or if you tend to breathe in your chest.

8. Intention

What would the ideal horse look like? How would he behave? What would be the perfect training level or health status? How would the perfect connection between you feel? Imagine your horse exactly how you want him to be every day, when you are brushing, leading, working over obstacles, or riding. Do this even when you are not with your horse.

Remember what we talked about early in this book: "Change your mind, change your horse." Visualizing the perfection in your horse is a powerful tool that allows you to stay in the present and avoid negativity and fear.

9. Feedback

Since horses cannot talk, you have to watch for the small signs they give with their bodies. Revisit the Fear and Trust Responses I listed in the section on *Body Exploration* in chapter 5 (p. 56). These responses will help you determine whether your horse is uncomfortable or comfortable with where and how you are using the *TTouches* (fig. 6.7). Read these responses and use them to help you know when to change the area you are working on, use a different *TTouch*, or adjust the speed or pressure to gain the horse's trust.

Circular TTouches

Many of the *Circular TTouches* not only have a pleasant physical effect but are also important because they help build trust and affect the communication of the body's cells (fig. 6.8). Young horses, as well as horses that have had bad experiences, have to learn to trust and feel safe. In my experience horses that are especially distrustful or aloof will very quickly come around

---

TTouch with the Back of Your Hand

If you find *Circular TTouches* with the inside of your hand uncomfortable, whether it is how you are oriented to the horse or because of specific physical abilities, you may prefer the *Chimp TTouch:* Keep your hand softly curled, folding your fingers toward your palm. You can now make circles with the flat surface of your fingers, between the second and third phalange, while keeping the wrist straight, but not tight.

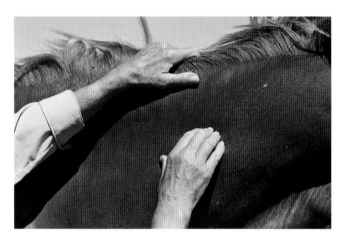

6.8 The *Circular TTouches* gently move the skin and tissue in a mindful, non-habitual way.

after experiencing the *Circular TTouches* and change their perception of people. Young horses will enjoy spending time with you and look forward to the contact. The connection that is established through *TTouch* is very different than one that is formed through dominance. Your horse will willingly give his best because he trusts you and enjoys a cooperative partnership.

Try the following *Circular TTouches* and see which are most effective for your horse.

Clouded Leopard TTouch

The *Clouded Leopard TTouch* is the "hallmark" *TTouch*. You use the tips of your fingers with a cupped hand in a smooth, circle-and-a-quarter motion (figs. 6.9 A & B). The thumb acts as an anchor and the heel of the hand does not rest on the horse as you move the tissue with your fingertips, without sliding across the skin. Allowing movement through all the joints in your hand will make this *TTouch* more fluid and effective.

6.9 A & B Clouded Leopard TTouch.

The Effect

The *Clouded Leopard TTouch* strengthens the horse's confidence, which is very important in young horses or those who need to be retrained. More confidence equals less fear, which allows horses to think and *act* rather than simply *react* to situations. It increases the horse's ability to learn, and he becomes more willing to cooperate. This *TTouch* creates a base of trusting cooperation.

Where to Use It

This *TTouch* has a focused feel that allows you to work in each place very specifically.

The *Clouded Leopard TTouch* is suitable for the upper neck and back all the way to the croup. It helps a sore back and tight muscles and gives the horse a new sense of his body. On the forehead, it promotes trust, and on the legs this *TTouch* helps the horse stay grounded, relaxed, and coordinated.

Lying Leopard TTouch

This *Circular TTouch* is done just like the *Clouded Leopard TTouch* but with a flatter hand, so more of your fingers are used to move the skin and the effect is more "diffused" (figs. 6.10 A & B). Using more of your hand means that

6.10 A & B *Lying Leopard TTouch.*

Connected TTouches

To give the horse a complete sense of his body, you can connect the *TTouches* by not lifting your hand after completing the circle-and-a-quarter but instead sliding it 2 to 3 inches in one direction and immediately starting the next circle-and-a-quarter. Use the *Connected TTouches* in parallel lines from front end to hind end, and they will also help your horse feel the connection between his head and tail.

you will be moving more tissue in a slightly less targeted way. The gentle connection with the whole of your fingers creates more warmth and contact with the skin. The thumb remains anchored and the heel of the hand does not rest on the horse.

The Effect

Through a larger area of contact, this *TTouch* warms, calms, and relaxes. It is suitable for nervous or tense horses, and helpful for horses that are afraid of the saddle or cinchy. The *Lying Leopard TTouch* reduces pain in acute injuries and can reduce swelling.

Where to Use It

Use this *TTouch* on the horse's face and jowls, the upper neck, shoulder, and barrel, including the horse's flanks. This is also a useful *TTouch* on the legs as it will teach your horse to stand quietly and improve his sense of connection to his legs.

Abalone TTouch

The *Abalone TTouch* is another *Circular TTouch* where the entire hand is softly touching the horse's body as you move the skin and tissue (figs. 6.11 A & B). The center of your hand is the center of the circle-and-a-quarter.

The Effect

This *TTouch*, when used over the entire back, is useful for preparing the young horse to carry the saddle. The even pressure prepares the horse for the girth and helps a cinchy horse to relax his tensed muscles and not be bothered by the pressure of the girth. The *Abalone TTouch* also encourages a horse to breathe more deeply.

Where to Use It

Use the *Abalone TTouch* on all heavily muscled body parts, such as the shoulders, croup, belly, and the inside of the thighs. It is a wonderful *TTouch* to use along the back and ribs to encourage a deeper breathing pattern. This *TTouch* can also be very useful when asking the horse to lower his head and relax his neck and back muscles (see p. 65).

6.11 A & B *Abalone TTouch.*

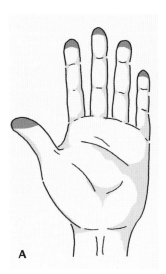

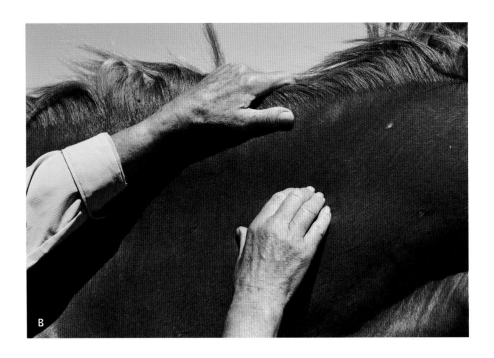

6.12 A & B *Raccoon TTouch.*

Raccoon TTouch

This is the lightest of all the *Circular TTouches* and is used with just the fingertips and very little pressure (figs. 6.12 A & B). The hand is held in the same way as when using the *Clouded Leopard TTouch*, but there is more of an arch through the hand. It is the easiest *TTouch* to use with a Pressure 1.

The Effect

Use the *Raccoon TTouch* to reduce swelling around wounds, to stimulate the healing process, and to promote circulation. *Raccoon TTouches* on the forehead build trust. Fearful or overly sensitive horses will calm down, fidgety horses will stand still, and horses that don't want to be caught will change their attitude toward people.

Where to Use It

The *Raccoon TTouch* is especially useful when working with the horse's face and around his eyes. Horses that are very tight in the poll often appreciate very light *Raccoon TTouches* all around the occipital joint and around the temporomandibular joint (TMJ). It is also recommended on the coronary band and around wounds.

Slide and Lift TTouches

The *Slide and Lift TTouches* are mindfully applied with one or both hands with or across the direction of the hair. (When using the *Lick of the Cow's Tongue* (see below) or *Zebra TTouch* (p. 96) your hand is used in lines along the horse's body.) These *TTouches* differ from the *Circular TTouches* because you are not moving the skin over the muscle—instead, the fingers slide across the horse's hair. These *TTouches* activate the circulation, create more body awareness, and are an excellent way to introduce the idea of mindful contact.

Lick of the Cow's Tongue TTouch

The *Lick of the Cow's Tongue* is an important *TTouch* for young horses because it helps them to feel the connection between their belly and their back more clearly (figs. 6.13 A–C). This improved body awareness will make it easier for the horse to accept and respond to the rider's aids.

The Effect

The *Lick of the Cow's Tongue* prepares the horse for the rider's leg, the saddle, and the girth. Horses that are overly sensitive and ticklish to the girth or rider's leg can learn to accept touch in this area and to understand signals given by the rider. Difficult horses benefit from *Lick of the Cow's Tongue* because it increases their confidence and improves gaits, coordination, and balance.

How to Use It

Start on the side your horse prefers to be touched. (Your *Body Exploration* practice should have provided an idea of which this is.) Stand at your horse's shoulder, and angle yourself slightly toward his barrel. Place your inactive hand comfortably on the horse's body, usually the chest or shoulder, depending on the size of the horse.

6.13 A–C *Lick of the Cow's Tongue.*

Try out different positions to find the one where it is easiest for you to be in balance.

Place your active hand, the one farthest from the horse's head, across the midline of the horse's belly. Be sure to keep your body at the shoulder in case your horse objects to being touched here. Now pull your hand with a soft, gentle, regular stroke across the hair toward the horse's spine. Your hand will have to turn halfway up the belly so your fingers point toward the spine. Push your hand farther upward, stroke past the spine, and end the TTouch there. Continue this motion from the horse's elbow as far back toward his flank as he is comfortable. Keeping your body closer to his shoulder will keep you safer.

Try different pressures and speeds and work both sides of the horse equally. Breathe calmly and keep your knees soft without locking them while using the *Lick of the Cow's Tongue TTouch*. If you find your horse finds this TTouch is too intense with your fingers curved, you can also use your flat hand. With extremely sensitive horses, use a flat hand and combine it with a *Lying Leopard* or *Abalone TTouch*, or even start by using the back of your hand under the horse's belly.

Zebra TTouch
The *Zebra TTouch* is a great technique to use when you are first introducing your horse to *TTouches* (fig. 6.14). Moving across the hairs, many horses really enjoy the contact, and it allows you to check in with all parts of the horse's body.

The Effect
This *TTouch* is a simple, easily applied way to improve the horse's awareness of his body. It is a perfect *TTouch* to prepare a young horse to accept the saddle or for having his croup touched, which is useful when using the *Dingo* leading position where a tap of the *Wand* encourages the horse to step forward (see p. 148). Horses that freeze when they experience the motion of the saddle on their backs can be helped to relax and breathe with the *Zebra TTouch*.

How to Use It
This *TTouch*, which consists of strokes in a zebra-stripe pattern, is mostly used across the back, neck, or croup with one or both hands. Two-handed

6.14 *Zebra TTouch.*

Zebra TTouches cover a width of about 12 inches with a flowing, back-and-forth rhythm.

Start by standing at the shoulder of the horse and place the hand nearest his head on the point of his shoulder. With your other hand, gently curve your fingers together and place them on the side of his shoulder. Starting the movement from your feet, rather than just your arm, start to send the hand with the curved fingers away from you, across the hair, allowing your fingertips to open as you move. As you reach the top of the horse's back, start to bring your hand back toward you, and allow the fingers to close again. Repeat this motion from shoulder to back, checking in with your horse to make sure he is comfortable with where you are touching him.

Troika TTouch

As I explained in the sidebar on page 84, most of the *TTouches* have animal names, but this one was named in honor of my grandfather, who was a race-horse trainer for the Russian Czar Nicolas II. A troika is a three-horse carriage that was typically used in pre-revolutionary Russia. The *Troika TTouch* consists of circular, sliding, and scratching movements over the skin.

6.15 *Troika TTouch.*

6.16 A–C *Tarantula Pulling the Plow.*

The Effect

Similar in effect to the *Zebra TTouch,* the *Troika* offers you an additional opportunity to make a first contact with a shy horse. It is a *TTouch* that promotes well-being and trust. The horse is already familiar with the scratching sensation you use from friendly mutual grooming with other horses. Horses that have lost their trust in humans and show no interest in connection will discover that contact with us is pleasurable.

How to Use It

Using the outside of the thumb, open and close your four fingers while moving them in circles over the hair at the same time. Sometimes it is useful to imagine that you are tracing a large, looping "@" symbol. The thumb and fingers meet at the end of the circle, which creates a small fold in the horse's skin. Continue in a rhythmical motion, finding areas where the horse enjoys the circular scratch, such as the withers and croup. For variety, you can move your fingers in larger circles, which will be more calming and improve circulation.

You can use the *Troika TTouch* on the entire body, especially itchy areas that are difficult for the horse to reach himself, such as under the belly, on the forehead, or behind the ears.

Tarantula Pulling the Plow TTouch

This *TTouch* was named after a giant, gentle California tarantula that lived in my office for a while. It is a nice way to connect a horse through his body and offers a non-invasive way to release tension in very tight, sensitive-skinned horses (figs. 6.16 A–C).

The Effect

This *TTouch* eliminates fear and builds trust. It builds a bridge for horses that are shy or don't like to be touched or groomed. It can help to make initial contact with a young horse or with one that is "blocked" toward people. *Tarantula Pulling the Plow* can give a horse new awareness in his body, improves circulation, and when used on the legs, allows horses to feel the ground under their feet, which calms nervous horses or those that startle easily. The *Tarantula Pulling the Plow TTouch* can also be used on itchy areas without irritating the skin.

How to Use It

Place both hands on the horse's rump, holding your fingers slightly curved. Let your thumb rest on the skin and keep your wrists straight so they do not touch the horse. It is best to start this *TTouch* with just one hand by letting your index and middle finger walk across the skin in small steps, making sure to go *with* the growth of the hair, not against it. The other fingers simply follow, and the thumb is pulled along as a "plow." You can use *Tarantula Pulling the Plow* with just one or both hands.

6.17 The *Jellyfish Jiggle*.

The *Tarantula Pulling the Plow TTouch* is great on the horse's midsection between the girth area and flank, as well as the neck and shoulder, and down the legs. You can string the TTouches together, starting on the horse's shoulder, moving up to the withers, then going down the leg all the way to the hoof. It is also helpful to use the *Tarantula Pulling the Plow* in long lines parallel to the horse's spine.

Jellyfish Jiggle TTouch

The wavelike motion of the *Jellyfish Jiggle TTouch* reminds one of the swimming motion of jellyfish as they glide through the ocean. The motion moves through your own arm and hand, to the horse's tissue (fig. 6.17). It can be a great way to help extremely tight areas of the horse's body release or to "wake up" a horse's nervous system.

The Effect

This *TTouch* relaxes and releases tensed muscles. It makes it easier for your horse to lower his head because you are taking away the tension in his neck and shoulders. When your young horse tightens his back or croup the first time he feels the saddle, you can use the *Jellyfish Jiggle* to help him release the tension.

How to Use It

Use both hands at the same time when applying the *Jellyfish Jiggle TTouch*. Place them side by side on a large muscle group, such as the croup. Using your fingers and hands, vibrate and send a gentle jiggle through the big muscles to create some movement. You will create a wavelike pattern that travels upward through the horse.

This *TTouch* is suitable for all the soft, larger muscles of the horse's hind end, neck, and base of the neck.

Python Lift TTouch

An 11-foot-long Burmese python named Joyce who lived in the San Diego Zoo inspired me to develop this *TTouch*, as well as the *Coiled Python* to follow (p. 105). These lifts relaxed her and were so enjoyable for her that she sought me out, seeking contact the next time I was in the same room with her. Done slowly on the legs, *Python Lifts* are relaxing; done quickly, they invigorate the horse (figs. 6.18 A–D).

> It is easier for your horse to lower his head when you take away the tension in his neck and shoulders.

6.18 A–D *Python Lift.*

The Effect

This *TTouch* is especially important for young horses because it improves their awareness of their legs. Horses that can feel their legs have an easier time standing still and are better balanced at liberty as well as under a rider. Horses in flight reflex have very little awareness of their legs. This *TTouch* helps bring that awareness and grounds the horse, too. Therefore, the horse can respond with more control and intelligence. By activating the circulation of the legs you can bring your excited horse "back to earth," and when you *Lower the Head* (p. 65) at the same time, the flight reflex will be eliminated and the horse can think again.

The *Python Lift TTouch* also improves coordination and reduces tension, which can improve stride length and cadence.

How to Use It

Place both hands on the top of the horse's leg just below the elbow, with full contact of your entire hand. Lift with enough pressure so that your hands do not slide over the hair but lift the skin. Exhale while you lift, pause for a few seconds, and then slowly allow the skin to slide back into its original position while you inhale, being careful not to drop the tissue too slowly.

Plan to lift less than the skin's maximum movement; most horses prefer a very subtle lift that may not feel very significant to the person applying the technique, but it can have a profound effect.

Start the next *Python Lift TTouch* about the width of your hand below the first and continue all the way down to the fetlock joint. As you work on the lower extremities, you need to change the position of your hands in order to keep as much of your hand's surface on the horse as possible; along the cannon bone, you will find that your fingertips overlap. Fold your body forward or squat beside the horse, but be extremely careful when around young or nervous horses.

Python Lift TTouches are mostly used on the horse's legs, neck, back, and the inside of the thighs. If your horse is too excitable and it is not safe for you to use *Python Lifts* on the legs, use your *Wand* to calmly stroke his legs, starting at the chest and slowly moving all the way down to the hooves while asking his head to lower.

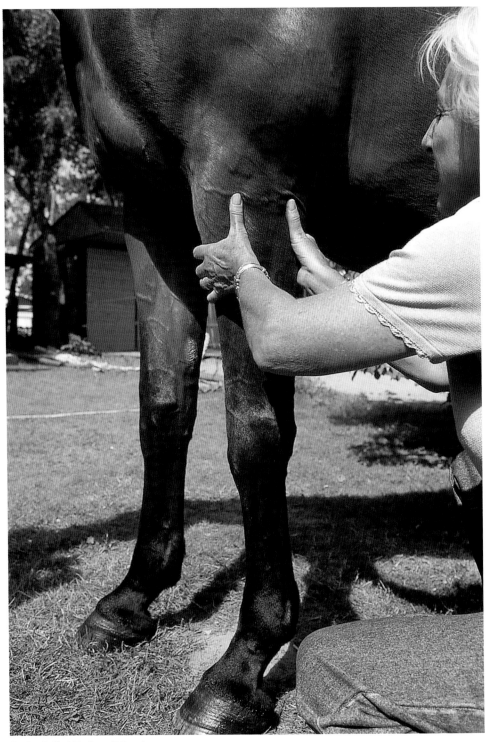

6.19 *Coiled Python TTouch.*

6.20 Gently working the extremities, including the tail, is a wonderful way to make a connection with your horse while helping him release tension and gain more awareness through his entire body. Most extremity exercises are very useful to practice before a ride.

Coiled Python TTouch

The *Coiled Python TTouch* (fig. 6.19) blends the relaxing effect of *Circular TTouches* and the increased awareness of the *Slides and Lifts*. It is a combination of the *Abalone* or *Lying Leopard TTouches* (pp. 92 and 91) that is finished with a *Python Lift TTouch* (p. 101).

The Effect

This *TTouch* improves coordination, increases confidence, and relaxes nervous horses.

How to Use It

Use one hand to apply the *Circular TTouch* of your choice, and then use both hands to lift, hold, and slowly release, following the description of the *Python Lifts* (p. 103).

Extremity TTouches

Extremity TTouches are done on specific parts of the horse's body (fig. 6.20). They are excellent tools for releasing tension, improving balance, and developing trust. Adding these into your daily grooming session can reap amazing results.

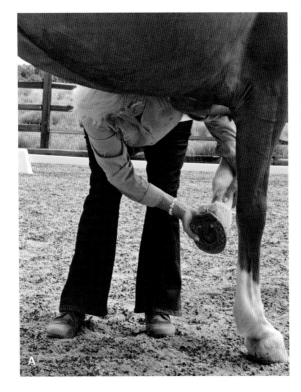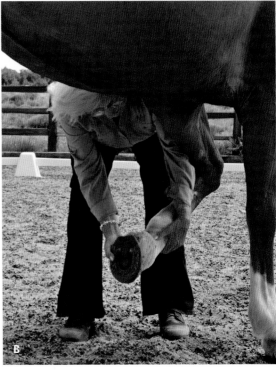

Front Leg Circles

The *Leg Circles TTouch* is a non-habitual movement for horses, which improves their awareness and ability to learn. It is also an excellent exercise to improve balance and range of movement through the shoulders and pelvis (figs. 6.21 A–D).

The Effect

Young horses need to develop a good sense of balance before carrying a rider, and the independent use of their legs is a good place to start. Beside balance, *Front Leg Circles* also improve surefootedness. The exercise relaxes the horse's shoulders, back and neck muscles, and can be a very effective, indirect way to start *Lowering the Head* (p. 65) and releasing the topline. Older horses will benefit from this exercise, too, with improved stride and enhanced freedom of movement in their shoulders and thoracic sling. *Leg Circles* is also an excellent exercise to prepare the horse for the farrier.

How to Use It

Stand beside your horse's front leg, facing his hind end. Stroke down the leg a few times and ask the horse to pick up his foot by gently scratching on the

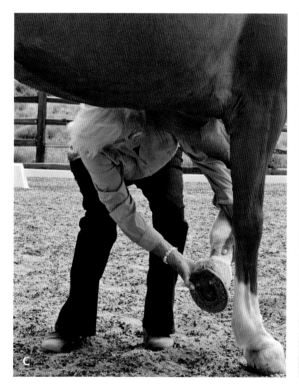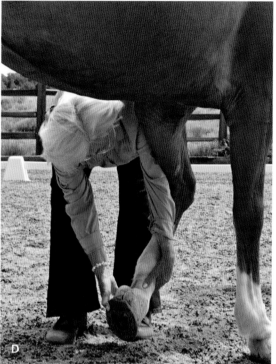

tendon above the fetlock or just below the knee. Count to three before asking again; it often takes a horse a moment to process the signal. Giving him a moment to respond will make him more responsive in the long run. Resist the urge to lean into your horse, which will just encourage an unbalanced horse to lean back.

Place your inside hand on the fetlock and your other hand on the hoof so your thumb points inward on the heel bulb, and the other fingers cup the hoof wall so the tip of the hoof points toward the ground. Maintaining the bottom of the hoof perpendicular to the ground keeps the pastern joint in a neutral position.

Starting the motion in your body rather than your arms, imagine you are drawing horizontal circles with the hoof in the air. Start the circles on the spot where the hoof had been on the ground before you picked it up and in the direction that is easiest. Be careful not to make the circles too large, especially when working with a young horse. Keep the hoof at a consistent height while drawing the first circle, so it resembles the blade of a helicopter. It is important to support the fetlock joint and the pastern as you circle the entire leg in a smooth, fluid motion. Try imagining that you

6.22 A–C *Hind Leg Circles.*

are tracing a large circle in the sand with your horse's toe.

After the first full rotation, circle the hoof in a downward spiral. Spiral down with every circle until you can place the tip of the hoof on the ground, which is a very non-habitual movement for the horse's front end. Lightly tap the tip of the hoof on the ground a few times, and then place the tip of the hoof on the ground about 8 to 10 inches farther back than where you had picked it up originally. You can now take light upward pressure on the tendon and rock the leg all the way to the shoulder.

When it is difficult for the horse to bring his leg all the way down, you can help him by placing the hoof on a platform or folded towel.

Notice how large or small the circle has to be for a round, easy movement. The idea is to show the horse's body what the possibilities are, not the limitations, so resist the urge to "stretch" his shoulder as you do this. Watch your own posture and use the strength of your pelvis by creating the circular movement through your bent knees, from your feet. This will protect your back, shoulders, and arms. You can also support your elbow on your outside knee.

Hind Leg Circles

Hind Leg Circles give you feedback about your horse's range of motion through the hind end while helping to improve his mobility (figs. 6.22 A–C). A horse that is unable to move his hind legs in very large circles is usually tight through the back and hindquarters. This tension can cause difficulties when being shod, lack of impulsion under saddle, spookiness, and trouble with canter departs and gait irregularities—to name a few.

The Effect

Hind Leg Circles TTouch improves the horse's balance as well as releases tension the horse may carry in his back and croup. It also helps to increase the horse's stride. Circling the leg under the belly helps horses become more fluid and flexible through the hind end. It is an excellent preparation for the farrier and will better enable horses for correct canter departs, lateral work, and flying lead changes.

How to Use It

Stand beside the horse's hind leg, facing the rear. To prepare him, use your hand to stroke down his leg a few times. Now ask him to lift his foot by scratching upward on both sides of the tendons using your fingernails. It is also helpful to use a voice command, such as "Up" or "Foot."

Take the hoof in your outside hand and hold it so your thumb points inward along the heel bulb and your fingers are cupped around the hoof wall. Your other hand supports the inside of the leg above the fetlock joint. Fold through your hips and knees. Support your outside elbow on your knee, which will stabilize your movement and make it easier to maintain the position.

Be sure to not inadvertently pull the horse's leg out to the side or stretch it out behind him. Support the leg at a comfortable height and start making small circles in the direction that is easiest for the horse. Use your whole body, not just your arm; this will make a more fluid circle and keep you and the horse in better balance.

See if it is easier for your horse to circle his legs clockwise or counterclockwise. Notice that there will be parts of the circle that are not as smooth as others. Be especially careful in those areas and make the circles smaller. If your horse tries to take his leg away, he is likely unbalanced or tight in the muscles. Instead of starting a wrestling match, take the leg you are circling

> The idea is to show the horse's body what the possibilities are, not the limitations.

6.23 With practice, your horse's range of motion will improve so you can bring the hind legs farther forward and under his barrel. Take the leg only as far forward as is comfortable for the horse.

closer to the supporting leg. This will help put the horse more over his center of balance, especially if you are accidentally pulling the leg too much out to the side. You may also find that wiggling the leg will help relax tension and bring the horse back into balance.

Once you have done six or seven circles (fewer if your horse is very unbalanced), start to spiral the hoof to the ground, resting the toe of the hoof on the ground about 6 to 8 inches behind the spot you picked it up from. Your horse will relax his hind end in this position—you can gently rock the leg to help encourage more release through the lumbar and sacro-iliac (SI) joint.

As your horse's range of motion improves in this *TTouch*, you can start experimenting by moving the leg more toward the midline under the belly (fig. 6.23). With practice, your horse's range of movement will expand dramatically, thus improving stride length and hind end flexibility.

Belly Lift

While I have long used this technique to reduce symptoms of colic because it relaxes the horse and helps increase movement through the digestive tract, *Belly Lifts* are also a great way to introduce the girth to a young horse or help reduce cinchiness in an older horse. It is ideal to have a helper on the other side of the horse to hold a towel that runs under the horse's belly (fig 6.24), but *Belly Lifts* can also be done on your own with a large sheet or towel folded into a narrow width (figs. 6.25 A & B).

The Effect

The *Belly Lift* is a wonderful preparation for young horses getting ready to carry the saddle and girth for the first time. Your horse will learn to relax instead of being surprised and feeling confined when he feels the girth, which can easily lead to him holding his breath and tensing his body. This *TTouch* is also useful for older horses that are apprehensive or defensive about saddling or are cinchy. It relaxes the horse's barrel and encourages deeper breathing.

How to Use It

When you have a helper for *Belly Lifts*, one of you stands on each side of the horse's barrel. Fold a large towel lengthwise so it is about 8 inches wide.

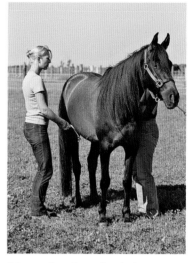

6.24 *Belly Lifts* with a helper.

6.25 A & B *Belly Lifts* on your own.

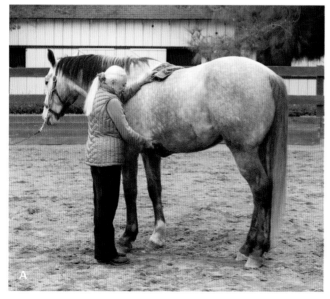

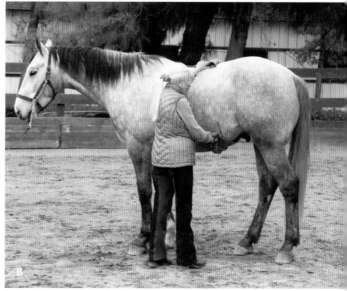

(A girth or surcingle can also be used.) Take the towel under the horse's belly and each person holds an end. Starting in the girth area, slowly lift the towel, hold about 10 seconds, and slowly release. The release should take about twice as long as the lift.

If you don't have a helper you can also do *Belly Lifts* by yourself using a bath towel or sheet that is long enough to wrap around the horse's barrel. Place the folded towel over the horse's back and pick up the opposite end under his belly. Your upper hand anchors one end near the withers while the lower hand actively lifts and supports.

Move the towel back on the barrel a hand-width and repeat the lift. Always work from the front to the back and go back as far toward the flank as is acceptable to the horse.

Remember to breathe slowly and deeply, keep your knees soft, and lift from your center to protect your back and shoulders. Be mindful to watch your horse's reaction. If your horse begins to fidget, move around, swish his tail, pin his ears, or act in any way agitated, use less pressure on the lift and slow down the motion. Listen to your horse and adjust your technique to find out what is acceptable to him. Paying attention to these small signs of discomfort or apprehension will go a long way to building your overall trust.

Some very sensitive horses find any kind of *Belly Lift* with a towel or girth too invasive. For horses that do not settle into *Belly Lifts*, no matter how little pressure you use or how slowly you go, try using an Ace bandage to do it at first. The elasticity of the bandage gives the horse a sense of the lifting and breathing without restricting his body. This is an example of chunking down an exercise to enhance the horse's trust and acceptance (see p. 20). Taking the extra time to allow for learning has more long-term benefits than simply "making" the horse accept it with more pressure or reprimands.

Back Lift

While the name and area of the body is similar, *Back Lifts* serve a very different purpose from *Belly Lifts*. *Back Lifts* actively ask the abdominal muscle to engage and lift the back. *Back Lifts* create a visible lift through the back and the withers, as opposed to the more passive *Belly Lifts* (figs. 6.26 A & B). You do not need anything other than your fingertips to do this exercise, and it is a great way to help your horse maintain good topline health—they can have a remarkable effect immediately. It can be helpful to have another

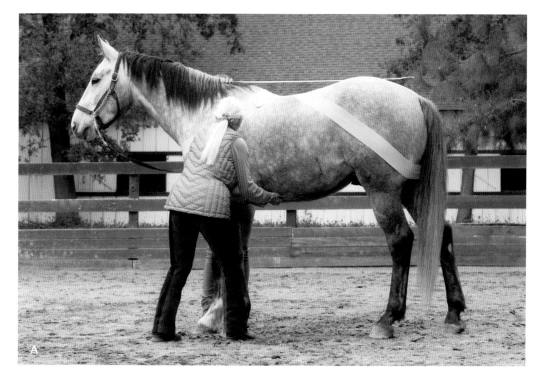

6.26 A & B *Back Lifts.* Note: The *Body Wrap* shown in these pictures is not required for this *TTouch.*

person around to let you know if she can see any lifting achieved. Sometimes it is difficult to tell if there has been a lift when you are standing so close to the horse.

The Effect

Raising the back is beneficial for young and inexperienced horses, and older, trained horses alike. For youngsters, it is a good idea to do *Back Lifts* after you have saddled them the first few times to help avoid a cold-backed reaction or have the feeling of the saddle surprise them. Older horses that tend to get cold-backed, tight in the thoracic vertebrae (behind the withers), or have the obvious effects of gravity with a dropped (swayed) back will be completely changed in the way they release and move. *Back Lifts* help encourage a healthier posture and show the horse how his abdominal muscles are connected through to the rest of the barrel.

How to Use It

When doing *Back Lifts*, it is always a good idea to start with the theory that "less is more." Some horses are sensitive along the midline and if a horse has held tension in his back, a substantial lift may be initially uncomfortable.

Begin by using *Zebra* (p. 96) and *Lick of the Cow's Tongue* (p. 95) *TTouches* to give the horse a feeling of connection from his belly up over his barrel and across the spine. Check your horse's responses to see that he is okay with contact on the belly.

Stand alongside the horse's barrel, behind his elbow, facing him. Fold through your knees and while closing your hip angle. Place your fingertips on the underside of his belly with one hand on either side of his midline. Make an upward motion through your feet and fingertips. You may have to repeat the motion. You should feel as though your horse has lifted his barrel and back; however, you may not be able to clearly see the results from your vantage point.

If your horse does not seem comfortable with this exercise, do less, or use the pads of your fingers instead of the tips. Most horses become more comfortable with this exercise as they do it more often. Horses that are very stiff or dropped through the back will show the most obvious change.

It pays to practice this on different horses. The more you do it and feel how to take the movement through your entire body, rather than just your fingers, the more effective you will be.

Ear TTouch

It is important that your horse is comfortable having his ears han-dled. In an emergency, *Ear TTouches* can help stabilize pulse and respiration, reduce the pain from colic or a severe injury while waiting for the vet, and can help to keep a horse from going into shock. According to traditional Chinese medicine, the triple-heater meridian runs along the base of the ear, which influences fertility, respiration, and digestion, making the area an important part of overall health and well-being. After an endurance ride or other riding competition, exhausted horses have been shown to recover more quickly with *Ear TTouches*.

In addition to the health benefits, horses that are not com-fortable about having their ears handled are often tight in the poll and TMJ areas. This translates into many other issues under sad-dle and on the ground, and inhibits overall performance. Related behavioral issues include: difficulty bridling, high-headedness, a tight topline, evading contact, and rushing, for example. *Ear TTouches* can help alleviate the tightness that leads to these com-mon problems (figs. 6.27 A & B).

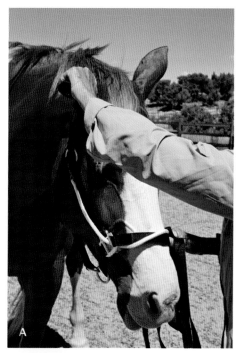

The Effect

For a young horse, *Ear TTouches* are useful to prepare him for the bridle being pulled over the ears and will start to reinforce a habitual posture of relaxation through the head and neck. It is also important as preparation for being comfortable with things above his head, such as a rider on his back.

When you have a difficult horse that does not like having his ears touched, you can teach him by *Lowering the Head* (p. 65) and *TTouching* the ears so he learns to accept something he previously feared.

How to Use It

Stand in front of your horse, just to one side of his midline, and ask him to *Lower the Head* (p. 65). Stabilize the halter with one hand while the other hand strokes one ear from the base to the tip. Do not try to pull the head down with your hand on the halter. Ideally the lowering comes as the horse relaxes from the release

6.27 A & B *Ear TTouches.*

The Ear Shy Horse

The most positive way to help a horse overcome a feared experience is to chunk down the exercise. Instead of using the palm of your hand to make contact with the ear, try using the back of your hand, or cover your hand with a sheepskin mitt or soft glove. Sometimes a *Head Wrap* (see p. 46) can work instantly. When your horse is very concerned about *Ear TTouches*, you may need to start the exercise with the back of the hand or *Chimp TTouch* (see p. 89) on the forehead, poll, and TMJ (fig. 6.28). As I mentioned, horses who are ear shy are often tight and locked in this area, making them apprehensive about having the area touched and handled.

6.28 Starting with the back of the hand or fingers is often a great way to help a horse feel more comfortable being touched around the ears and poll.

Some horses will be more comfortable when you stand behind their jowl, facing the same direction they are, and gently stroke the ear. Once your horse is confident that your touch is gentle and feels good, you will be able to stand in front of the horse to ask for the head to lower.

A pattern of tension or a postural habit that creates tension will be the most common reason a horse is fearful of having his ears handled. In some cases doing a few of the *Leading Exercises* (p. 132) first, and then coming back to *Ear TTouches* will release tension and help your horse be less fearful of having his ears touched. *Mane Slides* (p. 117) and even *Tail TTouches* (p. 118) can also help.

Remember that every time your horse learns to overcome a certain fear he will also learn to face other fears with more confidence. I imagine a balance scale. Every time the horse conquers a fear the confidence side gets heavier while the fears get lighter, and in the end, his confidence is so strong, or heavy, that the fear disappears.

6.29 A & B *Mane Slides.*

of tension in the poll area. You can also add some small *Raccoon TTouches* (p. 94) on the outside and inside of the ear, and when you come to the tip, let your thumb slide into the inside of the ear.

There is a reflexology point right behind the horse's ear. When you stroke this area, the horse will point his ears forward. This is called the *panniculus reflex*. This change in ear posture will also change the horse's attitude and behavior. Horses that are insecure will gain confidence and cooperate. I often compare this ear position in horses to a smile in people; everything is easier when you smile.

Mane Slides
Mane Slides are a deceptively simple technique that can have a huge impact on your horse's well-being and relaxation. Every strand of hair has a connection to the skin, cells, and fascia (figs. 6.29 A & B).

The Effect
Using mindful, gentle slides along the hair of the mane and forelock is a wonderful way to release tension along the crest and poll in a way that most horses love.

How to Use It
You can relax and settle your horse with *Mane Slides* on the forelock and mane. It is best to do this when you have asked your horse to *Lower the Head*

(see p. 65). Standing in front of your horse and slightly to one side, stroke the hair of the forelock with a soft, gentle movement from the root to the end of the hair, breathing and staying soft in your knees. If your horse has a very thick forelock you can divide it and do the *Slides* in sections.

You can also make small circles with a clump of mane or forelock and then let the hair slide between your thumb and index finger. Remember to breathe and maintain a soft, released posture in your body as you do each slide. For many horses, this is a good exercise to use before *Ear TTouches* (p. 115), especially when they tend to be tight in the poll or nervous about being touched around the ears or poll.

Tail TTouches

Tail TTouches are important for young horses, as well as those who need to be reeducated. You can tell by a clamped tail that a horse has tension throughout his entire body and *Tail TTouches* can release this tightness. Likewise, a horse that has a "wet-noodle" tail, one that feels like it will practically fall off in your hand, may be equally disconnected to his hind end and find any of the tail work that follows incredibly beneficial. A horse that is comfortable having his tail handled is more likely to be released through his entire topline all the way to the poll and maintain a healthy, supple, spine that can connect back to front (fig. 6.30).

The Effect

Tail Touches improve hindquarter awareness and help the horse that is afraid of noises and movement behind him. They help him feel and use his hind-quarters better, so he will have an easier time balancing the rider and engaging his hind end. Releasing tension through the tail can be an excellent way to indirectly release tension in the poll. In some cases, *Tail TTouch* is the key to helping a horse overcome fear around his ears and poll.

How to Use It

When you start *Tail TTouches*, always stand off to the side of the horse until you are absolutely sure that he does not feel threatened enough to kick out. Before working with the actual tail, run your flat hand all over the horse's hindquarters to feel if the muscles are tensed or relaxed and soft, and to see how your horse reacts to the contact. Is he relaxed? Does he lower his head and lift his tail? Or does he raise his head and tuck his tail when you work around the area?

> Releasing
> tension through
> the tail can be an
> excellent way to
> indirectly release
> tension in
> the poll.

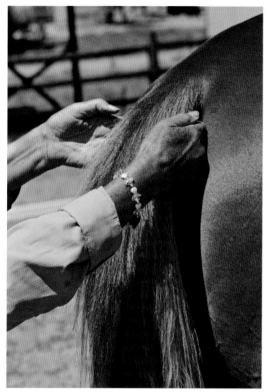

6.30 *Tail TTouch.*

6.31 Starting with light *Raccoon TTouches* around the base of the tail encourages a horse to release and lift his tail.

Start with a few *Circular TTouches* (see p. 89) over the entire hind end, along the thighs and right beside the tailbone. Pay special attention to the area around the loins, as nervous horses are often sore in this area. A young horse, especially, needs to be thoroughly prepared with other TTouches, such as the *Clouded Leopard* and *Zebra TTouches* (pp. 90 and 96) all over his body, then focusing on the hindquarters and tail with *Raccoon TTouches* (fig. 6.31). If you sense the horse is uneasy or fearful, wait on the *Tail TTouches* and come back to them later when your horse is more confident and has learned to trust you.

Take your time so the horse relaxes and enjoys the work over the hindquarters. Whenever your horse seems apprehensive, use the concept of chunking it down and work with the back of your hand with the *Chimp TTouch* (p. 89) or a sheepskin mitt. Also let him experience *Body Wraps* (p. 44) or go back to stroking the area with the *Wand* (p. 62).

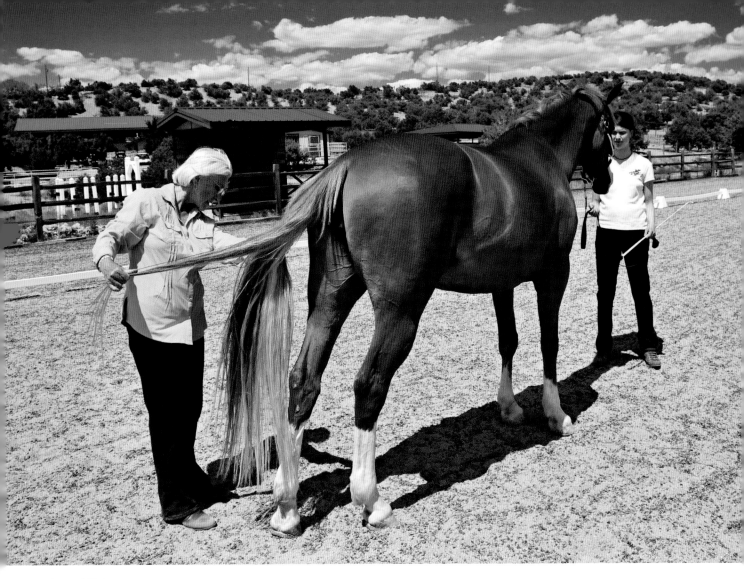

6.32 *Tail Slides* are a great way to help a horse feel more comfortable with being handled around the hind end. They offer the added benefit of releasing tension and encouraging relaxation.

Tail Slides

If your young horse or older horse is nervous having his tail touched, practice *Tail Slides*. Standing beside the horse, hold the tail in one hand and separate a few strands of hair with your other hand, sliding slowly from the root to the tip (fig. 6.32). Remember to breathe calmly and rhythmically while you stroke the tail strand by strand. Keep your fingers soft and flexible.

If you know the horse well and it is safe to stand behind him, try *Tail Slides* in that position. Alternate stroking a clump of hair to the right and left in a calm, rhythmical motion, letting your fingers slide to the ends of the hair. Only stroke the top third of the hair. This variation is most effective if you allow the motion to go through your entire body, not just your arms. It can be useful to think about shifting your weight from the right to left foot and back again, allowing your hand to slide along the tail hair with each shift of direction.

6.33 Keep the tail in the tail groove and gently rock back and forth to allow the horse to release the tail before you pick it up.

6.34 A & B I support the tail with both hands and gently circle it in both directions. This mare is very comfortable with *Tail Circles* and easily lifts her tail. If you are unsure about how your horse will react to the exercise, it is safer to stand slightly off to the side, perpendicular to the horse as in fig. 6.33, rather than facing him, as pictured here.

Tail Circles

Most horses love the feeling of careful movement through their tail. To be safe when trying *Tail Circles*, start by standing beside the horse, perpendicularly to the tail and croup. Place one hand on top of the tail and lift it slightly (fig. 6.33). Now slide the other hand under the tail near its base and lift the tail away from the body.

Let go of the tail hairs and support the underside of the tail with your hand closest to the horse. Lift gently. Take your other hand and support the bottom of the tailbone with your palm gently clasped around the tail. Lift with both hands so that the tail makes a gentle question mark shape, being sure that you are not forcing it into any position.

Circle the tail a few times in both directions, exploring the possibilities for easy, fluid movement (figs. 6.34 A & B). You never want to feel like you are forcing, stretching, or bending the tail. Be mindful and keep your knees soft; be balanced and breathe. Stabilize the tail between both of your hands

6.35 The *Tail Glide* is created by a gentle, steady backward shift of your weight. It relaxes the back and neck and gives the horse a new sense of his body.

so that you are not twisting it. The motion should be concentrated on where the tail attaches to the rump. Let the movement in your body move your arms—this will make the motion more fluid and it engages the entire spine.

Only make the motion as large or as small as seems easy for the tail to move; do not force the range of movement. Notice if clockwise and counter-clockwise are similarly fluid, or not, and whether you can see the motion move all the way along the horse's spine.

Tail Glides

When doing *Tail Glides*, you are ideally standing directly behind the horse. Only attempt this when you are really sure that the horse does not have a tendency to kick and you have practiced other variations of *Tail TTouches*, and other *TTouches*, too, all around the haunches. Always notice the horse's breathing, ear position, eye and nostril shape, as well as overall bearing while doing any *TTouches*, but especially when in a vulnerable position. Very few horses, if any, kick "out of the blue." Horses will generally try to give you plenty of warning when they are not comfortable with something before actually acting out.

Standing behind the horse, hold the tail with both hands close to its base. Place your feet one in front of the other, lift the tail, and shift your weight to your back foot so there is traction on the horse's tail, which will travel through his entire spine (fig. 6.35).

Hold for a few seconds, pause, and gently melt the pressure by shifting your weight to your front foot. Repeat this exercise two or three times and remember that you are expanding the horse's entire spine and connecting his front end with his hind end, thus improving body awareness and creating new possibilities for movement.

Do not "pull" the tail with your arms and shoulders, but create the movement by shifting your weight to your back foot. Remember to breathe regularly and calmly. Picture how the steady traction expands the horse's spine and takes pressure off each vertebra. Slowly support the tail back to its original position rather than just letting it go.

You can also improve the tail's connection to the rest of the body by keeping both hands close to the dock of the tail and gently pushing toward the spine. Keep the tail straight and follow the angle where the tail and croup meet.

Tail Pearling

For this variation of *Tail TTouches*, you must stand directly behind the horse. Again, only do so if you feel comfortable and safe. Take the tail in both hands so your fingers are underneath the tail with your thumbs on top.

6.36 A–C *Tail Pearling* is deceptively subtle but can give horses a great sense of release all the way from the withers to the pelvis.

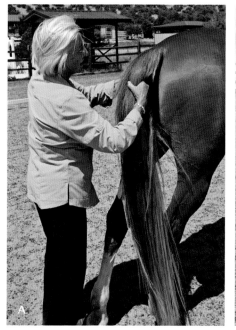

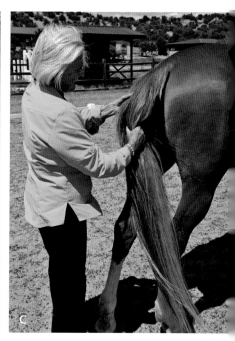

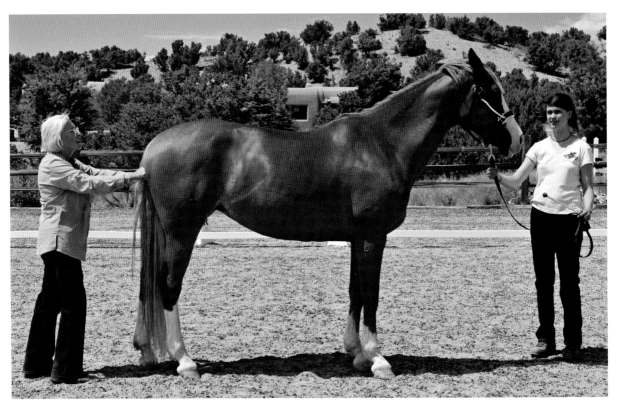

6.37 *Pelvic Tilt.*

Be aware that your thumbs are a little bit higher on the tail than the fingers, so they are not exactly opposite each other, which would make it harder to move the vertebrae in the tail—the point of this *T Touch*.

Move each vertebra in the tail up and down by gently pushing with your thumbs and lifting with your fingers. This is a non-habitual movement for the horse that he cannot do on his own. This motion allows for an increased sense of body awareness, releasing tension along the entire spine, and it encourages relaxation. Be mindful of the movement of each vertebra and pay attention as you are doing the work so the motion does not become mechanical. Halfway down the tail the vertebrae fuse so there will be less movement.

Pelvic Tilt

This *T Touch* can only be done when it is safe to stand directly behind your horse. The *Pelvic Tilt* is actually a very subtle movement. The motion should be more apparent on the slow release rather than the tilt. You may find it easier to stay soft with slightly bent elbows so the motion can come through your entire body (fig. 6.37).

The Effect

The *Pelvic Tilt* is an excellent exercise to encourage a horse to release through his pelvis, loins, and back while connecting the motion through the entire topline. Horses gain a new sense of body awareness and can improve the ability to engage through the hindquarters. This exercise is also helpful for horses who are nervous about things coming up behind them or who seem stiff through the loins.

How to Use It

Standing directly behind the horse, grasp a chunk of tail hair in each hand and place your fists slightly below the point of the buttocks, keeping your elbows bent and your feet shoulder-width apart. Shift your weight up and forward gently, in a scooping motion. Hold the pressure for a few seconds and slowly release. Imagine that the movement comes from your feet. Maintain softness in your joints, especially your knees and hip flexors.

Nostril TTouch

Always begin working around the muzzle area with the back of your hand. Once your horse is comfortable with gentle contact, you can move on to slowly stroking the flare of the nostril, either from the front, or while standing next to the horse's head, using your thumb on the outside of the flare (figs. 6.38.A & B)

The Effect

Doing mindful work around the horse's mouth and nostrils can positively affect the limbic system—the control center for emotions in the brain. When you affect the limbic system, and in turn, the parasympathetic nervous system, you can help the young or green horse overcome emotional responses, become more tolerant, and learn faster.

Difficult horses that have closed themselves off toward humans because of bad experiences often don't like having their mouth touched. The nostrils are therefore often a great place to start near the mouth but

6.38 A & B *Nostril TTouches.*

without setting up resistance in the horse who needs a restart. By learning to enjoy this *TTouch*, the horse becomes more open to new experiences and can change old behavior patterns.

How to Use It

Begin by doing some *Abalone TTouches* around the horse's muzzle (see p. 92). This will prepare your horse for his nostrils being touched and give you an idea of his level of acceptance. Note: With horses who are extremely sensitive around the muzzle you may have to start by diffusing the sensation with a cloth or sheepskin mitt over your hand.

Once your horse is comfortable being touched around the muzzle, stand next to his head and use your thumb and forefinger to gently slide down the flare of the nostril. It can be helpful to steady the halter with your hand nearest the horse and use your outside hand to stroke the nostril.

Most horses find this extremely relaxing once they know what to expect, and it can be a great way to increase trust and encourage relaxation.

Mouth TTouches

With horses that have behavior issues related to the mouth, I recommend having their teeth checked by a qualified professional to make sure

---

TTouches Around the Face

Mindfully and respectfully working all around a horse's face can be a good way to build rapport and trust. Most horses appreciate a slow approach around the head. Helping your horse become truly comfortable and happy about being touched around his head releases tension and reduces potential issues under saddle from a tight poll and jaw.

Too often, we are not aware or are "thinking about what to make for dinner" when we work with our horses. Always think about putting your mind in your hands and your hands on your horse when doing *TTouches*.

6.39 *Mouth TTouch.*

the problem is not caused by pain. *Mouth TTouches* provide many of the same benefits as *Nostril TTouches* (p. 125), as well as those more specific to the mouth. Begin with the flat of your hand, back of your hand, or cloth, depending on the level of your horse's acceptance (fig. 6.39).

The Effect

Mouth TTouches prepare young horses for carrying the bit and are excellent for older horses that are hard in the mouth, suck the tongue, stick the tongue out the side, are heavy on the bit, or fight being bridled. It is also an excellent exercise to prepare a young horse for deworming or any oral veterinary exam.

How to Use It

Stand facing the same way as the horse. Ask the horse to *Lower the Head* (p. 65), hold the halter with one hand, and use the other hand for *Lying Leopard*

6.40 A–C As your horse becomes comfortable with *Mouth TTouches,* slide your fingers under the lips, ensuring you gently pull the lips away from the teeth and jaw.

TTouches around the mouth, chin, and nostrils (see p. 91). Once your horse is comfortable with being touched, gently circle his upper lip and lower lip very slightly, using the palm of your hand to cup the chin and slide each lip around.

Steady the halter gently with your hand nearest the horse and slide the fingers of your outside hand between the horse's upper lip and the gums. Keep your fingers together and rub back and forth above the incisors where the gum and the lip meet with the length of your index finger staying parallel to the ground. Your fingers are pointing away from you, not upward. To work the bottom lip, cup the horse's chin with the palm of your hand and allow your thumb to slip inside the mouth and rub back and forth along where the gum and lip meet (figs. 6.40 A–C).

If the horse's mouth and gums are dry, wet your hands with water so they slide more easily. This makes mouth work more pleasant for horse and human. Note: It is a good idea to remove any large rings before placing your hands inside the horse's mouth.

Many horses will find this *TTouch* a little unusual at first. Initially, only work the mouth for a few moments before taking your hand away and giving your horse a chance to process what he is feeling. Once horses know what to expect, most really enjoy *Mouth TTouches.*

The Story of Indus

Indus came to me because he would not allow anyone to touch his mouth, and it was impossible to worm him. He avoided people by taking his head extremely high and not standing still. He had grown up in a large herd with very little handling by humans and had not been properly prepared to be wormed—a horse first needs to know how to stand still and enjoy human contact.

I put the gelding into the *Taming the Tiger* position (p. 68) to keep him from leaving me. This is a good leading position to teach young or inexperienced horses to be patient.

I started the session with *TTouches* on his shoulder, which was not threatening for Indus. He enjoyed them and at the end placed his head in my hands. This horse was fearful and not at all dominant. Indus was so frightened that he could not eat when we offered him some food. When you understand that a horse's reactions come from fear and lack of trust, you can approach with a different mindset. It is not about who is boss. My new questions were, "How can I help you to trust me? How can you learn to accept what you have to accept?"

I used *TTouches* on his entire body to improve his body awareness and led him over the *Ground Poles* of the *Playground for Higher Learning* (p. 175) to improve his balance and coordination. I placed a cloth over his muzzle, gave him a soft rope to chew on, and gently tickled his tongue.

By improving his physical balance you automatically increase a horse's mental and emotional balance. Indus learned in just one session to become balanced and accept having his mouth touched.

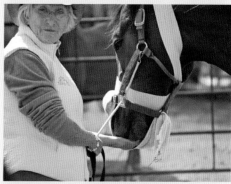

6.41 A–C A soft mitt helped to diffuse the feeling of my hand as a way to chunk down the process of being touched around the muzzle—and ultimately wormed (A). Sometimes, chunking down an exercise requires creativity and lateral thinking. Using your logic and intuition, you can help a horse like Indus change a previous expectation about an experience and replace it with a new, low-stress, positive one (B & C).

CHAPTER 7

Dance Steps

Leading Exercises

How you handle a horse on the ground has direct influence on habits and tendencies under saddle. Each of the following *Leading Exercises* is designed to help you become a clearer, more mindful leader, while bringing your horse into balance. A well-balanced horse with good self-carriage should be able to master each exercise, and the exercises in themselves help achieve this goal (fig. 7.1). If one exercise seems difficult for your horse, try another one, change which side you are leading from, incorporate some of the Elements from the *Playground for Higher Learning* (see chapter 8, p. 175), or take a moment to do a quick *TTouch* bodywork session.

It is a widely accepted fact that groundwork is an integral step in the preparation of any horse going under saddle. The Tellington Method uses a

7.1 Leading a horse from both sides as shown here is called the *Homing Pigeon* (p. 143) because it gets the horse to "home in" (focus), and it ends the flight reflex by giving the horse boundaries. With this horse, Big Surprise (see p. 234), the weight of the chain on the left side helps him *Lower the Head* (p. 65); on his right, the *Zephyr* lead helps provide that boundary.

7.2 Find a willing friend and practice your leading techniques on a human. This will provide valuable verbal feedback, as well as give you an opportunity to put yourself in the horse's shoes when you are the one being "led." This can be an eye-opening experience.

variety of *Leading Exercises* that are designed to logically prepare the horse for the skills he will need to safely and confidently carry a rider. All the exercises encourage healthy, functional postural habits that will physically and mentally prepare the horse for any discipline. A healthy posture helps horses maintain balance in the body, mind, and spirit, and reduces the instances of fear, reactivity, and tension.

These exercises do not necessarily need to be done repeatedly. They are steps in the learning process, teaching horses how to think and understand signals in a balanced way rather than simply be trained to do a specific exercise. They are best done with a considerable level of mindfulness on the handler's part. Every time you lead your horse you have the opportunity to provide him with positive—or negative—information. Paying attention to how you ask, how you allow for a response, and how you use your body language will improve communication, cooperation, and support a balance, relaxed posture (fig. 7.2).

Working with different leading positions allows you and your horse to be safer in difficult situations and become a harmonious unit. The

7.3 A–D Each of the leading positions are designed to help your horse develop balance and self-carriage: *Elegant Elephant* (A); *Grace of the Cheetah* (B); *Dingo* (C); and *Homing Pigeon* (D). Learning to respond to these light cues prepares the horse to understand your aids under saddle.

variations of the leading positions will challenge your own as well as your horse's coordination. All of them are used on both sides of the horse to promote straightness, concentration, and non-habitual movement. Whenever you lead a horse you can take the opportunity to promote a healthy, functional posture and begin to establish positive muscle memory for ridden work (figs. 7.3 A–D). It is important that the handler be as conscious of her own movement and posture as she is of the horse. The quality and subtly of the signal and communication is as important as the cooperation and result. Each exercise incorporates a clear signal, use of body language and voice to teach the horse and build a level of communication that will transfer to being ridden. The more precise you can become, the more acutely and quickly your horse will respond to you in all scenarios. If at first you feel uncoordinated, do not fret! Remember that throughout a horse's life he will have handlers who give slightly unclear signals. It is an educational experience in patience and tolerance for your horse to have a handler who is learning something new while he is.

In all of the *Leading Exercises,* use verbal cues as well. Verbal cues are extremely useful for young horses because they can be transferred to later use under saddle. I use "And…" before each request because it lets the horse know that a signal is coming and is less abrupt than simply saying, "Whoa," or "Walk on."

Once you are comfortable with each exercise, you can seamlessly change between any of them depending on the situation and what you are asking your horse to do. Remember that these exercises are not listed in any particular order. Each horse is an individual and should not be trained by one set recipe. Let your horse and your intuition lead you through the positions in the best order for you. If one exercise is too challenging or you or your horse feel unsuccessful, simply change which position you start with. Each one will highlight a horse's strengths or perhaps challenge him to learn balance, focus, and posture.

Here are a few specific recommendations, depending on your horse's stage of training:

FOAL OR WEANLING

1 For very young horses, the most useful and effective *Leading Exercise* is usually *Elegant Elephant* (p. 138) for getting from points A to B. The clear use of the *Wand,* your body position, and signal on the lead help the foal learn how to make smooth, balanced transitions from walk to halt and back again.

2 In some cases, it can be useful to teach a foal *Dingo* (p. 148); however, if you are not doing a lot of leading, you will probably find that *Elegant Elephant* is all you need.

3 Most foals will find *Homing Pigeon* (p. 143) to be too much stimulation, but if you feel the need to try it, have the second handler start by just walking in the position without a lead actually attached. This allows the foal to get used to the idea of people on both sides.

4 I do not recommend lungeing very young horses. It is more likely to do harm than provide benefit.

UNSTARTED THREE- OR FOUR-YEAR-OLD

1 Depending on how much your horse has been led already, you will probably find *Elegant Elephant* (p. 138) the easiest starting point. This Leading Exercise provides clear, concise signals and can be easy for the handler to master as well. Of course, there are exceptions to everything, so if the exercise feels "discombobulated," try a different position!

2 Establishing a clear understanding of *Dingo* (p. 148) will be invaluable for working in a variety of situations—on the ground and under saddle. Taking this skill to the *Cha Cha* (p. 156) will begin to create more self-carriage and increase the horse's ability to shift his weight in any direction.

Becoming an Ambidextrous Handler

Why is it considered "correct" to lead a horse from the left? Anyone who has gone through Pony Club or 4-H knows that leading a horse from the "far" or right side is considered incorrect. Horses are to be handled primarily from the "near" or left side. Unfortunately, this leftover military tradition is not particularly useful for your horse's overall straightness, flexibility, and balance. Leading horses from the left originated from the right-hand dominant military tradition of having the sword scabbard on the left side of the body. Leading and mounting horses from the left side meant that the sword was not in the way.

The result is that many horses are very one-sided and have a difficult time stopping without a left bend, or they might not be able to be led from the right at all. This tendency can be seen in unhandled foals, as they mimic their dam's posture, and is reinforced as they are primarily handled from the left side. Horses that rush on the lead will generally be turned in a circle as a way to slow them down, which increases imbalance to the left and often results in a tendency to drop the left shoulder and fall toward the handler.

Practicing leading and handling from *both* sides will go a long way to improve overall balance in posture and mentally accustom your horse to having a person on either side. It is also an excellent non-habitual exercise for handlers who, more often than not, are much less comfortable leading from the right.

3 If you have a second person to help, the *Homing Pigeon* (p. 143), even if only done once or twice, can have a huge impact. You will gain insight about how straight (or crooked) your horse is and help him develop confidence by giving him a positive, non-habitual experience in an unfamiliar situation.

4 As your horse gets more balanced and tuned in to your signals, work toward increasing the distance in *Grace of the Cheetah* (p. 141) and eventually *Dolphins Flickering Through the Waves* (p. 162). Trotting in hand once your horse is clear on the basics and calm about being asked to show different skills is an important step before lungeing and trotting under saddle.

5 It can be very interesting for you and your three- or four-year-old horse to practice these different *Dance Steps* as you incorporate Elements from the *Playground for Higher Learning* (p. 175). Each Element encourages you to practice halt, walk, turn, and wait—simple, effective ways to enhance balance and communication.

6 Once you can maintain distance in these positions and the walk cue is clear, work at even more of a distance on the lunge line. Consider lungeing to be a way to practice transitions and voice cues at a distance, and eventually, more trot work. Remember, it has been said that horses have a finite number of circles in them, so going around and around mindlessly is not productive. Keep the lunge work short and interesting.

REEDUCATING THE MATURE HORSE

1 For horses with a lot of history of being led, the *Leading Exercises* give them a new perspective on how they move in balance and use their body on the lead line. Regardless of which *Leading Exercise* you are practicing, pay attention to the older horse's posture in transitions and his overall demeanor.

2 The *Dingo* (p. 148) is useful, especially when the horse has a history of difficulty loading onto the trailer, going over obstacles, or moving forward easily under saddle.

3 Taking advantage of a friend to help you lead your horse in *Homing Pigeon* (p. 143) can be a fantastic experience for the horse. It is a very non-habitual exercise and shifts the horse's expectation of what being led is all about.

4 Some older horses have had unpleasant experiences being lunged, such as excessive stress and boring repetition. Change their perspective and incorporate some of the *Playground for Higher Learning* (p. 175) as you work at a distance with *Dolphins Flickering Through the Waves* (p. 162). Be sure to vary how you lead and what you ask for so you do not become repetitive or predictable.

Elegant Elephant

Named after the resemblance to the way an elephant handler might guide the animal's trunk with a small stick, this leading position is an excellent choice when first working with a horse on the ground. It allows the handler to provide clear, precise signals, and begins to show the horse how to move in balance and self-carriage through transitions and turns (fig. 7.4). This position will provide the most direct influence over the horse and the most control.

Basic Position

When first learning any *Leading Exercise*, it is often easiest to begin on the near (left) side of the horse because you are most accustomed to it. Once you are comfortable with the mechanics on the left, try it on the right.

Elegant Elephant places the handler near the horse's head, level with his eye. With the *Zephyr* lead attached over the noseband or up the side of the halter, the handler holds the knot end of the lead in her outside hand, with the excess line folded between the index and middle finger, as you might a lunge line.

Hold the *Wand* in your outside hand, resting in your palm, with the button end pointing up. Find the point where the *Wand* is best balanced in your hand with approximately one-third between your hand and the button end.

Take your hand nearest the horse and gently clasp the rope part of the *Zephyr* lead between your thumb and forefinger. You will be anywhere from very close to the side hardware of the halter to 12 inches away.

7.4 The *Elegant Elephant* is usually the easiest position to influence posture and straightness from the ground. The handler creates a clear signal with the *Wand*, lead, body position, and voice. The horse follows you, rather than being slightly ahead of you with you back by his shoulder, as is typically taught. In *Elegant Elephant,* the horse can actually see you.

Moving Forward

To ask the horse to come forward, move the *Wand*, which you hold level with the horse's nose, in a fluid motion forward in the direction you would like the horse to go. Allow your body to open as you make this movement.

Use the line to give a forward signal by gently sliding your fingers down the line as you say, "And waaalk." Give your horse a moment to respond to the signal before you start walking off so you do not just drag him forward. Ideally, the motion of your body and the *Wand*, combined with the signal on the lead and your voice, allows the horse to move forward without raising his head and tightening his back. Let the end of the *Wand* guide the horse where you would like him to go and at what level you would like his head. Be aware that the lead line does not tighten as you are walking.

Halting

To halt, begin by making a very small signal with the *Wand* to warn your horse that a cue is coming. Staying level with your horse's head, begin to quarter-turn your body slightly toward the horse as you say, "And whooooooa."

As you make the quarter-turn with your body and give the verbal cue, allow the *Wand* to quietly swoop toward the horse's off side shoulder as you give a slight up-and-outward signal and release on the lead. Touching the outside shoulder will help the horse halt by shifting his weight through his entire body and keeping him straight. Showing the horse how to halt by shifting his weight back in addition to a gentle signal on the lead begins to teach him halt without raising his head and neck, which is a key skill for later ridden work.

Be aware that your feet will likely be very obedient and halt as soon as you say, "And whoa." Override this habit and stay in motion until you feel your horse walking into the halt. If you simply stop your feet before your horse is organized enough to actually stop his forward motion, you will create crookedness by inadvertently turning the horse around you as a pivot point. The quarter-turn motion will help you stay level with his head to better achieve straightness and balance. As your horse becomes more balanced and tuned into your body language, your voice command will be more in sync with the actual halt.

Troubleshooting

If your horse is not halting easily, try touching him gently on the nose with the *Wand* before you bring it to his chest, and check that you are not falling too far back in your leading position. You may also check to see that your signal on the line is not too abrupt and that you give a clear ask and smooth release motion. Making some large turns left and right or using some of the obstacles in the *Playground for Higher Learning* (p. 175) will also help your horse find enough balance to stop in harmony. If none of these suggestions help your horse find a smooth halt, try one of the other *Leading Exercises* first, and come back to the *Elegant Elephant* later.

Turning

When guiding the horse through turns left and right in this position, think of yourself as the pencil on a compass in a geometry set. Staying level or slightly ahead of the horse's nose as you turn the horse away from you will create a correct, whole-body bend in your horse and avoid a dropped shoulder or rushing turn. When turning the horse toward you, be sure and have

7.5 The *Grace of the Cheetah* creates more distance between the handler and horse. The *Wand*, voice, and handler's body language are the primary signals. This leading position teaches the horse self-control and to listen to aids when you're at a distance.

the turn come through your body rather than just your arm and keep your feet moving so that you do not accidentally get stepped on.

Troubleshooting
When your horse is "stuck" through the turn, try taking the lead and your hand under the horse's chin toward the direction you are traveling.

Grace of the Cheetah
This leading position gives the horse more freedom than *Elegant Elephant*. It teaches the horse to follow the *Wand* and stay in his own space and balance (fig. 7.5). Horses that crowd their handler and only feel safe when they are close gain more confidence with this position and learn to keep their balance.

Basic Position
Stand as you would in *Elegant Elephant* (p. 138), even with the horse's head, holding the knot end of the lead and *Wand* in your outside hand, with your inside hand supporting the lead between your thumb and index finger,

approximately 12 to 24 inches from the halter. The *Wand* should be held so that your hand is at the button end and the tip is pointed away from you.

Troubleshooting

When leading at a distance the handler can tend to crowd the horse as much as the horse can crowd the handler. Be mindful that you establish and maintain your space away from the horse.

Moving Forward

To ask the horse to come forward, use the tip of the *Wand* to stroke the horse's nose once or twice as if you were applying paint with a soft paint brush. This brings the horse's attention to you and prepares him for a signal. Then move the *Wand* forward in a soft, flowing movement as you open your body in the direction you want to go. Keep the *Wand* at the same level you would like to see your horse's head. Combine this with the verbal cue, "And waaaalk," and a gentle, sliding signal along the lead with your hand nearest the horse.

Halting

To stop, slowly move the *Wand* up and down about 3 feet in front of the horse's nose to prepare for halt—it should be very precise and steady. Do not

7.6 To halt, the *Wand* touches the horse, and the handler stays level with the horse's head rather than moving back toward the shoulder.

move the *Wand* wildly. With a clear, purposeful motion, "swoop" the *Wand* toward the horse's chest and gently tap on it once or twice while saying, "And whoooooooa," as you make a quarter-turn toward the horse with your body (fig. 7.6). If your horse does not halt, add an "ask-and-release" signal, moving up and out with the lead. Avoid pulling backward.

Ideally, you and your horse will soon master this exercise to the point that the horse listens to your body language, voice, and *Wand* without the need to use a signal on the lead at all.

Troubleshooting

If your horse tends to crowd you in this position, try using the *Peacock* (p. 155) and the *Homing Pigeon* (below), or change which side you are leading from. Incorporating some of *Playground for Higher Learning* obstacles, such as the *Double Triangle* (p. 185), will also provide your horse with more focus and give him clear boundaries about where to stay. Remember that crowding is not a "dominance'" or "attitude" issue, it is a balance and body-awareness issue, usually the result of habitual crookedness or one-sidedness.

Homing Pigeon

The *Homing Pigeon* is an important step on the journey of turning your horse into a safe and reliable riding partner. The horse is led by two people, one on each side, which is a new experience for most horses (fig. 7.7). Handlers use the lead, *Wand*, voice, and body language to guide the horse between them.

The Effect

Homing Pigeon teaches the horse not to crowd and to maintain a specific distance to the handler. This is an important step in preparation for lungeing as it gives the horse confidence and improves his physical balance.

The *Homing Pigeon* gives your horse a safe "zone" in which to be introduced to new situations while staying calm. A horse that is under stress and excited can only respond instinctively and is not able to think and learn. The *Homing Pigeon* will help him override the flight instinct and think. Only then is the horse mentally and physically able to apply what he has learned and accept your guidance.

This *Leading Exercise* activates both sides of the horse's brain and helps the horse become more mentally and physically flexible. It improves the horse's ability to concentrate and have more than one handler working with him in a positive way. It is an ideal position for horses that are nervous around strangers or who do not like to have people on the right side.

Physically, *Homing Pigeon* is an excellent leading position to teach a young horse about straightness and self-carriage. Since most horses are inherently crooked or one-sided, being led between two handlers helps to encourage a straighter way of going. A horse that tends to crowd his handler, drop his shoulder, or get "pushy," for example, is likely crooked. By leading him in *Homing Pigeon,* the opposite handler can gently guide the horse to the middle and help him find a new way of going and using his body. Teaching a horse to use both sides of his body and brain is excellent preparation for work under saddle where he will be expected to listen to a right and left leg, seat, and rein.

Homing Pigeon is also an excellent leading exercise for horses that have a tendency to bite their handlers. Maintaining the horse balanced between the two handlers can keep everyone at a safe distance and teach the horse about boundaries and self-control without reactionary techniques.

Perhaps surprisingly, *Homing Pigeon* teaches the handlers as much as it does the horse. With two handlers, it is imperative to have clear

7.7 The *Homing Pigeon* provides clear parameters for the horse and enhances the handlers' communication and clarity. A handler stands on each side with a lead and a wand: one should be about 5 feet away, while the "primary" leader is about 14 inches from the horse. This leading position activates both hemispheres of the horse's brain.

communication, intention, and strategy to provide a good experience for the horse. Honing these skills is very useful for every other technique and exercise you will use in your training or retraining efforts, such as ground driving (fig. 7.8).

7.8 *Homing Pigeon* is a great technique to use when teaching a horse to ground-drive. It helps the horse maintain balance and straightness through turns and increases the clarity of the driver's signal.

How to Use It

For this *Leading Exercise*, you will need two *Wands* and two *TTouch* leads—usually two *Zephyr* leads. The lead of the "primary leader" generally goes onto the halter with the over-the-nose configuration (p. 42) and the opposite lead is attached to the side hardware or up the side of the halter. Avoid having both leads attached over the horse's nose. If you are concerned about how your horse will react to being led by two handlers, use a sliding line (an 18- to 22-foot driving line) threaded through one side of the halter. A sliding line is simply looped through the back top corner of the halter hardware and doubled-back to the second handler (see figs. 7.11 A & B, p. 149). This configuration means that if the primary handler has to take over, the secondary person can let go of one end of the line and allow it to slide free from the halter.

Since communication is so important, it is recommended that one person is designated the "Captain" and the other person is the "Co-Captain." The "Captain" is the one who decides when and where you will go, and

7.9 This young horse is kept in balance and learns to be grounded when hearing the sound of his hooves on the *Bridge* (p. 187) by the support of handlers on both sides in *Homing Pigeon*. A saddle pad held in place with an elastic girth, the *Promise Wrap* (p. 40) around the hindquarters, and the chest piece are like a "hug" and give a feeling of safe boundaries.

when you will stop and turn. Take turns with your partner because it really helps to improve the clarity of your signals and your mindfulness to play both roles (fig. 7.9). It makes a huge difference as to how well your horse understands what you are asking if you are sure of it yourself!

When leading a horse in *Homing Pigeon*, both handlers should be even with the horse's nose and can ideally see each other across the horse. Staying out to the side and slightly ahead will give you the most effective position to use your body language and help the horse stay in balance. If both handlers get caught back behind the horse's head, you may find yourselves imitating water skiers as you inadvertently drive the horse forward.

With Grace of the Cheetah

The primary leader and the helper can both be in the *Grace of the Cheetah* position (p. 141) to teach the horse to respond to the *Wand*, voice, and body signals. The tips of the *Wands* are pointed forward about 3 feet in front of the horse's nose and they create a focus point for the horse and a clear funnel for him to move between. Keep the *Wands* level with the desired head carriage of the horse. Make sure to give the horse enough space and stay about 3 feet away from his head (fig. 7.10).

With Elegant Elephant

When you need more control, the "Captain" can switch to the *Elegant Elephant* leading position (p. 138). Your hand is closer to the halter (about 3 inches from the horse's head) and can give precise signals. Hold the *Wand* so the button end points forward, and tap the horse's offside shoulder to slow as you steady the lead. The horse learns to slow down through your use of voice, body, the *Wand,* and the signal on the lead.

Note: You should never have both handlers in *Elegant Elephant* as it would crowd the horse and be counterproductive.

Communication Is Key

Mastering the *Homing Pigeon* is an exercise for the handlers as much as the horse. *Homing Pigeon* requires communication, planning, and clear use of your body language. If possible, try the *Homing Pigeon* with an older, experienced horse first. It can take a bit of practice and coordination until the two handlers are a fluid team, and it can be confusing for a young horse when the handlers are unsure. Even if you rarely have the opportunity to lead in this configuration, the experience enhances your clarity and intention in all aspects of handling and training.

7.10 The *Homing Pigeon* with both handlers in the *Grace of the Cheetah* position gives the horse space and requires clear body language to guide the horse through the exercise. Working through the *Labyrinth* (p. 179) in this way creates balance and focus.

Handler Combinations in *Homing Pigeon*

——————

➤ Both handlers walk forward in the *Grace of the Cheetah* position. This is the best position to teach balance and horse self-control.

➤ The Captain uses the *Dingo*, for example, when asking to go forward and activate the hindquarters, while the helper uses *Grace of the Cheetah.*

➤ The Captain uses *Elegant Elephant* to be more precise and have more control. The helper stays in *Grace of the Cheetah* to give the horse room.

Turning

Turning requires good communication between handlers. The inside handler signals the horse to actually create the amount of turn while the outside person is like the parameter of an outside rein. To avoid pulling back, the outside handler must stay ahead through the turn so she does not pull on the lead, which would confuse the horse. For this reason, it is a good idea to halt before the turn, or do a half-halt so the outside person has a chance to step ahead without having to run. If the outside person cannot get her body ahead, it often works to just think about keeping your hands forward through the turn. As soon as both of you are properly positioned, you can continue.

Troubleshooting

If the horse is fractious, shies, jumps to the side, or tends to rear, it is safer if one helper lets go and the primary person or Captain takes the horse herself. If you are concerned about how your horse may react to being led by two people, or one of your handlers is nervous, it is a good idea to start with a sliding line as the second lead (figs. 7.11 A & B and see p. 145).

Dingo

The *Dingo* leading position teaches the horse to respond to a light but clear forward signal on the lead, followed by a light scooping motion on the top of the croup by the *Wand*. *Dingo* teaches the horse to go forward and prepares him to accept the leg when asked to go forward on a signal under saddle. This leading position is also a basic and effective signal when teaching a horse to load into a trailer.

Once the forward signal for *Dingo* has been mastered, it is also a useful position for teaching basic lateral work from the ground, including side-pass, leg-yield, turn-on-the-forehand, and turn-on-the-haunches (as described in the *Cha Cha* exercise—p. 156).

Basic Position

Standing next to the horse's head, hold the lead line in your outside hand, folded as you would safely hold a lunge line, with your hand near the halter. Your hand nearest the horse holds the *Wand* so that the button end is resting next to your pinky finger. Allow your body to swivel slightly so you

7.11 A & B The *Homing Pigeon* with a sliding line gives a much more subtle signal than a fixed lead line. This can be used to calm a nervous horse and give him boundaries. For some horses, this may be too much confinement, and you may have to return to trust-building exercises and *TTouches* (pp. 53 and 77).

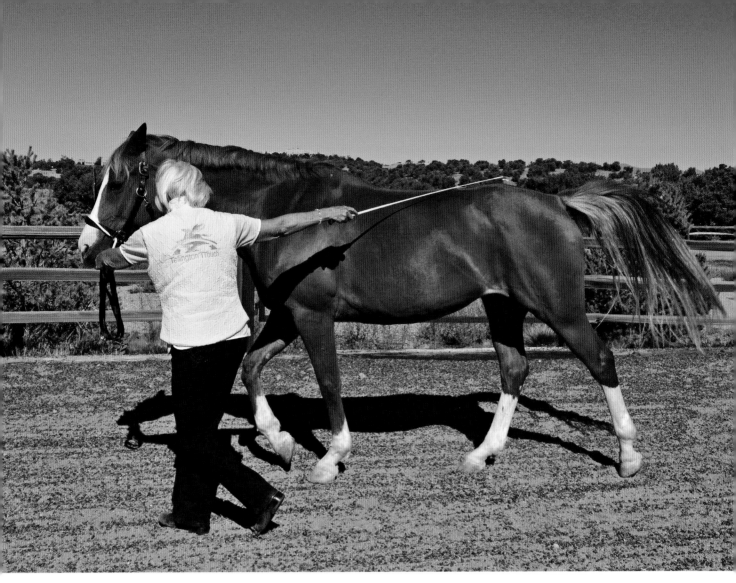

7.12 *Dingo* helps establish a "forward" cue for the horse. The handler's left hand at the horse's head asks the horse to go forward as her right hand reinforces the signal with a subtle but clear "scooping" motion at the top of the croup with the *Wand*. The handler's feet should be facing forward.

are angled toward the horse's shoulder, but your feet are ready to walk on forward (fig. 7.12).

Before you give a signal, stroke your horse all over the chest, back, legs, and croup with the *Wand* to prepare your horse for its use.

Moving Forward

There are four steps to the *Dingo* that flow together to create a clear, consistent signal for your horse:

1. Steady: With your lead hand near the halter, think of an up-and-back, "steady" signal from your body to shift your horse's weight off the forehand slightly and remain stationary (fig. 7.13).

2. Stroke: As you ask your horse to steady from the halter, take the *Wand* and stroke your horse from wither to croup two to three times (fig. 7.14).

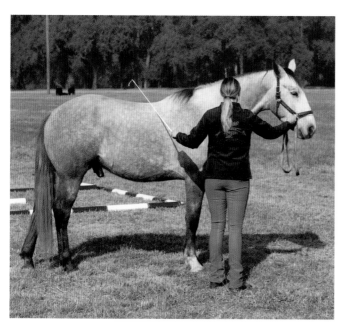 

7.13 The "steady" signal helps your horse learn to wait for the signal to move. It is important that you do not pull back with your hand but use an "ask-and-release" motion.

7.14 A stroke or two with the *Wand* along the horse's back lets him know a signal is imminent.

Make sure that the pressure is gentle but firm enough not to feel ticklish. This prepares the horse for a signal, connects his body, and ensures that he is not hypersensitive to touch along his topline.

3. Signal: Gently ask your horse to move forward with the lead, using an "ask-and-release" signal or by slowly sliding your hand a few inches down the line.

4. Tap: As you start the signal on the halter, take the *Wand* and gently tap the horse's croup twice. This should be a cue, not a punishment, so keep your hand soft to make an active, "scooping" tap rather than one that stings. Clearly say, "And waaalk," pausing for a moment to let your horse process the request. Be sure to wait for your horse's motion to begin before walking on yourself. This will ensure that you do not accidentally pull him forward. Like all the *Leading Exercises*, you want the horse to have a healthy posture and come forward without tightening his topline.

7.15 Teaching your horse *Dingo* is extremely useful for many different applications, such as trailer loading, going through narrow spaces, and as the initial signal to go forward under saddle.

The *Dingo* is a learned cue, not reflexive. At first, a horse will not necessarily understand that the tap on the croup means walk on (fig. 7.15). Initially, it may be the signal on the halter that creates movement more than the tap; however, a few times going through this process will link the tapping cue to "go forward" the horse's brain. Make sure that you pause after each signal so the horse has a moment to take in the information and respond to it before asking a second time.

Technically, *Dingo* is an exercise to teach a horse to move forward; it is not a leading position the handler maintains for long distances. Generally, the handler switches into *Elegant Elephant* (p. 138), *Grace of the Cheetah* (p. 141), or *Dolphins Flickering* (p. 162) once the horse is in motion.

Troubleshooting

If your horse is "sticky" or will not easily come forward, you can try asking him to come forward slightly to the right or left; this can release a planted foot and change his balance, or you may have to slide your hand farther down the line as you ask so he has more room.

Halting

When first teaching the horse *Dingo*, it is useful to ask for a few steps forward and then halt. This really helps the horse understand what the signal means and is an excellent exercise for shifting a horse off the forehand and carrying himself in a more functional posture. There are several choices when halting from the *Dingo* position:

Cueing the Camel

This is the most common way to halt a horse from the *Dingo* position and is very useful when only asking for one or two steps before halting. *Cueing the Camel* teaches horses to shift their weight up and back rather than putting all their weight on the forehand and dropping the back.

From the *Dingo* position, take the *Wand* across and behind the horse's hindquarters so that the *Wand* tip end is pointed directly opposite where the horse is facing. Pull your elbow backward as you bring the *Wand* between you and the horse's body, making sure the tip is pointing toward the ground. If you skim the ground with the *Wand*, simply make a larger backward motion through your elbow. Continue this U-shaped motion until the *Wand* is pointing in the same direction as the horse and can be brought in front of the horse's chest.

7.16 The horse is asked to back up by keeping the head level and straight. Hold the lead in the left hand and use an "ask-and-release" signal while tapping the horse's chest with the *Wand*.

Allow your body to quarter-turn toward the horse as you tap the *Wand* on the horse's chest, saying, "And whoooa." It can be helpful to think about shifting your weight and energy up and back as you do this, allowing for a small "ask-and-release" signal on the lead with this motion (fig. 7.16). Be sure to keep your lower back flat, not arched, and stay centered over the balls of your feet. Keep moving your feet until you feel your horse walk into the halt so you do not inadvertently bend the horse around you; ideally, the horse stops straight.

Boomer's Bound
Another way to stop the horse from the *Dingo* position is *Boomer's Bound* (figs. 7.17 A–D). This exercise prepares the horse for mounting by creating movement over his head. A lot of horses are scared the first time something moves above the head and back; *Boomer's Bound* teaches them not to feel threatened and to stay calm when you move in the saddle.

Before attempting this halting exercise, you will want to accustom your horse to the *Wand* over his head and back while stationary. Holding the line and *Wand* in the *Dingo* position, carefully but confidently motion the *Wand* over the back, neck, head, and ears. Once your horse is comfortable with this movement, you can try it from walk to halt.

As you ask your horse to halt from *Dingo*, bring the *Wand* forward and

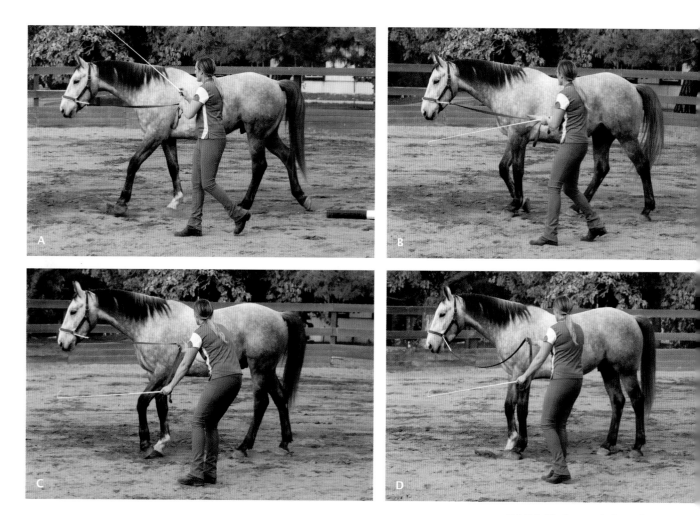

A

7.17 A–D *Boomer's Bound* helps familiarize horses with movement over the head in addition to being a practical way to halt a horse while keeping him straight.

over the neck and ears, over the horse's head and in front of his nose, as you say, "And whooooa," to signal a halt. If the horse does not stop with the visual aid of the *Wand* you may take the *Wand* to the chest as you give a small "ask-and-release" signal with the line and a quarter-turn with your body.

Peacock

This exercise helps to keep the horse at the desired distance and teaches him to be comfortable with motion around his body. It is also useful to employ when switching from *Dingo* to other leading positions on the fly.

While standing in the *Dingo* leading position, begin to move away from the horse, 3 feet or more, and carefully move the *Wand* back and forth between you and the horse as if it were windshield wipers on a car. Use

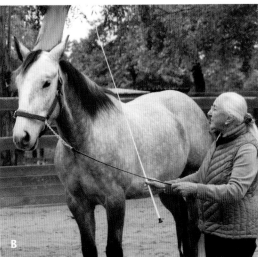

7.18 A & B The *Peacock* establishes a boundary between you and your horse, and teaches him to keep his distance from you while standing with his body in a straight line. You may use a light tap on the horse's neck to encourage him to keep an approximately 4-foot distance. Tapping on the neck also encourages the horse to keep his head and neck straight.

a steady and rhythmic motion with the *Wand*; it is not supposed to scare the horse away from you, but rather should clearly designate "your space" and "his space" (figs. 7.18 A & B). This prepares your horse to switch from *Dingo* to *Grace of the Cheetah* (p. 141) and *Dolphins Flickering Through the Waves* (p. 162). This motion can also be done while in *Grace of the Cheetah*, should your horse crowd you.

Cha Cha

Also known as *The Dance*, this exercise is a more advanced version of *Dingo*. It differentiates each of the horse's legs and where to move them: forward, back, and side to side (figs. 7.19 A–C).

7.19 A–C The *Cha Cha* begins like the Dingo; however, you only ask for one step at a time, differentiating which leg moves when.

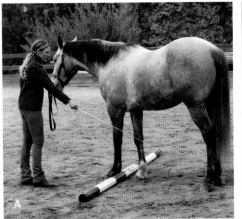
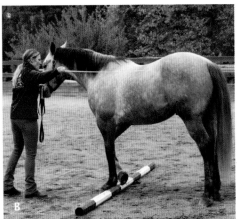

7.20 Using the *Wand* to stroke the leg and tap the hoof you would like to move helps increase awareness and clarifies the signal.

The Effect

Cha Cha is an introductory step toward lateral work and provides the handler with a way to quietly and systematically influence each foot. It helps to create greater balance, refines your signals, and encourages self-control and focus.

How to Use It

Once your horse is comfortable with *Dingo* and really understands the signal to go forward, you can begin to ask for one step forward with a specific leg. Decide which leg you would like to ask to move forward. Stroke the leg firmly all the way down to the hoof and tap the wall of the hoof (fig. 7.20). As you feel your horse shifting his weight forward, bring the *Wand* forward to ask for halt in *Cueing the Camel* position (see p. 153). It is important that you change to *Cueing the Camel* before your horse actually finishes the step so he does not commit to a second step.

Initially, ask for just one step forward and halt. Once you and your horse are comfortable with this, you can add to the complexity, such as adding one step back at a time. When asking a horse to back up, it is important to do so slowly (fig. 7.21). Teaching horses to back quickly can be very dangerous and does not teach them about their balance and self-control or put them into a good posture.

7.21 Teaching the horse to back using the *Cha Cha* prepares him to accept the rider's aids, whether going forward or backing up. To teach the horse to go straight back, keep the horse's head in line with his body by holding the lead 2 inches from the halter and cueing with light "ask-and-release" signals.

7.22 A & B When asking for any lateral movement, especially turn-on-the-forehand, be sure that you only ask for one step at time. Be sure to ask in a way that allows the horse to remain calm, and only ask as much as he can give comfortably. Do whatever you can to make the horse feel successful.

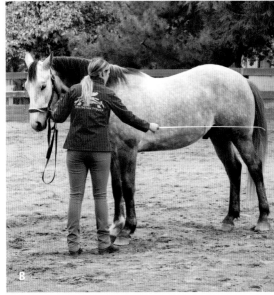

The most important thing to remember when you ask a horse to back up is to encourage a relaxed posture. Many horses put their head up and drop their back when backing. To encourage a more correct posture, most of the signal in the *Cha Cha* should be through the *Wand*, rather than the halter. A "tap, tap" on the horse's chest, point of the shoulder, or just below or above the knee can be very effective to signal a backing motion while maintaining a released topline.

Once your horse can slowly back with whatever leg you ask, you can start asking legs to move left or right independently, laying the groundwork for lateral exercises. *Cha Cha* can easily be used to teach turn-on-the-fore-hand, turn-on-the-haunches, and leg-yield from the ground. Use the same principles as the basic *Cha Cha*, asking for single steps, and focusing on balance and posture rather than speed (figs. 7.22 A & B).

Troubleshooting

Many horses will swing their haunches away from the *Wand* and essentially disengage their hindquarters. This is not a useful default. Ideally, the horse pushes off from the supporting leg and steps a single step across rather than scrambling sideways quickly (fig. 7.23).

7.23 Be mindful that the horse stays contained in his body while asking for lateral movement. A horse that is too flexible and is able to contort in all directions will lose much of the tensile strength required to truly carry a rider in self-carriage.

Trotting in Hand

Once your horse is familiar with *Dingo* (p. 148) and calmly and happily moves forward, it is time to introduce *Trotting in Hand* (fig. 7.24). For some horses it will be enough to simply use *Dingo* from the walk and allow them to naturally increase speed to the trot. Others, however, will require the steps to be broken down. No matter which way makes sense to your horse initially, it is important that he is not chased into trot and understands that it is a quiet, easy transition.

The Effect

Trotting in Hand helps reinforce verbal cues and familiarizes your horse with upward transitions.

7.24 Teaching your horse to quietly trot in hand is a great skill. Like any new exercise, pay special attention to your horse's posture and overall level of acceptance and comfort.

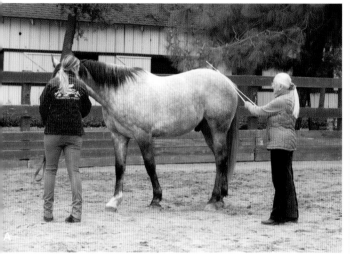

7.25 A & B The helper begins by letting the horse know that she is there by stroking the hindquarters with the *Wand* so that there are no surprises.

How to Use It

If your horse needs a clearer signal than *Dingo* from the walk, you may want to use a second person to help with this exercise. The use of the second person is not meant to push or scare the horse forward. The second handler simply helps clarify the signal forward.

Starting at the halt, the second person uses two *Wands* to quietly stroke the horse along the back and around the hindquarters. It is important to stand at a distance that makes you feel safe and where you are not able to be kicked, though this is unlikely if you are paying attention to your horse's body language and adding the signals in small steps. The person at the back should use her verbal cues as she uses the *Wands*, saying, "Aannnnnnnd…" as she strokes the horse, and then, "…waaaalllllk," as she taps the *Wands* together (figs. 7.25 A & B).

Once the horse is comfortable with the helper's position, she can ask the horse to go forward with a *Dingo* signal. The handler at the head simply helps reinforce the signal. Walk and halt a few times so the horse starts to listen to the helper. Make sure that the person at the back uses her verbal cues.

Now at the walk, the helper can ask for *Dingo* again. The handler at the head must not try and pull the horse forward. If the horse does not increase his speed at all, the helper should click the two *Wands* together to make a tapping noise above the croup. The handler at the head must make sure that she allows the forward motion to come from the signal at the back of the

7.26 Teaching your horse
to trot in hand is a practical
and fun exercise. You can
use the *Wand* as you have
in other *Leading Exercises*
to help with the cues.

horse and not the lead. Initially, let your stride get longer and "glide" into the trot so you do not surprise the horse by bouncing up and down.

The most important part, at first, is that the transition is a quiet one. Only ask for a few steps of trot and then ask for walk. Incrementally increase the length of the trot, watching for a relaxed posture and steady rhythm. When you are comfortable with the horse's understanding while using a helper, you can move on to *Trotting in Hand* on your own. The *Dingo* position and cue forward should let the horse know your intention (fig. 7.26).

Troubleshooting
It can be useful to trot toward the gate initially, just a few strides, if you are concerned about downward transitions, or if your horse needs a little more motivation.

Dolphins Flickering Through the Waves
Dolphins Flickering Through the Waves is a very useful step to prepare for lungeing while maintaining good posture and clear understanding. Initially,

many horses find being lunged—being sent forward in a lot of small circles—confusing. This exercise shows horses, in a step-by-step way, how to work at a distance from a handler in a healthy posture and a fun, reciprocal way (fig. 7.27).

The Effect

This exercise teaches your horse to keep his distance and stay in balance.

How to Use It

Dolphins Flickering Through the Waves is an extension of the *Dingo* position. Begin in the same leading position as you would for *Dingo* (p. 148). As you ask your horse to move forward with the "tap" on the croup and small signal on the halter, allow the lead to slide out through your fingers and send the horse out as you step away from his shoulder, adjusting your position so you are level with the horse's withers in a classical lungeing position. It is important that you allow the "forward" to come from the hind end and do not try to "pull" the horse forward with your hand. If you do this, you will often end up with your horse facing you.

Once your horse is moving forward, you can send him out with a gentle touch or tap at the shoulder, neck, behind the poll, and on the side of the halter, or on the lead to show him where he needs to be (figs. 7.28 A–D). Make sure to tap smoothly as if you were painting with a soft brush. Once

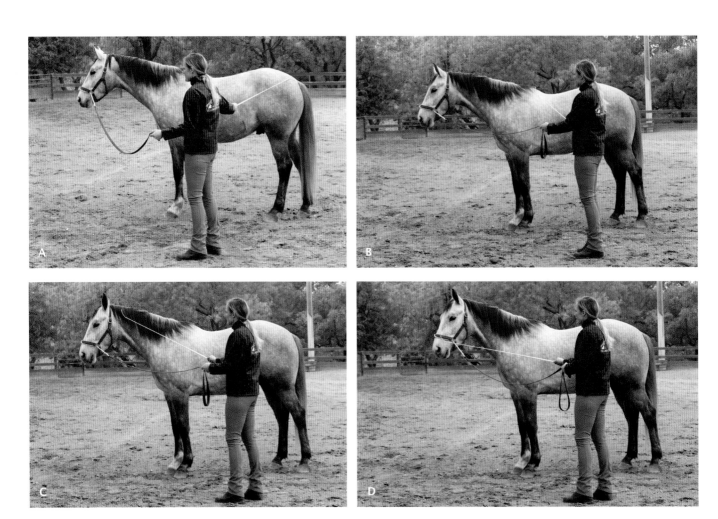

7.28 A–D Use the *Wand* to guide your horse in the direction that you would like to go. A signal on the croup starts the forward motion (A); a light signal on the withers (B), neck (C), or nose (D) helps send the horse away from the handler.

your horse has understood the exercise, you just need to point with the *Wand* and don't have to make a connection (fig. 7.29). To halt the horse, change to *Grace of the Cheetah* (p. 141), *Boomer's Bound* (p. 154), or *Cueing the Camel* (p. 153).

Troubleshooting

If you find that your horse is falling toward you, ask for a more purposeful walk or march before sending the horse out. The better the propulsion of the hind legs, the easier it will be for the horse to move out in balance.

Mindful Lungeing

Many trainers feel that lungeing with a saddle and bridle is an irreplaceable step when training a young horse. I would like to caution you that starting

7.29 As the horse understands the exercise, he is better able to maintain a steady distance and follow your voice and body language.

this exercise too early can cause a number of problems. A horse that is lunged with short side-reins, for example, can very quickly develop back problems, learn to overbend and shorten through the neck, and will not use his topline to its full extent. And repetitively moving a horse in a circle smaller than 20 meters can seriously damage the hocks and other joints. It takes a lot of experience and finesse to properly lunge a horse, and he can learn poor posture and negative behavior when it is done incorrectly. Unfortunately, it happens far too often—a horse gets going too fast on the lunge and ends up just running circles out of control. This can cause permanent physical damage and create crookedness, not to mention the fact that it can be psychologically traumatizing, too.

It is fairly common for a rider to lunge her horse so the horse can "get his bucks out" before mounting. In my opinion, this can really scare a horse and set the nervous system up to constantly repeat the behavior. When you prepare your horse properly for ridden work, and use the techniques in this book, it is very rare for a horse to buck. Lungeing a horse before getting on with the intent to get rid of excess energy will eventually just improve conditioning, so every time it will take longer to tire him out. Instead, take five minutes before getting on to do some *Ear TTouches* (p. 115), *Lower the Head* (p. 65), and use the *Lick of the Cow's Tongue* (p. 95) on his rump. Then lead the horse through the *Labyrinth* (p. 179) a few times, checking in with

Why They Buck

I see bucking as instinctual behavior, which is triggered by fear, stress, or pain, or as a symptom of imbalance. When young horses buck before they ever carry a rider, it is usually triggered by the unfamiliar pressure of the saddle and the restriction of a tight girth combined with a lack of balance. This can easily be avoided by preparing the horse with the *Troika TTouch* (p. 97), *Lick of the Cow's Tongue* (p. 65), and *Belly Lifts* (p. 111) before tightening the girth. Placing the girth gently and tightening it one hole at a time is the best insurance against bucking that is triggered by fear.

My initial approach to a horse who bucks is to check the reactivity in the girth area. Is he "goosey," meaning reactive to a direct 3 pressure behind the elbows? Or does he move away and throw his head up? These are clear signs of tension that can result in bucking. Go back to applying *Abalone TTouch* (p. 92) or *Coiled Python* (p. 105) in the girth area, and *Clouded Leopard TTouch* (p. 90)

along the back, followed by *Lick of the Cow's Tongue* (p. 95).

Many years ago, I met a young woman who brought a four-year-old Thoroughbred mare to a clinic in Calgary. This mare had been ridden for a year but still kept bucking her rider off. The first time she had been saddled was in a box stall without much preparation, as is often done with Thoroughbreds. This mare ended up bucking in the stall for an entire hour before the trainer was able to go in and take the saddle off.

In my opinion, the mare originally bucked because she had not been prepared for the sensation of the saddle on her back and the girth around her belly, and she held a lot of tension in these areas. It is not surprising for a young horse to be startled when, all of the sudden, there is something stuck on his back and a tight strap around his belly. He becomes frightened and bucks.

Once a horse learns to buck with a saddle, he will be more likely to resort to the behavior in times of stress. Most beings will default to what

Dingo (p. 148) to prepare the horse for riding and establishing clear communication. The horse learns to learn, to listen to you, and to be calm and attentive when you mount.

Teaching your horse to lunge in systematic steps, like using *Dolphins Flickering Through the Waves* (p. 162) and walking with the motion of the horse instead of standing as if cemented in one spot, reduces the chances of your horse responding to lungeing in an explosive manner. Using an oval shape rather than the usual round circle gives the handler more flexibility to

they learned first in times of extreme stress. These horses will have a much greater tendency to buck with the rider than horses that have been slowly and calmly introduced to the saddle and carrying a rider's weight.

To avoid bucking, always watch carefully that you take small steps and break the exercises in this book down into increments so that the horse is comfortable with the process and understands what is being asked of him. Use the Checklist (p. 285) to track his progress and revisit the areas that need attention. This way, training is fun for people and horses.

If this mare in Calgary had had the opportunity to be started under saddle with the help of *TTouches* and *Leading Exercises* and *Mindful Lungeing*, instead of feeling like she had to fight, she would have developed into a very different horse and would have had a much more stress-free and enjoyable life. But here she was—bucking had become a habit she resorted to as soon as she felt her

rider's demands were too difficult and she got tense and panicked.

I placed a rope around the base of the mare's neck and applied a bit of pressure in my direction to move her out of balance. Her immediate response was to buck as soon as she felt the slightest sideways pressure—she had never learned to balance herself. No wonder she bucked as soon as the rider shifted in the saddle. Being out of balance, especially when under the control of a human on the ground or when being ridden, can be incredibly frightening and cause a horse to react in explosive ways.

I used *TTouches* to release the mare's overall body tension and taught her in small steps to shift her weight and find her balance through the *Leading Exercises* and the *Playground for Higher Learning* (p. 175). As she became more comfortable in her body and able to maintain balance through changes of direction and transitions, the bucking stopped.

7.30 As you lunge your horse, pay attention to his overall posture. If your horse is bracing or leaning, you may want to use a *Body Wrap* (p. 44), the *Tellington Training Bit* (p. 278), or *Elements* from the *Playground of Higher Learning* (p. 175) to help correct him.

adjust varying distances, encourages the horse to go in straight lines as well as on a bending one, and can reduce the likelihood of the horse leaning to the outside (fig. 7.30). The transition from straight line to bend and bend to straight line helps create impulsion and focus.

The Effect

This is a very useful exercise because your horse learns to respond to voice commands before you sit in the saddle, and he becomes comfortable in transitions. Instead of just standing at a stationary center point while the horse runs in a circle around you, in *Mindful Lungeing* you walk about 30 feet, ask the horse for a half-circle, then walk another 10 feet, and do another half-circle. This teaches the horse to balance himself and think instead of just blindly running in a circle. The oval shape will give your horse the chance to learn about bending *and* straight lines, the combination of which allows for the development of impulsion and balance.

7.31 Working on an oval and walking parallel to your horse, rather than keeping your feet still in one spot, allows you more freedom for sending the horse out in larger figures and alternating between straight lines and curves.

Basic Position

To learn lungeing on an oval, start by leading the horse in *Dolphins Flickering Through the Waves* (p. 162) at a distance of about 6 feet. This teaches him to stay out of your space and listen to your signals to find the right distance, stop, and move forward when asked. You are a little farther away from the horse, but still close enough to be very effective and able to control him. Maintain a position directly in line with his shoulder and withers so you are not in a dangerous place, should he kick out in excitement or in a moment of imbalance.

Moving Forward

To create more forward energy in the horse I stand up straight, raise my hands to be level with the horse's back, and point the *Wand* an inch behind the tail (fig. 7.31). Your horse will quickly learn to respond to the level of your hands and willingly follow your signals to walk or trot on.

Lungeing with the Body Wrap
and Tellington Training Bit

7.32 A & B Ljori before (A) and after (B).

Try lungeing your horse with a *Body Wrap* (p. 44) and the *Tellington Training Bit* (p. 278—not shown here) under the halter. Attach the lead line to the halter and twist the reins of the bridle under the neck, securing them with the throatlatch. Carrying the *Training Bit* can release the horse's poll and TMJ, while encouraging soft chewing and salivating. Maintaining this freedom will encourage the horse's back to swing and the pelvis to engage, improving balance in all the gaits.

The *Body Wrap* can completely change the way your horse carries his body without causing any restrictions and can be a great way to develop self-carriage. The gelding shown here completely changed his way of going on the lunge immediately after wearing the *Body Wrap.* Once he experienced this new posture in *Mindful Lungeing,* he was able to find it more readily in the other *Leading Exercises,* under saddle, and even when he was free in the pasture.

Remember to keep your *Mindful Lungeing* session short and interesting. You can add poles for the horse to step over, and change the size of your oval so it does not become repetitive or predictable. Asking horses to carry themselves in bending lines as well as straight lines helps to build balance and self-carriage.

Halting

To slow the horse down, I lean slightly forward, lower my head, upper body, and both hands, and drop the *Wand* to point toward the hocks while the horse is about 18 feet from me. At the same time I use my verbal cue. You may also try taking the *Wand* into your front hand as you would with *Grace of the Cheetah* and using that as a cue to stop (p. 141). If you have prepared your horse with *Dolphins Flickering Through the Waves* (p. 162) you will likely have no problem halting the horse on the oval, rather than have him turn and face you as can often happen. Stopping on the oval, as opposed to turning to face you, teaches your horse to think rather than instinctively turn.

The Story of Lord Wendland

Lord Wendland—"Lord" for short—was bred for success. Success in the show jumping ring. International success. His pedigree contains all the great German jumping sires. Lord. Casall. Contender. Calypso. But then things went wrong…he just got too big. Successful international show jumpers are not extremely tall. Lord was lucky because his breeder gave him time to grow and play. He was only started at six years old, but his breeders soon realized that he just did not have the big jumping ability he was supposed to have.

Lord came from a flat part of Germany, and he had no idea what he was supposed to do with the hills all around the home he moved to. When his new owner walked him down his first hill, he just stopped. She coaxed him slowly down. When she turned him around to go back up the hill, again his body didn't have a single clue what to do—he even tried to jump it! His owner took him to do hill training four times a week until he eventually got the idea.

Under saddle, Lord was always way too short in his neck, even with a plain snaffle bit and very light hands. And whenever he was schooled over raised cavalletti or just trotting poles on the ground, he knocked them in every direction. Even with a lot of training and help from two thoughtful, professional trainers, he did not get better.

I met Lord's owner Daniela at Equitana in Germany, and she decided to try *TTouch* to see if it would help the gelding before his next jumping lesson. She performed a variety of *TTouches*, including *Python Lift* (p. 101) with an emphasis on the "pause" moment at the end of each movement, *Tail Circles* (p. 121), and *Leg Circles* (p. 106).

"What I found very interesting were the *Leg Circles*," said Daniela. She had performed them before on other horses. "So far all the horses I ever did *Leg Circles* with were really hard work. You have a heavy leg and are supposed to move it lightly and fluently, the movement coming from your complete body. I was very reluctant to try it on Lord because once you do one, you have to do all four legs. But I was surprised by Lord! His legs were extremely light, weighing nothing, moving very lightly, very loosely. They felt like they were not even attached to his body."

Daniela trailered him to the jump session directly following the *TTouch* bodywork and walked her horse for 10 minutes while her jumping trainer built a course. The trainer took him for his usual 30-minute warm-up, including trot poles…and Lord cleared them! It was the same with cavalletti at the trot and canter—the gelding had much better body awareness and control than any time before.

The next day, Daniela did hill work with Lord, this time using the *Balance Rein* (p. 275), and he reached down for the bit with long, relaxed steps and a swinging back and tail, even over the varying terrain.

Playground for
Higher Learning

Navigating the Elements

Any time you work with a horse, you want the experience to be engaging, interesting, and enriching. Incorporating the Tellington Method *Playground for Higher Learning* into your training and retraining sessions provides you and your horse with clear focus and specific exercises for balance and coordination. While they are not something you will necessarily repeat over and over, the *Elements* provide long-lasting learning for your horse, directly and indirectly preparing him for many lifelong skills and experiences.

For horses that have missed a good foundation from their previous training, the *Playground for Higher Learning* offers many possibilities in which to learn self-control and change old behaviors. These simple yet effective *Elements* (since obstacles are something that have to be overcome)

8.1 The *Elements* create clear, interesting points for horse and handler to navigate. Calmly mastering each of the *Elements* helps to build physical, mental, and emotional balance. The slow, mindful leading positions allow for improved self-carriage (physical balance), which, in turn, enhances self-confidence (mental balance) and allows for greater self-control (emotional balance).

are done fairly slowly and mindfully to enhance balance and concentration. The mindful, non-habitual movements used to navigate through the *Elements* improve the horse's ability to learn, refine communication between horse and handler as it becomes more clear and effective, and help the horse gain confidence as well as trust in the people around him. Nervous horses become calmer; horses that have "checked out" or "shut down" plug back in and start to enjoy working with you. Young and inexperienced horses will be engaged and gain self-confidence and trust in their handler through low-stress, mindful, positive experiences (fig. 8.1).

You can start by leading your horse through the different *Elements* in the *Playground for Higher Learning* and then progress with driving and riding through them. Make sure to lead your horse equally from both sides through the obstacles and use different leading positions (see *Dance Steps*, p. 131) to keep the work interesting and the horse balanced and flexible.

Here are a few recommendations for *Playground for Higher Learning* exercises for every stage of training or retraining:

FOAL OR WEANLING

1 If you are keen to introduce the *Playground for Higher Learning Elements* to your foal, start by letting him explore them while following his mother or at liberty with friends when weaned. Most foals are naturally curious and enjoy the playful aspect of discovering new items and scenarios. Note: Do not do this with the *Elements* made out of plastic.

2 A very confident foal that leads well can be led through some of the *Elements* with his mother or another calm, familiar horse present for reassurance. Keep the sessions short and do not ask him to stand around for long. Be careful to remain light with your hands so you can go with the foal's movement when he is surprised.

3 Plastic can be slowly introduced when leading, but be *very* cautious not to allow the foal to bite or nibble on it. If he were to bite on it and get scared by the movement or sound, he might not realize how to let go of it. This could cause a domino effect that is best avoided!

4 In most scenarios, a little goes a long way where foals are concerned. A well socialized, quietly handled foal that knows how to be a horse will

quickly learn these exercises as a three- or four-year-old, whether or not he has ever experienced them before.

UNSTARTED THREE- OR FOUR-YEAR-OLD

1 The *Playground for Higher Learning Elements* are ideal for any youngster being prepared for under saddle training. Navigate through all of the pole-based *Elements*, working up to walking over, between, and under plastic or other unusual items. The *Labyrinth* will likely become a cornerstone of the starting process for each stage of progression. Coming back to it with each additional piece of tack or new task helps to create a smooth progression by including the familiar, predictable exercise.

2 Mindfully mastering *any* of these exercises will help prepare your horse for his role as a confident, reliable, and happy riding horse.

REEDUCATING THE MATURE HORSE

1 It is a good idea to check in with all of the *Elements* when working with a mature horse. While they may seem like straightforward exercises, an unbalanced, tense, or crooked horse will have some difficulty navigating them with ease.

2 Horses that have issues such as spooking, bracing, tripping, difficulty crossing water, trouble trailer loading, or any number of other common issues will benefit from these exercises. Focus on precise communication through the *Elements* and encourage slow, mindful transitions and changes of direction. Enhancing balance and encouraging a healthy posture helps to relieve many of the tension patterns associated with challenging behavior.

3 In particular, mastering the plastic *Elements* in a low-stress, incremental way helps to build self-confidence and encourages learning and trust.

The Elements

Even if your horse appears to have no concern about any of the *Elements* that follow, going through them together will help build trust and communication and foster a better relationship.

The Labyrinth

A 1984 study with Anna Wise, the director of the Biofeedback Institute in Boulder, Colorado, showed that horses produce beta brainwaves when they turn the corner of a *Labyrinth* constructed of ground poles, using small, deliberate steps, and stopping frequently (fig. 8.2). Beta brainwaves are measurable in humans when they are using logical thinking!

The Use of Food

Sometimes I will offer the horse some food when he is fearful, holding his breath, throwing his head up, or is really tense. Food can also be very helpful with certain obstacles in the *Playground,* such as *Working with Plastic* (p. 190), or the first time the horse is mounted to establish a positive association and increase relaxation. I will either place the food on top of the plastic or offer it in a shallow dish. A horse that is chewing cannot hold his breath at the same time. By breathing and lowering his head, the horse relaxes and can think again. Chewing activates the parasympathetic nervous system while the sympathetic nervous system that triggers the flight reflex is reduced.

It is best to offer the horse grain, horse treats, or hay rather than pellets, because horses can choke on pellets. I offer horses that get too fixated on food a lower-value treat, such as grass or hay. Horses that are very stressed may not accept any food at all or will grab at the food anxiously.

Whether or not you choose to use food is up to the individual person and the horse. Unless you are using clearly defined methods of positive reinforcement training, food tends to be most beneficial with very sensitive or nervous horses. Horses that are very friendly or default to "fool-around" displacement behaviors when stressed can become overly fixated on food and may do best with a well-placed scratch or *TTouch*.

I have found that the *Labyrinth* teaches the horse to optimize his balance and increase self-control. He will find not only his physical balance, but his mental and emotional balance as well. Simple walk-halt transitions and left and right turns give the handler great feedback about where the horse is starting in terms of baseline understanding and help teach the horse in the process. When you first try the *Labyrinth* with a horse, it is interesting to pay attention to the following: Does he bend left and right evenly? Does the inside hind leg step under or does it make short steps? Does he rush out of the bend? All of these observations will give you information and help you notice changes in your horse's balance as you master more of the techniques outlined in this book.

Nervous horses often settle in the *Labyrinth* and it is easier for them to concentrate and respond to small signals while working with this obstacle. For many horses, the familiarity of the *Labyrinth* becomes calming and is a great tool to have when teaching new skills or using new equipment.

8.2 The *Labyrinth* is the hallmark *Element* in the *Playground for Higher Learning.* A horse that rushes, falls through turns, or has difficulty focusing will find this to be an invaluable exercise.

8.3 The *Labyrinth* (see fig. 8.2) can be adjusted as necessary with longer or shorter poles, depending on the needs of the horse. The *Open Labyrinth* shown here is another option that allows for wider turns should the horse find the exercise too challenging to stay in balance.

Equipment

Take six 12-foot poles and lay them on the ground with a distance of 4 feet between them in the shape of a maze (see fig. 8.2). Depending on the horse's size and flexibility, you can make the distance between poles larger or smaller. You can also make an *Open Labyrinth* that allows for bigger turns and different changes of direction (fig. 8.3).

How to Use It

The *Labyrinth* can be done using all the different leading positions. It is usually easiest to start in the *Elegant Elephant* (p. 138), which allows you to most precisely give halt and turning signals.

While you can go through the *Labyrinth* at a half-walk or without stopping at every corner, the "classic" way to use this *Element* in a mindful manner is to halt before each turn. As you approach the *Labyrinth*, halt before you enter, and put yourself in a position level with the horse's eye. Ask the horse to walk forward and allow motion to start for a step before you direct him through the turn. Prepare to halt for the next corner almost as soon as you have started walking. It is important to start asking to halt before you are at the place you would like to be stationary so your horse has a chance to respond smoothly. Continue this process throughout the rest of the *Labyrinth* (fig. 8.4).

For some horses, *Dingo* (p. 148) will be an excellent leading position to use. The *Dingo* helps to create more propulsion in the walk and encourages a better step under and through with the inside hind leg through the corners. As you take your horse through the corner of the *Labyrinth*, allow your horse enough room to make a wide, balanced bend rather than pulling him onto his inside shoulder.

8.4 The *Labyrinth* gives the handler a lot of information about the horse's balance and straightness; at the same time, it teaches the horse how to bend and rebalance in and out of turns.

Troubleshooting

While on the outside of a corner, the handler needs to think about sending her hands forward, much like the pencil making a circle on a geometry compass. This will avoid inadvertently pulling backward when you are on the outside of the turn.

The Zebra

The *Zebra* is a simple element that gives horses and handlers (or riders) a clear parameter between two sets of poles (fig. 8.5). The gentle changes of direction help horses learn how to subtly shift their weight and offer a change of bend.

Equipment

Six to eight 10- to 12-foot poles are ideal, set up in a zigzag "chute" (see fig. 8.5).

How to Use It

The *Zebra* can be used in virtually any leading position, while ground driving, or riding. It can be used to create some parameters and distance with your horse or to simply give him the experience of gently turning left and right while maintaining forward motion.

The Fan

Practicing the *Fan* is a way to help improve hoof-eye coordination and the horse's ability to judge distances. The arcing nature of this *Element* helps to create a clear bend through the horse's body, which allows for more articulation through the hocks and encourages a dynamic shift of weight (fig. 8.6). Horses that are stiff through the body,

8.5 The *Zebra* is an easy *Element* to create and can be modified, depending on the number of poles at your disposal.

8.6 The *Fan* encourages a balanced bend through the horse's body, as well as concentration and coordination.

8.7 The spacing between the poles in the *Fan* can be adjusted for the needs of the individual horse. Mounting blocks, wooden stumps, straw bales, tires, and crates are all potential risers for the poles. Always check to make sure that the poles do not roll too easily should they be knocked down.

Step by Step

When your horse is having trouble with an *Element*, make it easier for him. For example, if he stumbles over the poles while in the *Fan*, start by leading him over just one pole at first. Ask him to stop before the pole and again after the front feet have stepped over it. Stroke the legs firmly with the *Wand*, tapping each hoof with the button end. Increase the level of difficulty (the number of poles navigated, for example) gradually, possibly over several sessions.

heavy on the forehand, or have a tendency to trip will benefit from mastering the *Fan*.

Equipment

Four or five 12-foot heavy poles and something solid one end of each pole can rest on, such as one or two tires or a bale of straw (fig. 8.7).

How to Use It

Choose a leading position where you are a little bit farther away from the horse. This allows your horse enough room to see the poles and find his balance. Start in the *Grace of the Cheetah* (p. 141) and later you can add *Dolphins Flickering Through the Waves* (p. 162), and *Homing Pigeon* (p. 143). You can use this *Element* for all *Ground driving* techniques, and once confident, under saddle, as well.

Initially plan to halt before the first pole so you can regroup and help your horse go forward in a calm, relaxed manner. You may stroke the legs and tap the hooves with the *Wand* to help increase awareness and remind your horse where his feet are.

Keep the exercise simple in the beginning and use *Grace of the Cheetah* to walk over the low end of the poles. Then take the horse though the center of the poles, watching two poles ahead of the horse to be sure he has enough room, and that he can see the poles and judge the height. Lead the horse from both sides. When you are leading on the side that puts you on the high end, it is safest to walk around the outside rather than over the poles.

If your horse has a hard time navigating the poles, experiment with different heights and distances to make it easier until he finds his coordination.

Pick-Up Sticks

Pick-Up Sticks improves sure-footedness and coordination (fig. 8.8). The horse learns to lower his head to better judge where to place his feet instead of rushing over an unfamiliar obstacle. Young horses gain confidence and those who are being retrained learn to concentrate and develop a positive attitude toward new challenges.

8.8 *Pick-Up Sticks* helps horses become more aware of their feet while encouraging focus and coordination. This is a great *Element* to incorporate for the horse that is not careful on the trail, or the horse that tends to rush and trip, and for where footing is uneven.

Equipment

You will need four to six poles. Square poles are ideal but can be hard to come by; two-by-fours can be substituted. Crisscross them at random on the ground in a single pile.

How to Use It

Start with the *Elegant Elephant* (p. 138) leading position to ensure the horse moves slowly and is concentrating as you navigate around and over the *Pick-Up Sticks* from various directions. Later on, you can switch to *Grace of the Cheetah* (p. 141) to give the horse more room to see where he places his feet.

Double Triangle

The *Double Triangle* is a wonderful element for teaching the *Leading Exercises* with more space between horse and handler (p. 185) and when *Ground Driving* (p. 209). The configuration of poles allows for bending lines and provides clear spatial boundaries. It is also a great element to use under saddle for clear and fun changes of direction and transitions.

Equipment

You will need six poles. If possible, three pairs of different colors are best. Set them up with one smaller triangle surrounded by another larger, open-sided triangle (see fig. 8.9).

How to Use It

The *Double Triangle* can be used simply as poles to walk over; however, it is

8.9 Use the shape of the *Double Triangle* to put yourself on the inside of one set of poles and your horse on the other. This creates a clear visual barrier for your horse and yourself. As he understands the signals, you can change the size of the triangular space, spiraling in and out as you like.

an excellent *Element* to use when teaching horses to lead in *Dolphins Flickering Through the Waves* (p. 162). Having the horse walk around the outer triangle while the handler stays on the inside helps clarify the exercise and teaches the horse how to stay at a distance.

For driving and riding, the poles can be used in a clover-leaf pattern to encourage bending and turning. Using different colors makes it a great *Element* to use when working with another person because it is easier to plan and describe where you want to direct the horse.

The *Double Triangle* is fun to use in riding lessons and can even be set up as small jumps or cavalletti as skills increase.

8.10 Simple poles or slightly raised *Poles and Cavalletti* can be used to increase awareness, balance, and focus in the horse you are training or retraining.

Poles and Cavalletti

Poles and Cavalletti can be used in many different ways and configurations, especially for *Trotting in Hand* (p. 160). Start slowly and gradually increase the speed you travel and number of poles once your horse is confident and relaxed with the *Element* (fig. 8.10).

Equipment

Several 10- to 12-foot poles and safe risers to prop up the poles' ends (optional). These can be set up in standard sequences and lines, with spacing appropriate for your horse's stride.

How to Use It

Use the poles at a variety of distances and heights to improve your horse's balance, focus, and coordination. They can be used at the walk and the trot. You may also enjoy the challenge of asking your horse to step forward and backward over them with each foot in turn, using the *Cha Cha* (p. 156).

The Platform and the Bridge

Working with a *Platform* increases the horse's confidence and balance. It is preparation for teaching the horse to load into a trailer as it shows him it is safe to walk over a surface he may not trust at first due to the hollow sound. This will persuade the horse that he can rely on your guidance. It is a good

8.11 A horse that is comfortable walking onto the *Platform* or *Bridge* will be willing to stand quietly and not rush off.

way to practice your *Dingo* (p. 148) skills and has a lot of practical uses that translate into many everyday situations.

Equipment

Platform: Use a piece of 1-inch-thick plywood or another "platform" that is 3 feet by 6 feet and strong enough so the horse cannot break it when standing on it. Large pieces of cardboard or rubber stall mats are also suitable to teach the horse to walk on different surfaces.

Bridge: You can raise the plywood or platform into a "bridge" by placing three or four 4 x 4s underneath. This will make the surface sound hollow, similar to the loading ramp of a horse trailer. Once your horse is comfortable with the *Bridge*, it can be a fun step to convert it into a teeter-totter with each side raising or lowering as the horse crosses it. Check that all surfaces have good traction and are not slippery.

How to Use It

The *Dingo* leading position is ideal for working with the *Platform* or the *Bridge*. Start with the *Platform*, letting the horse lower his head and examine the unfamiliar surface. You can place a little bit of grain on the surface to encourage him to chew and breathe.

When asking your horse to navigate any obstacle he is unsure of, it is important you are ready to give him enough space. Staying level with his nose and being ready to slide out on the lead will ensure you do not get bumped or stepped on should the horse take a big step or leap over a strange surface.

Tap the croup to ask the horse to come step by step onto the *Platform*, slowly. Be sure to breathe and allow your horse enough time to pause and respond between your requests.

Troubleshooting

Most horses are not too worried about walking across plywood or a similar

---

Backing Up:
Preparing for Trailering

Mastering the *Platform* or *Bridge* has obvious links to successful trailer loading; however, it is important to teach horses how to load *and unload*. Many horses who are uncomfortable in the trailer are actually as anxious about the unloading process as they are the loading.

To prepare for trailer loading, it is very important to also back the horse off the *Platform* or *Bridge* so he will be able to back out of the trailer without panicking and scrambling. This should be done a step at a time in a balanced, controlled, and relaxed manner. Be mindful of your horse's posture as you ask him to back so he does not learn to throw his head up. Backing slowly, one step at a time, with a released posture is very important and will help prevent a horse from rushing back as soon as the trailer door opens.

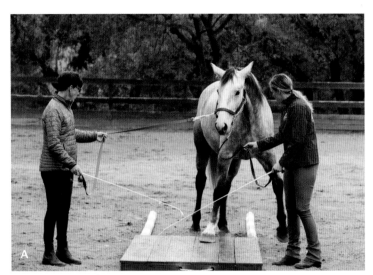

8.12 A & B Chimera is wary of the newly painted *Bridge* (A). Instead of pressuring him until he is resigned to stepping onto it, we break the exercise into low-stress pieces and start where he is comfortable, walking *across* as opposed to walking *lengthwise* (B). This helps his self-confidence and trust, and makes walking lengthwise a non-event.

surface. If your horse is, simply follow the steps for *Working with Plastic* (see below), substituting two pieces of plywood for the plastic.

If it is difficult for the horse to cross the *Platform* or *Bridge* lengthwise, try going *across* it to start with until your horse gains enough confidence (figs. 8.12 A & B). It can also be helpful to use a second leader in *Homing Pigeon* (p. 143) to give your horse more space while maintaining clear parameters (fig. 8.13). There is no good reason to force a horse through a situation that scares him. Chunking down an exercise into small steps allows the horse to be successful, increases his trust in his handler, and usually creates longer-lasting results.

Working with Plastic

Imagine you are out on the trail and come to a small creek. Your horse plants all four feet, throws his head up, and refuses to take another step. Now what?

Should you use a whip to get the horse to move? Make him do it? I am sure you have heard many times that in these situations you have to show the horse who is the boss and that you cannot let him "win." If he does not cross the creek you will have "lost," the horse will remember the moment and never go through a creek in the future. This belief causes a lot of people to use methods they don't usually condone because "there was no other way." However, there *is* another way that is safe for the horse and you while being fun and successful.

8.13 When your horse understands *Dingo*, asking him to calmly step forward is easy and low-stress. Here, Chimera is in *Homing Pigeon* to help him stay straight.

When you try to force the horse across the creek in this situation, you teach him to fight against the rider and to resist. This is not just unpleasant, but can also be very dangerous. While you may be able to eventually get him across, it does not necessarily mean that he has learned anything or that you will not have to repeat the entire process the next time you come to a creek.

A horse that refuses to cross the creek has not been prepared properly; the same is true for a horse that refuses to load in the trailer. Neither have learned how to approach and respond to a new and potentially scary situation—in balance and with a responsive and trusting state of mind.

Working with Plastic and other surfaces is an excellent way to begin to chunk down the instinctive aversion to strange-looking objects. Teaching your horse how to navigate over, under, and between plastic on the ground will improve his self-confidence and trust in you, which will translate to a safer, more cooperative riding horse.

Equipment

A heavy tarpaulin or old shower curtain works well for this exercise. You may want poles, tires, or rocks to help secure the plastic to the ground. Poles and standards or barrels can help create an alleyway.

Prerequisites for Working with Plastic

"Desensitizing" a horse to scary things is not a new concept, and it can work for many horses, but what does it teach them? For some horses, it teaches them to freeze and "suck it up"—not to actually be comfortable with whatever they are experiencing. When you introduce *Working with Plastic* in the *Playground for Higher Learning*, you are aiming to "familiar-ize" the horse with strange and unusual things so he can learn to *act* rather than *react* by breaking the exercise into small steps to make the horse successful and facilitate the optimal learning process (fig. 8.14). Taking the time to help a horse be really accepting and comfortable over, under,

The Second Time Counts

When working with horses and potentially "stressful" objects or requests, it is important to observe how a horse handles the experience the *second time*. Horses will sometimes blindly do what you ask simply because they are amenable. I have seen many young horses happily march into a trailer the first time they are asked, only to be "stubborn" about loading the second time. For many horses the reaction they give you the second or third time tells you how comfortable they actually were with it the first time.

Just because we can push a horse through something does not mean we should or that it necessarily teaches him anything. This is why we always come back to the idea of chunking down the exercise. If you keep the process low-stress for the horse, he better understands what is happening and can better cope with the situation instead of freezing or fleeing the stressor.

8.14 Taking the time to introduce plastic with small, simple steps takes the drama and pressure out of the process. While it may not be as "exciting" to watch, it goes a long way to create confidence and trust. Adding a little food helps to activate the parasympathetic nervous system, or the "thinking" part of the brain.

between, and around plastic will lay the groundwork for a successful outcome whenever life throws a creek, or other unfamiliar obstacles, into your horse's way.

When first introducing plastic, make sure you are in an enclosed space on a calm, quiet day. Beginning *Work with Plastic* on a blustery day is a recipe for disaster. Always plan to set yourself up for success. While you may be able to "make" it work, there is no reason to start with adrenaline and excessive stress when there is always another day.

First, your horse has to know how to quietly move forward from a signal. This sounds simple, but many horses have never learned to truly work with their handler from the ground. Teaching your horse to really understand *Dingo* (p. 148) will become an invaluable tool in a variety of circumstances. He understands that it is a signal, not a punishment, so his adrenaline and cortisol levels do not increase when you have to use the exercise in a potentially scary scenario. He knows a clear signal to come

forward when you give it—and I don't mean that he just follows you when you are walking, but that he pays attention, is willing, and follows your signals through a thought process. If your horse is not able to do this yet, have another go at the *Dingo Leading Exercise*, as well as the *Elegant Elephant* (p. 138) and the *Grace of the Cheetah* (p. 141).

Remember: Your horse can only truly learn when he does not feel threatened or fearful. It is important not to ask too much of him, because he will fall back into his instinctive behavior, such as freezing, avoiding, or backing up. Learning cannot take place when the stress threshold is too

high. This is not about getting the horse over the sheet of plastic "by any means necessary." How the horse goes over or under or through the plastic and approaches it is much more important than how quickly you can accomplish this goal (figs. 8.15 A–F). I want to see the horse move slowly and in a controlled way. This means I can ask him to take one step at a time, forward and backward, and stop him at any time. Rushing forward in an uncontrolled manner is not considered intelligent behavior but an instinctual reaction.

We don't get our horses used to something they are afraid of simply through repetition, but by instead helping them to see the obstacle differently and to change their expectations. This teaches them to think, and this ability will be invaluable for you and your horse in many situations in the future. This is why the *Working with Plastic* is such an important part of the *Playground for Higher Learning*.

Walking Over Plastic

Start with two sheets of plastic folded twice placed on the ground in a "V" shape, with the tip of the "V" open and still quite far apart. Lead your horse through the "V" starting at the wide end. Stop a few feet before the plastic so the horse gets a good chance to have a look (fig. 8.16). Watch that he keeps his head low and ask him to lower it if he is unsure (p. 65). Be sure and stay level with the horse's nose or ahead to allow enough space. You may step on the plastic but do so quietly.

8.15 A–F Walking under the plastic was too much for this horse (A). Following chunk-it-down principles, we pared back the exercise to walking under wands, which was still stressful (B). Instead of pushing the horse through or making the right thing easy and the wrong thing hard, we just made it easier and went back to simply walking between people, then between people standing on blocks. Adding a little food helped change the horse's perception about the situation, and physiologically, made it easier for him to think (C & D). Adding the *Homing Pigeon* (p. 143) helped the horse stay straighter and keep the handlers at a distance, which allowed the horse to relax and walk through the area of concern calmly (E). Finally, we re-introduced plastic (F).

8.16 When your horse has not seen plastic before or seems concerned about the new object, allow him to walk past it. When introducing new things, it is always a good idea to put yourself between the horse and the potentially scary object in case he tries to take a wide berth.

Lead him through the opening between the plastic pieces. If the horse is still concerned, place the tarps farther apart until he can calmly walk between the two tarps lying on the ground. Offer him some food when he is hesitant to encourage him to chew and breathe, which will help him think and override the flight reflex (figs. 8.17 A–C). You can offer the food from a shallow dish or sprinkle it directly on the plastic. It is very important that you do not allow a horse to grab the tarp between his teeth.

Once your horse is able to calmly walk through the plastic, halt on the other side between the two pieces. Now you can start to bring the plastic closer together. Reduce the distance between the two tarps little by little until he steps over the closed tip of the "V" and calmly onto the plastic. Soon he be able to walk over the entire length of the plastic calmly and with confidence (figs. 8.18 A–C).

8.17 A–C A little food can go a long way in giving your horse a positive experience. A great way to check to see how comfortable your horse is with the exercise is by asking for a halt after walking through. A horse that rushes through or does not like to stop with something behind him is displaying fear or anxiety about the exercise.

The Bitterroot Ranch by Mandy Pretty

Since the mid-1980s, the Bitterroot Ranch in Dubois, Wyoming, has been host to a Starting the Young Horse with the Tellington Method workshop. During this six-day workshop, participants from all over the world have helped prepare ranch-bred Arabians, Andalusian-draft crosses, and the occasional Quarter Horse for their future career as a safe, fun guest horse.

Owners Mel and Bayard Fox were first drawn to Linda after having a horrific experience sending a mare out to be trained. Mel has long been a passionate Arabian horse enthusiast with an extensive history of breeding athletic, sound-minded horses. In the early eighties, she sent a quiet, six-year-old Arabian mare to be started under saddle. The mare had been calmly handled, she led well, and was generally cooperative and straightforward in nature. The trainer ran the mare around a round pen to prepare her, added the saddle and bridle, and then swung a leg over her back. As he mounted, the mare reared and went over backward, hitting her head on the fence. She died right in front of Mel's eyes. From that moment, Mel was determined to find a way to have her horses started with respect, compassion, and safety.

Today the horses raised at the ranch are taken through the exercises outlined throughout this book. They arrive on the first morning of the clinic having been taught to lead as a weanling, with little else done to them aside from trims and dewormings done quietly in a catch pen. By the end of the week, they are leading pros, comfortable with *Ground Driving,* crossing a *Bridge,* wearing a saddle, and when they are ready, carrying a rider calmly.

I worked as a wrangler at the ranch for a number of years. During this time, I continued

on with the horses after their initial experience at the clinic. Each horse was unique, and I had to make some adjustments, break down the steps, or think outside the box more than once. However, their interest in learning and their willingness to try was practically universal. I believe that their "clean slates" and quiet, reasonable handling were a core reason for this.

Much of the time I was working alone down in an arena a mile away from the main ranch center. This isolation made me extremely aware of staying safe and taking things slowly. In all the years I started horses, I can happily say that I did not come off once while getting the youngsters going under saddle. This is not because I have a Velcro seat that can ride out anything; it is a testament to the fact that I let each horse tell me what he was really comfortable with—that is, not just putting up with what I was asking. And I did not have a time limit. The end result was horses that were quiet and happily responsive—and a rider without broken bones and bruises.

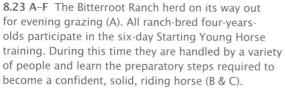

8.23 A–F The Bitterroot Ranch herd on its way out for evening grazing (A). All ranch-bred four-years-olds participate in the six-day Starting Young Horse training. During this time they are handled by a variety of people and learn the preparatory steps required to become a confident, solid, riding horse (B & C).

By the end of the course, many are ready to be backed or will be backed after more sessions of groundwork with the ranch wranglers (D). The youngsters have handlers from the ground initially to help make the transition easy and clear (E). As they gain more confidence, the horses are ridden solo (F).

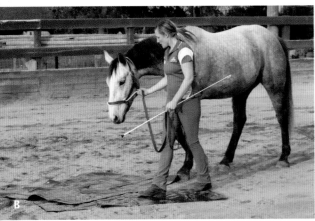

8.18 A–C As your horse is confident about walking between the "V" of plastic, incrementally move the pieces closer together until you are walking right over it. For most horses, introducing plastic in this way is a non-event and helps boost their confidence and trust in you as a handler.

Walking Between Plastic

Using two poles and four jump standards or barrels, create an "alley" for the horse to go through—sometimes a fence on one side can be used. Check that the horse is comfortable walking through this before adding plastic draped over the poles or barrels or fence. If you notice that your horse seems concerned or at all anxious, practice the principles of chunking the exercise down (figs. 8.19 A–C). Some horses will want to start by walking next to just one side of the alley with you between him and the object in question. Incrementally add small steps to move forward. Make the aisle wide enough so the horse can comfortably walk through and stop in the middle before making it narrower. Be sure and stay far enough ahead when leading so you are in a safe position. Taking the time to really break down the steps into manageable, low-stress pieces will help your horse build confidence and truly learn from the experience rather than just "get through it."

Walking Between People and Under Objects

One of the steps I like to take a horse through before he has a rider on his back is to walk between and under taller objects, like people standing on mounting blocks. Getting horses really comfortable with things above and behind them is a logical step toward happily accepting a rider. As with all Tellington Method exercises, this is done incrementally, starting with people standing on the ground, then standing on mounting blocks or bales of straw, and advancing toward walking under two wands or pool noodles held between the two people.

Equipment

In an ideal world, you have two extra helpers to act as your "walk between." If this is not possible, one person will certainly work. Each person needs a mounting block or bale of hay (covered with a towel or blanket to avoid temptation), or some other sturdy, slightly elevated object. Two *Wands* or pool noodles are also needed.

8.19 A–C *Walking Between Plastic* uses the same incremental idea as walking over it. As long as you listen to your horse's small signs of concern, most horses quickly master this exercise with confidence. In the long term, many small steps achieve long-term success much more quickly than going straight to the goal of the exercise.

How to Do It

Place the blocks about six feet apart. Use the *Elegant Elephant* (p. 138) or *Grace of the Cheetah* (p. 141) to lead your horse between the blocks. Notice if he rushes at all or if his walk stays consistent. Then take him through but halt right before the blocks, and ask your horse to walk forward and halt with the blocks lined up on either side of him, and again when the blocks are behind him. If this is at all challenging, chunk it down. Try it with one block, move them farther apart, or change the side you are leading from—use your imagination to break the process into small, manageable pieces.

More Preparation for Trailer Loading

Horses that are afraid of things above them are often difficult to load into the horse trailer because they are fearful of the confinement. When I prepare a horse to be loaded, I do so by breaking the exercise into small steps. The horse learns to stand still on and walk forward over plastic, through a narrow alley with plastic on either side, and under it, too. You can add a *Platform* or a *Bridge* to the plastic alley: Ask the horse to step on, walk over, and back off the *Platform* and your horse has mastered the necessary steps for loading into the trailer. Add a clear understanding of *Dingo* (p. 148) and *Cha Cha* (p. 156) cues, and you are well on your way to a low-stress, trailer-loading experience.

Note: If you find that a previous "easy loader" is suddenly resistant, it's time to play detective. Sometimes a driver is too quick to brake or accelerate, goes round turns too fast, or the trailer is exceptionally noisy. We have even known of several circumstances where a horse that has always loaded suddenly refuses to go in. Later it was discovered that the trailer's floorboards had become dangerously weak. A big change in behavior is a key way a horse tries to communicate with you. So, it is up to you to figure out exactly what he is trying to tell you.

8.20 Taking the time to help your horse be completely comfortable with walking between people and unusual objects is a fantastic exercise to prepare him for standing at the mounting block, having a rider above him, trailer loading, and trail riding.

For most horses, this will not be a particularly difficult exercise but they all react differently.

Once your horse is comfortable standing between the blocks, repeat the exercise but first with a person standing next to a block, and then, have your helper(s) stand *on* the blocks.

Some horses will find that they are more comfortable with a person on one side rather than the other. If your horse can quietly stand between the two helpers, add some *TTouches* or offer a small bite of hay from one side. Having your helpers mindfully do some *Zebra* or *Troika TTouches* (pp. 96 and 97) along your horse's topline is a nice way to make standing at the mounting block pleasant and relaxing, and helps him get used to the sensation of a person reaching over him from above. If you find that your horse is holding his breath or is in a "freeze," try having one helper offer a little food. Ask your horse to keep his feet still and turn his neck to receive the offering.

8.21 Many horses are never really comfortable with things above them, rider included, so taking the time to walk under different objects calmly and quietly is a wonderful learning experience.

As your horse becomes totally comfortable standing between the blocks and being touched on both sides, you can add the concept of walking under things. Using the same process as you did with the blocks, add one *Wand* or dressage whip at a time and let your horse walk through. As he masters the element, add the pool noodles.

Walking under strange obstacles is an important skill that every riding horse should be comfortable with (fig. 8.21). Besides being a useful skill for trail riding, trailer loading, or life around the barn, it is a great way to introduce the idea of something being above your horse's ear level—such as a rider! Without preparation, many horses are surprised by the motion of a rider mounting for the first time. Familiarizing your horse with walking under two *Wands* or pool noodles is a great first step. Have your two helpers stand on mounting blocks or straw/hay bales placed approximately 4 to 6 feet apart.

If there are enough people on-hand to help, *Homing Pigeon* (p. 143) is a great leading position to help keep the horse balanced and straight through the exercise. Lead him to the obstacle and allow him to see the people standing above him. Initially they should hold the *Wands* upright. The handlers should walk between the blocks first, asking the horse to wait, before signaling him forward. If the horse rushes through and cannot halt on the other side or between the blocks, you may need to place the blocks farther apart. If the horse seems relaxed, go through again, this time with the helpers on the blocks holding the *Wands* together to make an archway. As the horse grows comfortable with this obstacle, the people standing on the blocks can bring the *Wands* lower and lower so that the horse actually has to lower his head to go under and may feel the *Wands* touching his neck and back as he goes through. Only proceed as the horse is really comfortable with the process. A horse that can halt under the obstacle and right after it is a horse that is confident and relaxed (figs. 8.22 A–C).

Once the horse is comfortable with the *Wands* or pool noodles, you can go on with the exercise. Hold a folded tarp for the horse to walk under, or any number of things that your imagination can dream up: tree branches, dangling plastic bottles tied to a small rail—the possibilities are endless. The most important thing is to watch your horse for signs of anxiety and be prepared to scale back the exercise into more manageable steps.

Taking the time to go through these exercises is a great way to boost your horse's self-confidence and ability to navigate unusual situations and trust your requests. Once you have led your horse through these steps you can try it while *Ground Driving* (p. 209) and adding a *Platform* or *Bridge* to enhance the exercise.

8.22 A–C Chunking down the pool noodles allows the horse to approach the obstacle in manageable steps, eventually feeling comfortable with them crossed above him as he stands calmly beneath.

The Story of Heartbreaker

The *Playground for Higher Learning* (p. 175) and the *TTouches* (p. 78) can create huge changes in a horse already going under saddle, as was shown by the six-year-old grey gelding Heartbreaker. Mandy Zimmer is a student of the former trainer of the German Olympic Dressage team, Klaus Balkenhol. Heartbreaker was chosen to participate in a seminar I was teaching because he always got scared at horse shows when the crowd applauded. He was also afraid of the horse trailer. The gelding tucked his tail in and had a very tight neck, which made me think he connected riding in the trailer with the stress of the show grounds.

I did *Tail TTouches* (p. 118) and led him over the *Bridge* (p. 187) that we built from a large piece of plywood in the *Playground for Higher Learning* (p. 175). He was afraid of the *Bridge* and startled even when we padded it with rubber mats from his stall. A horse that cannot walk over the *Bridge* usually cannot be loaded into a trailer.

When I asked Heartbreaker to step off the *Bridge*, he stopped and just looked out the window of the arena, not paying me any attention. A clinic spectator asked me why I allowed him to ignore me, as it was clear that he was not "with" me at that moment. His distant facial expression showed me he was nervous and concerned about stepping off the ramp of the *Bridge*. I had the sense he was telling me that he would much rather be somewhere else. So I gave him a little bit of time to think, stroked him with the *Wand* and applied some *Lick of the Cow's Tongue TTouches* (p. 95). Because I did not punish the gelding, I gained a lot of his trust.

Within a very short period of time, the 160 clinic auditors could clap around Heartbreaker without causing him to be afraid. He trotted and cantered in perfect rhythm and did not tuck his tail. The horse's improved body awareness and newly found trust in his rider helped him not to shy any more.

Horses learn to think and let go of deeply rooted fears through Tellington Training. The method offers new solutions for problems that have previously taken years of work under saddle to solve. I'd rather work with the horse's intelligence than his muscle any day.

8.24 Mandy Zimmer and Heartbreaker.

CHAPTER 9

Ground Driving

In the Driver's Seat

Once you have established good communication leading your horse, the next step is *Ground Driving*—an important skill that will help the introduction or reintroduction to riding become clear in a calm and straightforward manner.

It is usually best to have confidently navigated the *Playground for Higher Learning* (p. 175) through several different *Elements* and done some *Trotting in Hand* (p. 160) before moving on to driving; however, there are always some exceptions. I have known horses that had a terrible time halting in balance when doing work on the ground until they experienced *Chest Line Driving* (p. 213). So give yourself permission for earlier groundwork not to be perfect before you continue on; you can always go back to those exercises.

9.1 *Ground Driving* is one of the most important exercises for preparing a horse to accept being ridden.

Before starting *Ground Driving*, you do want to make sure that your horse is reasonably comfortable being touched around the barrel, hindquarters, and tail with a variety of *TTouches* and the *Wand*. This prepares your horse for the sensation of the driving lines touching him and increases the benefits of the exercises.

One of the most useful tools for preparing a horse to be quietly started under saddle is *Ground Driving* (fig. 9.1). It teaches horses to listen to signals behind them, respond to rein and leg cues, and ensures they are comfortable with motion behind—and beside—the body. *Ground Driving* is also a good way to expose your horse to new places and obstacles. In the Introduction, I told you about ground driving horses when I was a young girl (see p. 7). In the past decades, I have developed the techniques I began with into a method that I finely tuned with hundreds of horses. While many people do some sort of long lining in preparation for riding, the Tellington Method approach differs in a few respects.

The most unique aspect of how I start a horse to be ground driven is that I do not attach lines to his head. Starting a horse with *Chest Line Driving* (p. 213) is very different from traditional long lining techniques, and it gives the horse a completely different sense about shifting his weight off his forehand and finding self-carriage while remaining completely free through his head and neck.

The second difference from traditional methods is that I attach the lines to the halter rather than to a bit. It takes years to attain the finesse and skill necessary to drive from the bit—the weight of the lines make signals much heavier than you realize, especially if just run through a stirrup—and many horses become overbent and behind the vertical. Unless you have a very skilled hand, it is difficult to be soft enough to drive off the bit. The other advantage to driving from the halter is that you can use the lines against the horse's body to give a signal at the place where the rider's leg will be so the horse starts to learn this cue before you are ever in the saddle.

The process of *Ground Driving* is really broken down into two exercises: *Chest Line Driving* and *Ground Driving* proper. Both are excellent exercises and provide some different benefits and learning experiences. *Chest Line Driving* can be an amazing exercise to use on horses that are being restarted and have a negative association with ropes and lines, or ones that have learned to use the head and neck in a braced posture. You can combine both exercises once the driver has a handle on one set of lines, since combining

> The most unique aspect of how I start a horse to be ground driven is that I do not attach lines to his head.

both driving techniques requires four ropes. Using a double set of lines is incredibly useful for a horse that tightens his head and neck as soon as he feels the weight of the lines on the halter or when re-educating an older horse with a deeply engrained tension pattern.

Some thoughts on how *Ground Driving* exercises can be incorporated into your horse's training, depending on his stage and situation:

FOAL OR WEANLING

1 A horse of this age would not typically be taken through the steps of *Ground Driving*. What can be useful, however, is to use the concept of the *Balance Rope* (p. 215) to teach a high-headed or tense foal how to halt through his entire body and not brace through the head and neck.

2 It can also be a good idea to introduce the *Pig Tail* (p. 218) in small sessions to help familiarize the foal to ropes around the body and legs.

UNSTARTED THREE- OR FOUR-YEAR-OLD

1 In my experience, it is invaluable taking a not-yet-started horse through all the steps of *Ground Driving*. Taking the time to go from *Balance Rope*, *Pig Tail*, *Chest Line Driving*, through to *Ground Driving* will help prepare your horse by giving him many of the skills necessary to become a confident, calm mount.

2 Some horses at this age will breeze through the steps, while others need time to process and will take several sessions to really understand the concept. There is no need to put a timeline on it; your horse is ready when he is ready. The progression should be as low-stress as possible for everyone involved.

REEDUCATING THE MATURE HORSE

1 Going through the steps of *Ground Driving* can be invaluable for every riding horse. The driving exercises help to make ridden signals and aids clearer, and set you and the horse up for a safer, more successful experience.

2 Whether you know the horse's history or not, it is a good idea to take him through all the outlined steps to ensure a safe and positive session.

9.2 Here you can see some of the basic equipment needed for *Chest Line Driving*, one step in my *Ground Driving* method.

Taking a few extra steps to "check in" (see p. 60) to see how comfortable your horse is with the exercise is definitely worth the added minutes and usually has lasting, positive results.

Equipment

You will need a flat nylon or leather halter that does not slide or collapse, a helper at the horse's head with a lead, a *Wand*, two 21-foot ropes about 9 mm in diameter that will be attached to the horse's neck and chest, and two 21-foot ropes about 7 mm in diameter that will be attached to the halter as your driving lines. It is helpful to have the two sets of ropes in different colors so it is easier to tell them apart (fig. 9.2).

A surcingle with a breastplate or a saddle with double-ended snaps and rings is ideal for running the lines through and reducing some of the weight of the lines attached to the halter. It can be best to use a *Body Wrap* (p. 44) with younger horses so they are not surprised by the contact of the lines.

I advise handlers to wear gloves when *Ground Driving*.

Chest Line Driving

For most horses, it is a good idea to begin with driving from lines attached

9.3 *Chest Line Driving* is a fantastic exercise for horses not yet started and previously trained horses alike. It is a very non-habitual exercise that allows horses to explore the freedom of the head and neck while connecting with the hind end.

to the chest only. Besides chunking down the exercise for the horse, it also helps a new driver get the hang of two lines before adding a second pair. For some horses the weight of the lines attached to the halter can make them feel claustrophobic and tense if the process is not broken down into small, easy steps. The freedom of the head and neck in *Chest Line Driving* starts to allow your horse to find self-carriage and balance without tension (fig. 9.3).

9.4 A driving line can make a *Balance Rope* in a pinch (it is also suitable for use as a *Balance Rein* when riding—see p. 275). Take the line and "crochet" or "daisy chain" it, leaving approximately 12 to 18 inches at either end. Snug the end of the line so it does not release and tie the two ends into a square knot.

9.5 *The Balance Rope* is a good check-in step before attaching the driving lines and running them to the back of the horse. It also helps the horse get used to receiving signals closer to where the rider will be.

Balance Rope

The *Balance Rope* is an exercise to prepare your horse for the signals used when *Chest Line Driving* or later riding with a *Balance Rein* (see p. 275). "Crochet" a circle (fig. 9.4 A–C) or simply fold a driving line in half if you want something temporary (in thirds for a smaller horse). With a person leading at the horse's head, place the driving line around the base of the horse's neck, and hold it while standing beside the horse's shoulder, facing forward. Your hand nearest the horse should rest below the withers, so you do not have to reach over them, while your outside hand holds the line that comes around the base of the neck.

The person at the horse's shoulder gives the verbal signals and makes the plan. The leader at the horse's head asks the horse to move forward and steers, and will help reinforce the signal to halt until the horse understands the signal from the chest (fig. 9.5).

To Walk: The handler at the shoulder allows the *Balance Rope* to be slack, no pressure on the chest, and says, "And waaaalk." The handler at the head uses the *Wand*, lead rope, and body language to ask the horse to walk. It is important that the leader stays far enough ahead so that the person at the shoulder does not step on her heels.

Many horses will be hesitant, at least initially, to move forward with a person at their shoulder. Give the horse a moment to respond to the request. If necessary, the person at the shoulder may reach back and gently use her fingers to give a *Dingo* cue on the croup (p. 148).

9.7 Teaching a horse to turn his neck to look at something is much safer, and more practical, than teaching a horse to face up to anything he is unsure of. Remember that whatever you teach the horse on the ground should transfer to when you're in the saddle.

Nothing to Fear

It is a good idea to make sure your horse associates any movement behind him with something positive. A quick and easy way to check in with this is to ask the horse to halt as a person with a food reward in hand briskly walks up from behind and says, "Whoooa." The person coming up from behind should be doing so in a safe place where she can see the horse's eye as opposed to directly behind the horse. The leader reinforces the halt initially, but it does not take most horses very long to figure out something nice is coming! It is very handy to have "stop" become a horse's default when something surprises or worries him, or when he is simply confused.

Always ask for his head and neck to turn back to see the person with the food while his feet stay still. This helps prevent a tense posture often associated with horses "facing up." It is also very inconvenient and potentially unsafe to have your horse spin quickly to face anything that surprises him.

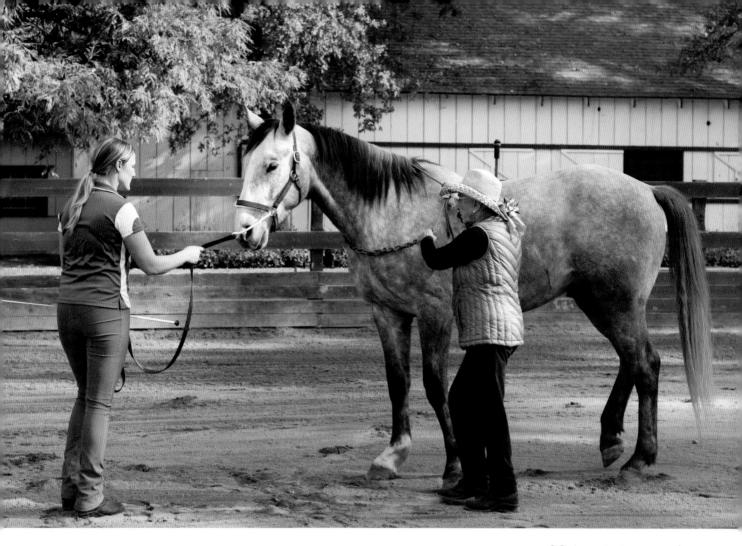

To Halt: As the handler at the shoulder asks the horse to halt, she should start by taking a breath and relaxing through her back, taking up the slack in the *Balance Rope* so it touches the horse's chest right above the point of the shoulder. She clearly says, "And whoooooa," so that she is taking up the slack as she says, "And," while adding the signal as she says, "Whoooa." The signal should go up the line of the horse's scapula rather than straight back toward his tail. Allow your body to make a slight quarter-turn toward the horse as you signal (fig. 9.6). Be sure to release a moment as you allow the horse to step into the halt.

Initially the handler at the horse's head may need to help reinforce this new cue, but most horses pick up on it very quickly.

Backing Up: Use the same cue as in the halt but really focus on thinking of an up-and-back motion through your signal so you imagine shifting the horse's weight up toward his croup. This is a good exercise for teaching horses to back in a more functional posture. Learning to do this from the *Balance Rope* will easily transfer under saddle when riding with a *Balance Rein* (p. 275).

9.6 A quarter-turn toward the horse helps create a clear signal to halt without using a lot of pressure in your hands. If your horse does not halt immediately, release the signal on the *Balance Rope*, and ask again more slowly with help from the leader.

9.8 A & B Always give your horse the opportunity to see what new piece of equipment is being added. This helps you slow down and acknowledges that you are listening to the horse and *working with* him rather than just "doing things to" him.

Introducing the Lines

Once your horse understands what the *Balance Rope* exercise entails, it is time to add the next step: the driving lines. As with any new object or piece of equipment, it is considerate and wise to let your horse know that it is not a threat (figs. 9.8 A & B). For safety reasons it is best to have the handler on the same side as you are, or lead with the *Homing Pigeon* (p. 143).

Pig Tail

The *Pig Tail* is a small but important step to any work with lines around a horse's body and legs. This simple check-in is great insurance to prevent any unnecessary drama or fearful reactions.

While a handler stands at the horse's head, a second helper checks in with the driving line, calmly stroking the horse with the line folded in her hand to introduce the rope (fig. 9.9). Begin on the chest or shoulder on the same side as the handler and allow the horse to turn his head and sniff the rope.

Next thread one end of the driving line through a few of the chained links of the *Balance Rope*. Take a *Wand* and wind it around the rope so you have a 3-to-5 foot "drape" in the rope between the *Wand* and the horse. Should your horse seem concerned about this, make the drape shorter and chunk down the exercise into smaller steps. Use the combination of *Wand* and line to stroke the horse all over his body and legs, gently introducing the line.

The *Pig Tail* allows the handler to stay a safe distance from the horse should he react to the lines touching his legs, and it provides a good indicator of how comfortable the horse is with ropes. Your horse should be okay with the *Wand* being stroked all over his body before trying this step.

Initially, I highly recommend simply threading the rope through the *Balance Rope* but not tying it to any young or very nervous horses (figs. 9.10 A & B). The lines will simply come loose if the horse has a reaction, and he can walk out of the situation without having the source of concern (the

9.9 *The Pig Tail* is a simple check-in step to gauge your horse's acceptance about ropes and being touched all over. Watch for the smallest signs of concern and pause if you notice any. Change in facial expression, respiration, and overall tension are all small but clear signs. These small checks are your insurance policy. It pays to take more time making sure your horse is really comfortable before attaching the driving lines.

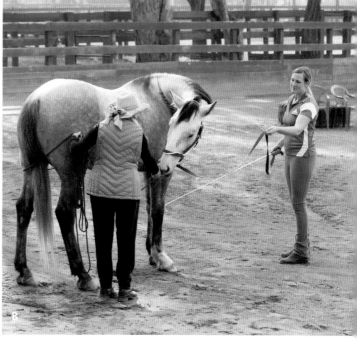

9.10 A & B Starting with the driving line threaded through the *Balance Rope* but not tied means that you can allow the horse to simply walk out of the lines if he gets nervous or scoots forward. Once you feel the horse is ready, you can attach the line with a quick-release knot.

9.11 Hold the line in the hand closest to the horse so it stays parallel to the barrel. I am slowly stroking Chimera as I move back to a driving position. Checking in with your horse at each step is insurance for avoiding surprising behaviors.

lines…you) dragging behind him. This step is an excellent way to chunk down the process and ensure a safe, positive experience.

Using the Lines

One Line

Begin with one driving line and stay at a comfortable distance from the horse's hind end. Hold the line in the hand closest to the horse so it stays parallel to his barrel. The line should sit just above the point of the shoulder and right behind the withers.

Also for safety, it is best to have the handler on the same side as you are, or lead with two extra handlers and the *Homing Pigeon* (p. 143).

Take the line attached to the rope around the horse's neck and keep it in your hand closest to the horse's body. This will ensure that the line stays along the horse's side and keeps you, the "driver," following the track of his inside hind leg. Start at the horse's barrel and gently stroke the horse's side. The handler in the front should allow the horse to turn his head to look at you. Be sure to check in with your horse's ears, eyes, and respiration as you continue with this exercise.

Make sure your horse is comfortable being touched on both sides and around the hindquarters. It is important that you do not allow the line to get caught under the tail or drop lower than the hocks. For safety, all handlers must be paying attention and watching the horse's reaction.

To Walk: Once your horse is comfortable with you moving around him while the line is touching him, you can ask for a walk. Walking and halting with only one line attached initially is a valuable check to see how comfortable your horse is with lines touching him and makes for an easy, and safer, step before adding a second line. With the line attached on the same side as your handler (moot if you have two handlers in the *Homing Pigeon* position—p. 143), stand so you are just to the inside of your horse's footfall. This ensures that you can observe your horse's eye and allows your horse to see you. Hold the line with your hand that is closest to the horse, so the line stays parallel to the barrel, and quietly stroke the line on the side of the barrel. This will prepare the horse for a signal but prevents hypersensitivity. Remember that at this point he should still be standing quietly. If your horse starts to walk forward when you simply stroke the line on his side, have the handler help to steady him with the lead and *Wand* so the horse understands that it is not a signal to go forward. To ask for walk, stroke the barrel twice as you say, "Aaaand," then give a gentle "tap-tap" with the line to simulate a light leg aid, as you say, "Waaaalk."

Many horses will not initially understand this signal to go forward. Be patient. Do not immediately repeat the signal, but give the horse a chance to process and respond to the request. If he doesn't start moving, ask one more time and have the handler help to reinforce the cue with a signal from the head and with the *Wand*.

As you walk, be mindful that you have no pressure on the horse's neck and are thinking about maintaining "supported slack" or "float" on the line. It can be useful to remember the image of pushing a baby carriage or a lawn mower as you follow with your horse.

To Halt: Once your horse understands the idea of going forward, ask for a halt. When you only have one line attached, most of the signal may come from the handler at the head. However, it is a good place to practice. Take a breath and gently pick up the slack from the line as you say, "Aaaand," then take a feel on the line as you say, "Whooooa." Remember to slow your feet into the halt rather than suddenly stop them, and keep your joints and lower back released and soft. Initially, you may have to repeat the cue and have the handler help to reinforce it.

When you have checked in with walk and halt a couple of times, and your horse has remained calm and confident in the exercise, you can change the line to the other side. Horses can be very different about experiences on the right or left side of the body, so it is worth the few extra minutes to do these steps on both sides before progressing. Remember: It is safest to thread the lines for a check-in, before tying them. For some horses a single line is more challenging than having two lines, so adjust the exercise as appropriate.

Two Lines

When you and your horse are ready to add the second driving line, take a moment to ensure that you and your horse are comfortable with you flipping the lines to one side of him in a single, smooth movement (fig. 9.12). If something were to scare your horse, it is very important to be able to get both lines to the inside and step forward into a typical lungeing position. This will allow you and the handler to diffuse the situation and regroup.

Food, or a well-placed scratch, can be very useful when introducing your horse to the feeling of the lines around his hindquarters. Always be

9.12 Always check that your horse is comfortable with having the lines flipped over his body so both lines are on the same side. This is incredibly important if you plan on *Ground Driving* extensively and in unusual places. Anytime you feel like your horse is tense or very nervous, simply flip the lines to one side so you are in a place of better control and less potential to create more forward energy than you want.

9.13 A & B The signal for walk is a two-part request. First, the driver strokes the barrel with one line in a downward motion as she says, "Annnnnddd." Then, the line makes a gentle "tap-tap" signal on the barrel, followed by a pause, as the driver says, "Waalllllllk."

aware of where the lines are sitting—not too high, not too low—and make sure that your horse is not in "freeze" or "checked out." Walk around your horse, mindfully allowing the lines to touch around the hindquarters, while you keep the lines high enough that they cannot get stuck under the tail. If you have a very sensitive horse, it can be a good idea to start with the two lines crossed over the croup. This will reduce how much line the horse feels on his sides and give him a chance to get used to a line on either side without having them hang too low. In this configuration, you are simply following the horse and letting the leader give all the signals.

Once you have both lines attached, carry on with the walk, halt, and then backing signals, as well as *Chest Line Driving* through a variety of obstacles (figs. 9.13 A & B). With two lines, you will still only ask for walk with one line at a time—it's not a chuck wagon race! Stay slightly to the inside track—as with one line, it ensures that the horse can see you and that you can really watch his expression.

Turning is not especially clear for horses when initially *Chest Line Driving*, so the emphasis in the exercise is on walk, halt, and being completely relaxed and comfortable with the lines around them while maintaining freedom through the head and neck (fig. 9.14).

How to Hold the Driving Lines

1 Hold the lines in your left hand with your index finger between the right and left line (fig. 9.15 A).

2 Pick up the dangling ends of the lines with the pinky finger of your right hand and hold them between your pinky and ring finger or ring and middle finger, whichever is most comfortable for you (9.15 B).

3 Reach forward with your right hand to take hold of the right rein from your left hand, creating a "bridge" between the two lines with the ends held by your pinky. The bridge connects your hands and improves your balance. It allows you to keep a clearer connection to the horse and helps you to use the reins in unison (9.15 C).

4 Hold the line on the right side of the horse in your right hand and the line on the horse's left in your left hand. Keep your hands about as far apart as the width of your horse's hind end. Some sensitive horses will require a wider hand span when asking for a halt.

  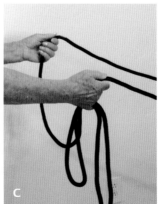 

9.14 When *Chest Line Driving* it is up to the handler at the horse's head to really clarify turning left and right. Practicing turns, even if the driver cannot initiate them, is a great way to let your horse feel the lines along the barrel and haunches.

5 Practice changing both lines from right to left and vice versa. To turn left, place the lines in your right hand, with your index finger separating them, and then slide up the left line with your left hand. This creates a clear turning signal. To turn right, place the lines in your left hand with your index finger separating the lines, and slide up the right line with your right hand.

6 When driving from both the chest and the halter with four lines (see p. 00), take all four lines into your left hand, keeping the thinner lines on top between your bent index finger and thumb, and the thicker lines between your index and middle finger. Hold the dangling end of the lines between your little and ring fingers of your right hand (figs. 9.15 D & E). Practice holding the same configuration with all four reins in your right hand, and then two reins in each hand (figs. 9.15 F & G).

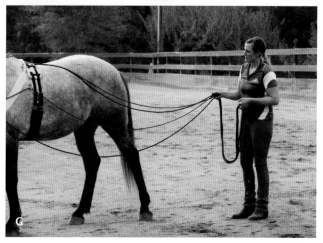

9.15 A–G Holding the driving lines—one set, two sets, and in the left and right hands.

Ground Driving from the Halter

Once your horse is comfortable driving from the chest, it is time to add the lines to the halter. The safest practice is to check in with your horse and add the lines one side at a time, as you did with *Chest Line Driving*. This will only take an extra minute or two and is a worthwhile step.

Ground Driving puts you at some distance from the point of contact with the horse (fig. 9.16). As a result, the weight of the lines on the halter is heavier than you would think, even though the lines used here are much lighter than practically any other options on the market. This means that it is very important to have a point of support, either in the form of a surcingle or saddle, to run the lines through. The added benefit is that it gives your horse practice wearing tack and moving comfortably with a girth done up.

9.16 *Ground Driving* from the halter helps horses understand a rein signal before having the added input of a rider's weight.

Introducing the Surcingle

Before you attach the lines to the halter, you need to "dress" your horse. How you apply the surcingle or saddle for the first time is an incredibly

important step that can shape the way your horse views the experience long term, and it provides you with valuable information about how comfortable your horse is around the girth area, ribs, and back.

Always take it slowly when introducing new pieces of tack. Present a new object to your horse from the side so he is able to turn his head to sniff it. This puts him in a position to visually inspect it in a relaxed posture. When you show things to horses directly in front of them, they are less able to see it and are more likely to raise the head and tighten the back when they are concerned. (If you are using a saddle rather than a surcingle, please refer to "Introducing the Saddle," p. 246, for more detailed information.)

Once your horse has had a chance to see what you are putting on his back, gently place it where you want it to sit. It is important to be mindful about how you place the tack down—*set* it rather than dropping it on the back. If your horse has not worn tack before or is not happy about having the girth done up from previous experience, it is important to do *Belly Lifts* (p. 111) as gentle preparation. It is also helpful to use a breastplate so that the girth does not have to be done up as tightly to ensure it is stable. A too tight girth can actually make it difficult for a horse to breathe comfortably and creates tension in the body.

When you do tighten the girth, always pull down on the billets as you use your other hand to fasten the girth hardware. This reduces how much pressure is applied and helps ease the tightening process. This is a good rule any time you tighten a girth.

When your horse is young and new to the concept of "wearing" anything, it is a good idea to lead the horse around in the surcingle before moving on to driving. Some horses have a sense of being disconnected to the hind end once a girth is done up, and they can act more surprised by things touching the hindquarters than they would be without tack. Quietly navigate the *Playground for Higher Learning* in tack. Going back to predictable requests that the horse is familiar and confident with is a good way to help him transition each time you add a new piece to his training.

Once your horse is comfortable with walking, turning, and halting in the tack, *Trot in Hand* (p. 160). The movement of the added tack can surprise a horse when he is trotting for the first time, and you want to make the exercise as uneventful as possible. Ask for a few steps of trot in an enclosed area, focusing on relaxed, smooth transitions, using your voice and the *Wand*. Do this several times. If your horse seems to have a similar

> **A too tight girth can make it difficult for a horse to breathe comfortably and creates tension in the body.**

Ground Driving Solo

While driving with a handler as leader is ideal and much easier for horse and person to understand, it is not always possible. Teaching a horse to *Ground Drive* without a leader is certainly doable and is easier the more skilled the driver is. It is not a good idea to learn how to drive with a green horse on your own. The mixed signals can confuse the horse, and if he is not totally comfortable with the lines, you can get into trouble.

To drive by yourself it is important to have a contained space, but not so contained that there is nowhere interesting for your horse to go. When your horse is very sensitive, you want to introduce the lines in a safe, small area so he does not get moving too much and scare himself. Introduce the lines in a similar way as you would with a handler helping at his head. Check in that your horse is comfortable with the lines all over his body, on both sides (see p. 220).

It is important that your horse is comfortable with having the lines flipped over his croup as you change positions, so practice this motion in a confined space first. The lines should only be around his hindquarters when you are in—or almost in—a *Ground Driving* position. When you move out to the side, more like a lungeing position, keep the lines over the horse's back. As mentioned earlier, this is also a key safety feature: If, at any point, you feel as if your horse is unsure or tense, simply flipping a line over and stepping to the inside puts you in a place where you can help calm and reassure the horse.

When *Ground Driving* on your own, it can be very helpful to have the *Playground for Higher Learning* set up so it gives both you and the horse *Elements* to focus on, and it makes going forward comprehensible to the horse.

trot rhythm to when he trots without tack and does not rush or brace, he is probably comfortable with the added noise and movement. When you are using a saddle, start with the stirrups run up and secured, and slowly work up to having the stirrups down while trotting a few steps at a time.

Attaching the Lines

When your horse has moved out with the saddle or surcingle, you are ready to go on to the next step of *Ground Driving*—attaching the lines to the halter. Depending on your horse's general temperament and acceptance of new things, you may want to choose to repeat the same steps for adding one and then two lines that you did with *Chest Line Driving*. It does not hurt and only takes a few extra moments that help to ensure a seamless transition to the halter.

From personal experience, it is much easier to thread the line to the halter last, taking the line from the back of the surcingle or saddle forward to the halter (fig. 9.18). The line should thread through the surcingle (or

9.17 The movement of the tack hardware and its noise, whether it is a saddle or surcingle, can be surprising for some horses at first. *Trotting in Hand* (p. 160) as you add each new piece of tack can be a good insurance policy to make sure the horse is comfortable with movement on his back.

9.18 For ease, take one end of the driving line through the ring on your surcingle, or stirrup if you are using a saddle, and then bring it forward to the halter hardware. This will save you from having to thread the entire length of the line through the surcingle ring. Tie the line with a quick-release knot (see p. 71).

the stirrup iron when you are *Ground Driving* with a saddle) to reduce the amount of slack weight placed on the head. In either case, it is useful to add a double-ended snap with a ring or carabiner to run the line through. This reduces the amount of leverage placed on the line and makes for a softer, more refined signal from the driver.

There are a few things to consider when you *Ground Drive* the horse with a saddle: If you are using an English saddle, keep the stirrups pushed up high on the saddle and thread the lines through the stirrups. Again, use a soft breastplate so the girth does not have to be tight. When you are using a Western saddle, tie the stirrups up so the lines do not run too low and swing too much when turning.

When you attach the line to the halter, it is best to tie the line to the upper back corner of the halter hardware. This will prevent the hardware from tipping into the side of the horse's mouth when you give signals to turn, making it more comfortable for the horse.

9.19 Going back to familiar *Elements* in the *Playground for Higher Learning* (p. 175) and the addition of a *Body Wrap* (p. 44) can help make the progression to driving from the halter calm and uneventful.

For many horses, *Ground Driving* with the addition of a *Body Wrap* (p. 44) is incredibly helpful for balance, coordination, confidence, and overall awareness. When your horse is sensitive to the lines touching his sides, a *Body Wrap* is very important (fig. 9.19).

Ground Driving from the halter allows the "driver" to influence all the signals for turning in either direction as well as halt. When turning, it is important to slide up on the inside line and follow the inside hind of the horse. Your outside line must "give" enough not to confuse the horse. Always start with less is more as far as signals are concerned. Most horses have a bit of lag time initially because there is a considerable distance between where the signal starts, at the driver, and the halter. As you and your horse become more skilled, the handler at the front should be able to do less and less until all the signals are coming from the driver (fig. 9.20).

Once walk, halt, and turning in both directions are clear, you may want to add trot and backing up into the mix. When trotting in a *Ground Driving* position, you want to be sure that you are ready for the upward transition and do not accidentally pull back as the horse goes forward. Choosing a contained area and short transition will help this to be successful. As with all of these exercises, it is important to have clear communication between the driver and the handler.

Why All the Lines?

*C*hest Line Driving is an exercise unique to the Tellington Method. The signal at the base of the neck is an effective way to show horses how to stay balanced through transitions and understand how to maintain a functional posture when external signals are added. For many horses, pressure on lines to the head initially causes a high-headed, bracing posture that is not balanced or relaxed. Using the chest lines, along with lines to the halter, gives the handler tools to help her horse learn how to respond to the signal on the halter with the same released, relaxed posture. If your horse is comfortable with a signal to the halter and he can maintain a good posture and balance through transitions, you can certainly *Ground Drive* without the *Balance Rope* and second set of lines. For most horses, however, the extra lines are extremely beneficial for supporting their balance and overall self-carriage.

9.21 A & B
Having two sets of lines when driving encourages freedom of the head and neck and helps horses accept the feeling of a signal on the head. Light pressure at the base of the neck can activate the "seeking reflex" and helps avoid bracing and tension.

9.20 Driving with two sets of lines, including one attached to the halter, helps to encourage a released neck and relaxed posture. As the horse becomes more accustomed to listening to the driver's signals, the handler at the horse's head should slowly step away and reduce how quickly she reinforces the signals.

To ask for a step or two back, use the same signals that you would use for the halt, slowly adding a connection to the lines, pausing and then slowly releasing whether or not the horse has responded. If the horse does not respond, ask again, and then have the handler at the head ask in a way the horse understands, using a touch of the *Wand* on the chest or the legs. When your horse does not respond to the driver after a few attempts, check that you are not "squeezing" them forward with the lines by spreading your hands apart. It is also important that you are breathing and relaxed in your posture.

After a bit of practice you can soon master all the *Elements* from the *Playground for Higher Learning* (p. 175), which will give you and your horse new ways to engage. Driving through the various *Elements* helps reinforce verbal cues as well as those from the lines.

The Story of Big Surprise

Big Surprise was a 16-hand, 16-year-old Warmblood brought to one of my clinics in Europe. It was my twelfth year giving this particular clinic in Italy, hosted by my co-teachers, Silvia Torresani and Massimo Da Re, both long-time Tellington TTouch teachers and both veterinarians. Big Surprise was dangerously spooky in the arena and couldn't be ridden with other horses, as he would shy and bolt at any movement. He simply was not safe to ride.

As he entered the arena on Day One, it was easy to see he was high-headed, holding his breath, and had a worried eye. He was (big surprise!) completely out of balance mentally, emotionally, and physically. His front legs were widened and braced, and he really didn't want to be touched (figs.

9.22 A–T As he came into the arena on Day One, Big Surprise was high-headed, tense, and holding his breath. By the end of the three-day clinic, he had been transformed.

9.22 A & B). And interestingly, he had tiny black flies swarming about his face, probably from sweat caused by stress hormones. None of the other horses had flies around them.

I asked for the tack to be removed (saddle and his usual Pessoa snaffle bit) so I could take him into the *Labyrinth* (p. 179), ask him to *Lower the Head* (p. 65), and encourage him to focus (fig. 9.22 C). I replaced the bridle with a well-fitting, flat leather halter. He stood in a lateral, unbalanced posture, but I hoped he would become more diagonal after a few trips through the *Labyrinth* with a lowered head, combined with a variety of *TTouches*. I have found through the years it's far easier for a horse to lower his head while he's moving rather than simply standing.

Big Surprise began to focus and bring his head down as he navigated the *Labyrinth* (figs. 9.22 D–F). I used a chain lead (p. 70) up the side of the halter (not over the nose) to add a bit of weight and encourage the horse to lower his head. I held the Wand ahead of his nose so he could see and follow

it. I also stroked him on the nose with it. As he began to lower his head, I released the lead as he stepped forward, and I kept a mental picture of him with his head down.

If he couldn't do it—and many horses can't in the beginning—I would seek another way for him to be successful. There are multiple ways to help a horse say, "Yes," to a request. For example, with a high-headed horse such as Big Surprise, I would use *Back Lifts* (p. 112) to bring his back up and lower his head.

Next, I lightly cupped his eye with my hand to calm him. As his head came down, I was able to do *Ear TTouches* (p. 115) and soon after, for the first time, he extended his nose to make a clear connection to me of his own accord (figs. 9.22 G & H). This is so important, as I do not wish to train horses to respond by rote but instead want them to feel safe enough to reach out to me. The result is a cooperative, willing, and safe equine partner.

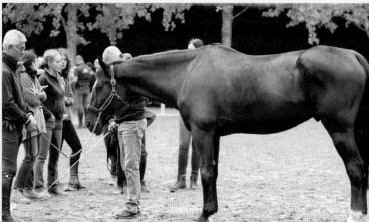

It was time to put his tack back on and ride him. His regular saddle went on, but instead of his usual snaffle, I replaced it with the *Tellington Training Bit* (p. 278), making sure to keep the lower rein loose. As I rode him through the *Labyrinth*, his head progressively telescoped down (figs. 9.22 I–K).

Already we had progressed from spooky to calm—Big Surprise and I trotted, relaxed and forward, through plastic sheets, under an arch of *Wands* and other once-scary items on light contact (fig. 9.22 L). By the end of Day One, the gelding's trainer could ride the horse at a soft, forward, engaged canter with draped reins.

On Day Two Silvia and I led Big Surprise in the *Homing Pigeon* (p. 143) through the *Labyrinth* to give him a new level of confidence. He "homed in," signaling the end of the flight reflex (fig. 9.22 M). I followed this with *Hind Leg Circles* (p. 106) and *Tail TTouches* (p. 118) to further help him let go of tension and soften his hindquarters. Big Surprise clearly enjoyed the bodywork

and turned his head to observe what was happening behind him (figs. 9.22 N & O). It's so important to give horses the freedom to participate in their training—to have a say in what is happening—and to honor their intelligence.

By the end of Day Two, Big Surprise was standing quietly, head lowered and relaxed, surrounded by participants from the clinic. We gave him time to further relax and rebalance on Sure Foot® Equine Stability Pads, developed by Wendy Murdoch (fig. 9.22 P). I highly recommend these pads as a great addition to the Tellington Method (see www.murdochmethod.com).

On Day Three we moved to the indoor arena due to rain. I put Big Surprise's regular snaffle bridle back on, along with the *Liberty Neck Ring* (p. 277) and *Promise Wrap* (p. 49), to help the horse maintain his newly balanced posture (fig. 9.22 Q). The gelding's trainer then rode him between plastic sheets and beneath pool noodles (see *Working with Plastic*, p. 190), all designed to help the horse overcome fear of things behind and above, and to develop trust, confidence, and a feeling of safety (figs. 9.22 R & S). At the end of Day Three, Big Surprise went over a low jump in a beautifully balanced posture (fig. 9.22 T). It was a huge and wonderful shock to this horse's trainer and rider how dramatically Big Surprise changed over the course of our three days together.

Two weeks later, Big Surprise went to his first show and jumped wonderfully with no spooking or "surprises." He was as good as he had been at the clinic.

PART III

Happy Progress

CHAPTER 10

Time to Saddle Up!

Introducing a Rider Calmly and Quietly

Your horse is now comfortable with a wide variety of *TTouches* and can be led through the *Playground of Higher Learning's* various *Elements* with confidence. *Chest Line Driving* and *Ground Driving* have helped him learn to listen to your cues from behind his shoulder, and he is familiar with movement around his hindquarters. The next step is the transition to carrying a rider.

The time has arrived! Your horse is about to graduate to work under saddle! All of your preparation has paid off and the slow, mindful exercises on the ground will result in a smooth and uneventful transition to work under saddle. A few specific considerations as to this stage of training:

FOAL OR WEANLING

Do not do the exercises in this chapter with foals.

UNSTARTED THREE- OR FOUR-YEAR-OLD

1 The outlined steps that follow, introducing the saddle, bridle, and rider, were developed with the horse who has not been ridden in mind. Take the time to go through all the incremental steps as an insurance policy for a safer, more confident early riding experience for you and your horse.

2 If your horse is slow in maturing or just does not seem quite ready, wait to get on for the first time. There is much more to be gained than lost when it comes to waiting to ride a young horse. In my experience, waiting an extra year can often make the introduction to more extensive ridden work go faster because the horse is that much more mature—mentally and physically.

3 Should you decide to start your three-year-old under saddle, keep the work to a minimum and focus on short, slow, positive experiences. You may even consider doing a couple of sessions then giving him a long break. This allows for more physical development, which will make for a more able, willing horse.

4 Even at four years, I recommend waiting to do a lot of intense work until he is at least five. Let his first experiences being a riding horse be fun, interesting, and easy. You are setting him up for the rest of his ridden career, so it is worth taking extra time to make sure he is confident and keen.

REEDUCATING THE MATURE HORSE

1 As with *Ground Driving* (p. 209), it is worth going through the early steps of this chapter as if your horse has never been ridden before. If you are restarting him, there are presumably some gaps in his education or ineffectual habits in his ridden tendencies. Going through these small steps can help change his expectations about what kind of experience he will have carrying a rider and give you some clues about where he is lacking understanding or harboring anxiety.

Saddling for the First Time

Each new lesson in this book has been introduced in small steps, and saddling for the first time is no exception. Once the horse has mastered all the small nuances comfortably, he understands the new task and can master it. This keeps the work fun for everybody.

You have already prepared the horse for the feeling of the girth with the *Abalone TTouch* (p. 92), *Belly Lifts* (p. 111), and the *Lick of the Cow's Tongue* (p. 95). You know he is not extremely ticklish or overly sensitive. The horse has learned to be touched all over and enjoys *TTouches* on his back, belly, and girth area. The *Belly Lifts* and *Ground Driving* with a surcingle have introduced your horse to the pressure of the girth under his belly and on his back. These have helped him be comfortable moving without feeling restricted. You have led the horse with the surcingle at the walk and trot and he stayed quiet and relaxed.

Sliding the Saddle Pad Exercise
You can now get the horse used to a saddle pad. Your helper holds the horse with a halter and lead and has a *Wand*.

10.1 A–D Show the horse the pad before placing it on his back (A). Use *Zebra TTouches* (p. 96) under it to add a pleasurable sensation (B). I find that showing a horse a new object from the side allows him to better see and sniff it. It also reinforces the idea of keeping his feet still while he turns his head to look at something unusual (C). Place some food on the pad when it slides to the ground to encourage the "whoa" (D).

Equipment
Saddle pad, lead, *Wand*, and some food for reinforcement.

How to Do It
This exercise is your "insurance policy" for any time down the road something falls off the saddle or slides off the horse's back, reinforcing a halt reaction rather than a startle.

Show the horse the saddle pad, let him sniff it, and offer him some food off the pad. Now place it on his back and offer him food while encouraging him to turn his head toward the pad. Make sure to do this from both

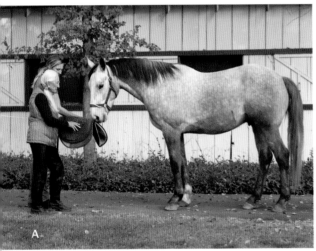

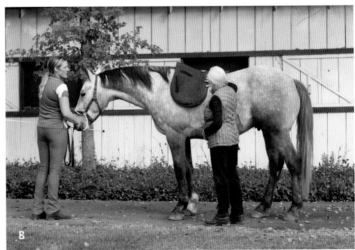

sides. If your horse seems concerned about the saddle pad, try starting with something smaller—a hand towel, for instance—and see if that makes it easier. Include a few *Zebra TTouches* (p. 96) underneath and around the pad to help the horse enjoy the new feeling on his back and encourage good breathing.

After establishing that your horse is comfortable wearing the saddle pad, you want to teach him how to react should it slide off his back (figs. 10.1 A–D). Begin by standing near the horse's shoulder, on the same side as the handler, if you have one, and quietly slide the pad to the ground, saying, "And whoooooa," Place some food on the pad while the handler shows the

When Theory Goes into Practice

On more than one occasion, I have found the *Sliding Saddle Pad* exercise to be invaluable. One memorable experience was on a confident, five-year-old gelding. We generally very lightly started our horses as four-year-olds, then put them back out with the herds and continued their education as five-year-olds. This particular horse was very ready to become a "big boy"; he was always waiting at the gate and was engaged with every lesson.

On one of our first hacks out I got to experience how long-lasting some lessons really are. As the gelding calmly led the way back to the farm, I was riding him on the buckle, allowing him to march along in a lovely, forward walk. Because he was so confident and relaxed about the new surroundings, I let myself get a little too casual. As

I turned around to speak to my riding partner, my horse stumbled and stopped suddenly, unseating me over his left shoulder. Not my finest hour. My unexpected dismount was very smooth, and I simply rolled and found myself, relatively comfortably, on the ground. And since the gelding was a youngster, on his way home, experiencing his first time parting ways with a rider, my first thought was that I would be walking home.

Instead of rushing toward the barn, surprised by my sudden movement, my horse put on the brakes, turned around, and started gently snuffling me. I had to laugh. The extra 20 minutes I had put in the previous year were really paying off. I remounted and we continued our ride without incident.

10.2 A–C This simple exercise has great benefits. Start slowly and gradually make the exercise more involved, working up to the trot, and having the pad slide off both sides of the horse's back. Take your time, working your way up to using a raincoat or other noisy and potentially scary items in this exercise.

horse that there is something interesting to be had. Do this once or twice on each side before continuing.

If your horse startled, you need to repeat the exercise in even smaller steps. You can take the pad off carefully and place it on the ground slowly while giving the horse a sense of security with the *Body Wrap* (p. 44) and more *TTouches* (p. 78).

When your horse is ready, have your handler ask the horse to walk. Walk alongside and quietly slide the saddle pad off so it falls on the ground as you say, "Aaaaand whoa," and place a treat on the pad. The handler asks the horse to halt and turns him to investigate the saddle pad on the ground (figs. 10.2 A–C).

After a couple of tries, most horses understand this exercise and start to halt on their own as soon as they feel the saddle pad begin to slide off. Do this exercise on both sides. It is really worthwhile taking the time to work up to having the horse *Trot in Hand* (p. 160) and allowing the pad to slide off on its own.

Note: You may have to adjust the type of food used in this exercise according to the horse's personality. Nervous, tense horses that lack self-confidence can usually have higher value treats, like a small horse cookie or piece of carrot, without becoming consumed by the food. Relaxed, more gregarious personalities often do better with lower value treats such as hay or picked grass. Of course, it is often the thought that counts more than the actual treat or volume of treat!

Introducing the Saddle

After your horse has mastered the *Sliding Saddle Pad* exercise, you can introduce the saddle itself. Allow your horse to sniff or investigate the saddle politely before placing it on his back. If you have a helper available, have her stand at your horse's head, stroking his front legs with a *Wand* as you saddle for the first time (fig. 10.3). Be mindful not to drop the saddle onto the horse's back or catch his withers as

you place it. Once the saddle is set, allow the horse to turn his head to look at it. When introducing any new item to a young or inexperienced horse, it is a good idea to keep the notion of "casual consciousness" at the front of your mind. This is the difference between being careful yet relaxed about something rather than just being slow. Being casually conscious means that you breathe and stay relaxed while being completely observant and mindful about how the horse is feeling in the exercise.

Attach the girth to one side and do a few *Belly Lifts* (p. 111) before actually securing it. A *Belly Lift* is the most useful tool you can use when introducing the saddle; doing them can prevent lifelong issues with "girthiness." *Belly Lifts* help your horse relax, which can prevent him from "blowing out" or being "cold-backed," as well.

10.3 Even if your horse seems completely at ease, it is a nice courtesy to let him sniff the saddle as you approach. Being mindful about how you tighten the girth should become a habit with horses of all ages and experience levels.

10.4 Whether your horse has never worn a saddle or is a seasoned veteran, *Belly Lifts* with the girth and saddle is a polite, considerate exercise to practice any time you tack up. It gives the horse a chance to relax rather than anticipate the feeling of a girth being tightened and helps to reduce overreaction to the process.

For *Belly Lifts* using the girth, take the end of the girth in one hand while the other hand supports the girth billets to act as a counterbalance (fig. 10.4). Gently lift up on the girth while the handler encourages the horse to *Lower the Head* (p. 65) or look at you. Count two or three, pause, then slowly release the pressure. Ideally your horse will be familiar with this exercise from his experience in *Ground Driving* with the surcingle, so it should not be a new sensation. Repeat this several times, watching for the smallest hint of concern, whether it's the flick of an ear, tightening of the eye, swish of the tail, or shallow breathing. Given any of these signs, pause, and reduce the pressure slightly.

When you do up the girth, do so incrementally and without using a lot of leverage to tighten it. "Casually but consciously" drop the flaps, move the stirrups, and let the horse feel some movement around the saddle. Lead the horse through the different *Elements* of the *Playground for Higher Learning*—turning, walking, and halting (fig. 10.5). This small step helps you ensure that the horse is not concerned with wearing the saddle and can potentially avoid any reactive behavior as you continue the training process.

10.5 Returning to a familiar exercise makes the addition of a new exercise or concept, such as wearing a saddle, seamless and low-stress for your horse.

If he is anxious or wary, take more time doing easy, familiar exercises and end the session. Once he seems comfortable wearing the saddle, you can use the *Dolphins Flickering Through the Waves* leading position (p. 162) to ask for trot at a distance. Note: When you are using an English saddle make sure the stirrups are secured so they cannot slide down and bump the horse's sides the first time he is asked to trot.

Watch for Reactions

➤ Always look for subtle signs of apprehension, tension, or confusion as you carry on with each step.

➤ Notice the horse's posture. Does he keep his head and neck relaxed or does the addition of the saddle create tension?

➤ Does his respiration change?

➤ How does his back feel?

➤ Does he maintain the same swing through the body when walking and rhythm in his stride, or is there tension?

➤ Does he move forward freely or seem insecure when he has a saddle on his back?

➤ How does he deal with being led through already familiar obstacles?

➤ Does he trip or is he well balanced and coordinated when he steps over cavalletti and ground poles?

Dealing with Biting

There are a lot of different opinions on how to deal with a horse that bites. I understood 30 years ago that aggression stems from fear. Instead of punishing the horse I will look for the reason behind the biting, knowing that the behavior is simply communication. Some horses threaten and bite the air without connecting with the person. Others hit the person with their teeth and mouth wide open without biting down. There are also horses that will truly bite and leave an open wound or a severe bruise, but they are the minority. Few horses truly bite for the sake of biting.

It is important to recognize the different triggers for biting and look at them from a new perspective. Some horses—young ones in particular—constantly want to lick, nibble, and chew on the lead rope or rein, or suck or twist their tongue. These are signs of stress, not a horse with a bad attitude. We need to evaluate the situation that causes the horse to bite. Biting is often triggered by brushing a horse when he is really sensitive or sore, as well as tightening the girth. These situations put the horse under added pressure and stress. A horse will usually try to subtly tell us he is not comfortable with something by a change of expression—holding his breath or flicking his ears or tail—but we are taught to ignore this language. When a horse's "whispers" are constantly ignored, we leave him with little choice but to shout!

When the horse bites the air while you do up the girth, he has no intention of hurting you, but is showing us that our doing up the girth is very uncomfortable for him. Often, the horse will respond the same way even when you are very careful with the girth. He remembers the discomfort from previous experiences and may already start biting when he sees the saddle coming toward him. We can only change this

➤ Can he easily navigate the turns in the *Labyrinth*?

➤ Does he suddenly start to get mouthy or "goofy" with an additional step?

➤ Is your horse "too" still or in freeze (see sidebar, p. 34)?

All of these are large indicators that the horse is not comfortable, and the more experience you have the more quickly you will find the really subtle hints: a slight hardening of the eye and lack of movement of the ears, for example. The more quickly you learn to recognize these signals, the more

behavior if we truly listen to his body language and understand the root of it. Think or say, "I understand what you are trying to tell me," instead of punishing him. Tighten the girth very slowly and gently, or change the routine and expectations by removing the saddle once or twice before actually tightening the girth, and prepare him with some *Abalone TTouches* (p. 92) and *Belly Lifts* (p. 111) to release his tension. Sometimes, it also helps to saddle the horse from the right side because it changes the pattern of expectations.

If none of these suggestions seem to change a horse that is defensive about the girth, you likely need to address saddle fit or chat with your vet about the possibility of his having ulcers.

During my Feldenkrais training, I learned from an Israeli neurologist that the mouth has a direct connection to the limbic system. This discovery led me to develop the *Mouth TTouches* for horses (p. 126). These *TTouches* have helped many horses to stop biting. If your horse truly bites and is dangerous, I recommend *Taming the Tiger* (p. 68) while working with him: Hold the lines in such a way that he cannot reach you with his mouth. With your free hand, carefully start some *TTouches* on the outside of his mouth. He can learn not to react instinctively but to concentrate and think instead. Through the *Mouth TTouches* you will trigger new learning on an emotional level. The horse learns to trust you and can learn to enjoy the *Mouth TTouches*. Through these *TTouches* the horse quickly loses his tendency to bite and learns to change his behavior.

To understand why the horse bites does not mean that you are condoning it. It is up to you to find a way to change the behavior in your approach and understanding of it.

quickly you can reassure the horse. As horses begin to realize that you are listening to their "whispers" (their smallest indicators of concern), their trust in you will grow.

Troubleshooting

If your horse seems insecure, you can attach a *Body Wrap* (p. 44), stroke the chest and legs with the *Wand*, and do some *TTouches* around the body. Take a mindful breath and repeat the *Elements* of the *Playground for Higher Learning* with more purpose and attention to your own signals and posture.

The horse is only ready to be mounted when he can manage these *Elements* in a well-balanced manner while maintaining normal respiration and a relaxed frame of mind and body.

Where to Start?

As you have seen, many of the exercises in this book can be done at a young age. They help develop many skills that can be directly transferred to ridden work. Generally, I recommend using *TTouches* when the horse is still a foal. Foals should learn to trust people, be touched all over the body without fear, and stand quietly and let the handler lift all four feet. Of course, being willing to be led and stand still are also important basic lessons for any young horse.

Young horses will benefit from work with the *Elements* from the *Playground for Higher Learning*, but it is important not to overdo it. Foals and young horses learn a lot when they work about once a month. Sometimes, you will find that they have made a huge progression even when left to their own devices.

Depending on the breed of your horse, you can do the initial backing at about three years of age, but I recommend not asking too much until he is four—and there are some horses that do best when left until five years old. It is a very individual thing that depends on mental and physical maturity and balance.

I don't agree with starting horses at two because they are physically, mentally, and emotionally not yet ready for the demands. Many horses that have been started early are already "used up" when they are five or six years old, and are no longer rideable.

10.6 It is a good idea to introduce a piece of riding equipment from the ground first. Here, Mandy asks Chimera to stop from the signal on the nose of the *Lindell Sidepull* (p. 275). Teaching your horse this signal before you are on his back simplifies learning and is a safer way to assess the clarity of your cues.

Introducing the Bridle

I always start horses without a bit, initially. For most horses, the bit is very distracting and takes a long time to be fully understood. Beginning their riding education without a bit means that they are able to clearly understand turning and halting as they learn to balance with a rider, without potentially creating resistance to the bit—a resistance that will later have to be undone.

The *Lindell Sidepull*—which I describe in detail on p. 275—is a well-designed piece of equipment that I like to use because it creates a very clear turning aid and encourages lateral flexibility without causing the head to tip (fig. 10.6). When fitting a *Lindell* or any snaffle bridle or sidepull it is vital that the noseband is not fitted too tightly. It is so important for horses to have the full use of the jaw to lick and chew when being ridden. A tightly fitted noseband will inhibit the jaw and cause tension in the entire body.

Ask your horse to *Lower the Head* (p. 65) each time you go to bridle him; this will set up a positive habit that can carry through the rest of his ridden life and helps to keep the bridling process relaxed and cooperative. Assuming

10.7 Adding the snaffle underneath the *Lindell Sidepull* makes for an easy transition and gives the rider the ability to create clear, understandable signals for the horse who is not familiar with the bit, or to reeducate the horse that does not understand or feel comfortable with a bit.

your horse is comfortable with the preparatory *T Touches* around his poll and ears (p. 115), he will not likely be concerned about the crownpiece of the bridle coming over his ears. If for some reason he is worried about this step, go back to doing some more *T Touches* around the area, and consider adding a *Head Wrap* and *Body Wrap* before you try it again (pp. 46 and 44).

Once your horse is comfortable with wearing the bridle, add the *Balance Rein,* which lies around the horse's neck like the *Balance Rope* we used in *Chest Line Driving* (p. 215). I use the *Balance Rein* as a second rein to help the horse, young or old, find his balance. It assists in rounding the horse's back and lengthening and rounding the neck while helping him shift his weight off the forehand. (Find more information about the *Balance Rein* on p. 278.) Practice taking the reins and *Balance Rein* back and forth over your horse's head so you can make sure he is okay with movement above him.

Depending on your own personal philosophy or your horse's future career, you can decide to add a snaffle bridle to the *Lindell Sidepull-Balance Rein* configuration (fig. 10.7). If you plan on riding the horse with a bit, add

Behavior Is Just Communication

If you have spent enough time in the horse world, you will have likely heard of a horse "testing his rider." You will see this in school horses, green horses, or any horse that has the difficult job of carrying different riders. An experienced rider will get on and have no trouble, while a new, often less skilled rider gets on, and all of the sudden, the horse does not respond the same way but acts "naughty" or "resistant."

In my experience, this is not necessarily an "attitude" problem on the part of the horse; it's one of clarity or a deeper physical issue.

Every rider, no matter how much she tries, gives slightly different signals to the horse. Think of yourself when you get into a rental car. Doesn't it take a bit of time to figure out the different steering, pedal sensitivity, or realize where the blind spots are? And a car doesn't have a brain and nervous system!

When a horse has a physical imbalance or crookedness, mild chronic pain, or some other deeply rooted physical issue, it is far easier to ignore the symptoms with a skilled, balanced rider who innately compensates for any weakness in the horse. A less experienced rider will be more of a "passenger" and be less able to help support the horse. This will often result in the "testing" of the rider, when in fact it is really a case of the horse lacking the support he needs to do the job that is being asked.

I had this happen with a homebred horse at my farm. This lovely gelding was practically born trained. As a four-year-old with ten rides under his belt, he would safely carry a four-year-old child like a pro. He was calm, well-balanced, and an overall fantastic horse. Then one summer he started to "test" his riders. Lesson students found that he would turn around and try to go to the gate. On a trail ride, he would be "barn sour" for newer riders and want to go home. Because none of these things happened with a more skilled rider, it was chalked up to him "taking advantage" of beginners.

When a skilled diagnostic vet came to the farm, I decided to have him checked out, just in case. He was not lame or uneven to the naked eye; however, after days of tests, lungeing, flexions, ultrasounds, and X-rays, it became apparent that he had a very serious tear in his hind suspensory ligament. *Ding ding ding ding ding!* No other hints other than his intermittent reluctance to haul beginners. What a saint of a horse. He was one of my greatest teachers: Whenever something like that pops up, I always remember my experience with him and look deeper, because there is *always* a reason for behavior.

the snaffle bridle (without a cavesson) underneath the *Lindell*, fitting the *Lindell* noseband appropriately. As you introduce the action of the snaffle, you can vary how much connection is on the *Lindell* reins and how much is on the snaffle reins, making a gradual transition to snaffle cues clear for your horse. Note: Always have your horse's teeth checked by a professional before introducing the bit.

Mounting for the First Time

The moment you have been preparing for (fig. 10.8)! Thanks to the *TTouches* (p. 78), your horse has good body awareness and relaxation. You have improved his balance, coordination, and ability to learn while building a foundation of trust. Your horse knows and understands the different leading positions (p. 132) and has mastered the *Playground for Higher Learning* obstacles (p. 175). He is familiar with the *Body Wrap* (p. 44) and is not concerned about movement and sounds behind him. *Working with Plastic* is not an issue; he can be led with the saddle at the walk and trot, and be lunged on an oval. Your horse has been *Ground Driven* (p. 209) and happily understands your voice, rein, and body-language cues.

These steps have helped your horse to override the flight instinct and to develop self-control. He stops and thinks instead of instinctively reacting when confronted with a new situation. Through the stages of his education, you have gained a trusting relationship with him. You now have a partner who is willing to work with you and happy to be spending time with you.

Equipment
When you are ready to get on, you need a well-fitted saddle, a *Lindell Sidepull* (p. 275), a *Body Wrap* (optional, p. 44), *Zephyr* lead (p. 40), and a *Wand* (p. 62), as well as a contained space—ideally rectangular or square rather than round.

How to Do It
Always visualize the outcome that you want rather than think of the worst-case scenario. If you feel yourself becoming tense before mounting your horse, or if you are holding your breath or feeling fearful, it may be a good idea to wait or have a more confident, experienced person step in.

10.8 Mounting a horse should be a calm, quiet event, not a rodeo. If your horse is extremely anxious or nervous about a rider on his back, it is best to go back a few steps or chunk down the exercise even more. If a horse continues to find the weight of a rider to be very stressful, it is worth ruling out any physical issue with your vet.

Pick a nice day with no wind when you feel well, and have lots of time, patience, and a friendly helper. Brush your horse with feeling that day and treat him to some of his favorite *TTouches*. A few minutes of *Ear TTouch* (p. 115) and some stroking with the *Wand* down the chest and legs will help your horse to concentrate. Calmly saddle the horse and put the *Lindell Sidepull* on (p. 275). Attach a *Zephyr* lead (p. 40) to the sidepull, and place a *Balance Rein* (p. 275) around your horse's neck. Walk your horse through the *Labyrinth* (p. 179) and a few other obstacles to check in with your communication and his concentration level.

You need a solid mounting block that is truly secure. You can also use bales of straw. It is important for the mounting block to be safe. Having a helper is ideal. It enhances safety and gives your horse a familiar, predictable request from the ground. If you do not have a helper, you should be an extremely experienced trainer and rider to proceed on your own. The mindset of your helper is very important. Having a person who is present, aware, relaxed, and observant is necessary. A nervous or unaware person on the ground is less helpful than having no helper at all.

Once you have the site prepared, your helper leads the horse next to the mounting block. A *Body Wrap* (p. 44) can improve his balance and give him an added sense of security.

Step onto the mounting block at your horse's left side while your handler holds the horse with the *Zephyr* lead and a *Wand*. The horse should stand quietly as you step up and get organized, and he should remain totally unconcerned as your footsteps make a sound on the block or your stirrup leathers make a flapping noise. Stroke him all over his body with the *Wand* and use a few calming *TTouches* on his neck and croup while you are standing on the block. Remember to touch your horse behind the saddle. Some horses seem to get "disconnected" from their hindquarters when wearing a saddle, and you want to make sure that they know where their body begins and ends. If you find that your horse is surprised by your touch, you may want to add a *Promise Wrap* (p. 49) or do some *Tail TTouches* (p. 118). Ask your horse to turn his head to you and offer him a treat or a handful of hay (figs. 10.9 A–C). For some horses, a scratch in their favorite spot may be more appropriate. If your horse rips the food out of your hand, you know he is holding his breath. In this case, you need to do more preparation before stepping into the saddle.

Repeat the exercise on the other side of the horse. When you get the sense that the horse is concerned, repeat this exercise a few times from both sides until he is completely comfortable, calm, with regular breathing, and he is interested in what you are doing. Remember to

10.9 A–C It is worth every moment you spend practicing standing calmly at the mounting block. Creating a positive association at the start goes a long way to creating good long-term habits about the mounting process. If your horse suddenly stops standing quietly for mounting after a few rides, you will want to check that he is not sore or carrying excess body tension.

touch him along the neck, croup, and girth area to check in and remind him about being present in his own body.

Cavalry Style

The cavalry style of mounting is the best way to help maintain a horse's balance and keep the saddle in place while allowing for a seamless transition to the horse's back. If you have never mounted this way before, practice on an older, trained horse first, mastering it from the left and the right side.

For mounting from the horse's left side, stand on the block facing the horse's head—not his tail, as you might be used to doing. Take the reins in both hands with the left hand anchored in the mane; hold the offside saddle flap with your right hand. This transfers your weight over the horse and prevents the saddle from slipping. Put your left foot into the stirrup, watching that your toes are pointing toward your horse's head. This keeps you from accidentally poking your horse with the tip of your boot, which could startle him. Place the inside of your left knee against the saddle.

Gently and gracefully push your right foot up and lean over the saddle so your head is on the right side of the horse. In this position, you are not in the center of the horse, but diagonally over the saddle (figs. 10.10 A–C). This distributes your body weight evenly over the horse's right and left sides and allows him to balance. From here, it is easy to smoothly bring your right leg in a flowing movement over the horse's back without putting strain on your own back.

10.10 A–C Mounting mindfully should be a habit whether it is your first time or five hundredth. The cavalry style of mounting, facing forward, placing your offside hand on the opposite flap helps steady the saddle and avoids putting excessive pressure on the withers and spine.

10.11 Offering a treat or well-placed scratch once you are in the saddle is an easy way to reinforce a good halt at the mounting block. Once a horse is hopeful that a reward is coming, he finds it much easier to quietly stand in anticipation while the rider settles herself. It also helps makes the entire experience positive and encourages a nervous horse to breathe and chew.

Be aware of your own breathing while you are mounting. Try getting into the saddle on an exhale, because this helps keep your back released and allows for a smooth motion. Gently set yourself into the saddle and slowly sit up straight as you place your right foot into the stirrup.

Ask the horse to turn his head and take a treat from your hand. As you reach forward, be aware of maintaining an independent seat so that you do not inadvertently slide your leg back toward his flank. Apply a few *T Touches* on his neck and behind the saddle while your helper should stroke the horse's chest and front legs with the *Wand* (fig. 10.11).

Do not leave the horse standing over the mounting block if it is a portable device. Once you are settled in the saddle, your helper should quietly remove the block from underfoot—it should be picked up rather than

10.12 Dismounting is an important step. You want to ensure it is a calm, positive experience for your horse. Some horses can be surprised by your sudden presence on the ground so use the same level of mindfulness as you do when mounting.

dragged so you do not surprise the horse that is likely focused on the new task of carrying your weight.

Dismounting

Now it is time to prepare for the dismount. Offer your horse another treat so he is not surprised when you swing off. It is safest to take both feet out of the stirrups and slide to the ground with a smooth, flowing movement. Remind your helper and yourself to keep breathing and have the horse keep his head and neck at chest level. Your helper can also give the horse a treat while you carefully slide out of the saddle to make sure the horse keeps breathing. I like to add a verbal cue, "Aaand whoooa," as I dismount to help reinforce the halt (fig. 10.12). Always dismount before you feel like you and the horse have had enough. Your first few mounted sessions may only last minutes; however, giving your horse short, manageable experiences helps boost his confidence and lays the foundation for success as you increase what is expected of him. Do not forget to praise your horse, and end the session with a few *TTouches*.

Mounting Blocks

The benefits of a mounting block have recently become more formally acknowledged by studies. While it is a good idea to have the ability to mount from the ground, always choose a block or raised object to mount from when you have the option. Besides being much easier on *your* body, mounting from an object higher than the ground is much easier on your horse, especially on the right side of the withers and spine.

10.13 The leader on the ground should be calm and aware, paying attention to the horse's reactions and communicating clearly with the rider. In all the years I have started countless horses, I can only think of one that was extremely uncomfortable with his first mounted experience. As it turned out, he was extremely weak in the stifles and had difficulty carrying weight prior to on-the-ground strengthening exercises. Carrying a rider need not be dramatic, and with quiet preparation, rarely is.

First Steps Under the Saddle

Like the first experience mounting, your horse's first steps forward with a rider should be calm and uneventful. If your horse is comfortable carrying the saddle, you have done all the preparations such as *Ground Driving* (p. 209) at the walk and trot, mastered all of the *Playground of Higher Learning* (p. 175), and have mounted and dismounted a few times, your horse is ready to take his first steps with a rider.

Your horse should know the *Dingo* leading position really well before you step forward under saddle for the first time. It is best to have a helper to be the "leader" from the ground who gives the horse an added sense of security (fig. 10.13). She helps the horse to understand the rider's signals because she can combine them with her own signals. For the first ride, I like the horse to be dressed in a *Lindell Sidepull* and *Zephyr* lead, a *Balance Rein*, saddle, and possibly a *Body Wrap*.

Always sit lightly on a young horse's back, and remember that the back muscles that are needed to carry you have not yet been developed. Some young horses can become tense if they are worked too hard too soon and can tighten the back when the rider sits too heavily or is very braced and stiff through the back and ankles. Some young horses pin their ears and

10.14 A & B Take the time to touch your horse in front of and behind the saddle before asking for walk. Be mindful not to surprise your horse. Start with your hand in a familiar place like along the crest or the shoulder.

refuse to take even a single step when the rider sits too heavily on her seat. Offer some *TTouches* in front of and behind the saddle (figs. 10.14 A & B).

Signal to Step Forward

Lighten your weight in the saddle by about 5 to 10 percent, stroke the horse's croup, then gently tap the horse with the *Wand* on top of the croup and give him the voice signal he is familiar with, "And waaaalk," while the leader gives a forward signal with the lead. If your horse hesitates, do not worry, he is likely processing the information and figuring out how to balance (figs. 10.15 A & B). Give him a moment, and if necessary, repeat the cues. It is best for the helper to ask the horse to walk fairly straight rather than on an immediate turn; however, if a horse is very "stuck," he may need to take a

10.15 A & B It is important to help your horse connect to his entire body. Carrying the weight of the rider must be a very disorienting sensation for a horse at first, so help him the best you can. Teaching your horse the *Dingo* (p. 148), along with clear verbal cues, on the ground will make for a smooth transition under saddle. The helper is there to clarify the signal, but she must give the horse a chance to respond before she adds to the cues. Too often we ask again without giving the horse a chance to process the information and respond.

10.16 A & B To ask for the halt, be prepared to allow your horse to walk into it as opposed to "slamming on the brakes" the moment you think about halting. A smooth, balanced halt that takes a step or two is better than an abrupt one that is unbalanced and tense.

step off to one side in order to shift his weight into balance.

Signals for Stopping

To halt, lighten your seat in the saddle, pick up the *Balance Rein* (p. 275), and exhale, being careful to not ask the horse to move forward with your lower leg. Use the *Lindell Sidepull* and *Balance Rein* to give the horse the signals to stop, using the *Balance Rein* 55 percent and the *Lindell* reins 45 percent (figs. 10.16 A & B). Use a smooth signal on the reins as you pick them

10.17 As you and your horse progress, his posture should stay relaxed and he should be comfortable with being touched all over the body.

up, and resist the urge to pull. Horses will halt on the release of the aid, not the pull, so it is imperative to ask and release when you use the reins. As you engage these signals, use your voice to clearly say, "And whoooooooa," as you did when leading him on the ground. In addition to being a consistent cue that the horse knows from earlier work, it also prevents *you* from holding your breath!

If your horse feels like he is not going to stop from these signals, the leader can add to your signal with one of her own on the lead, and by touching the *Wand* to the horse's chest. This links the signals that the horse has learned on the ground to the ones you are teaching him under saddle. Most horses that have difficulty stopping or going under saddle are simply lacking balance and have not yet learned how to organize themselves with the added weight of the rider. Using a leader means that you are chunking down the process for your horse and keeping him within his comfort zone. By using a helper as a leader for several sessions you will go a long way in promoting confidence and a quiet transition to work under saddle.

At the walk, ride through the *Playground for Higher Learning* obstacles and, during each session, add a lot of slaloms, turns, circles, and ovals, *TTouching* the horse all over his body and maintaining a relaxed posture (fig. 10.17). Keep the sessions short at first and gradually increase them.

The Half-Walk

At the *Half-Walk* the horse shortens his stride by shifting his center to his hindquarters. He needs to raise the base of his neck to achieve this, so it may be necessary to think slightly "up-and-back" through the reins and *Balance Rein* as you lighten your seat in the saddle. Five or six steps at the *Half-Walk* are enough; then give the horse the rein and let him walk on with his head and neck free and extended. Repeat this exercise three to four times per riding session. The *Half-Walk* produces amazing changes in horses that are rushing or slow horses that are out of balance.

First Trot

Once your horse has found his balance after a few rides at the walk and understands the signals to stop and go forward easily, and you have had some solo rides at the walk without the support of your helper, you can ask for a trot. In the beginning, just a few steps—maybe 10—are enough! The main goal is for a quiet, balanced, upward transition, not the *quantity* of trot that you get. Your experienced helper should lead the horse the first few times you trot (and the horse must already be comfortable trotting on the ground without a rider).

Keep your *Wand* behind your leg, and with the reins of the *Lindell* and *Balance Rein* loose, lighten your seat, and stroke then tap the horse with your *Wand* on the croup (fig. 10.18). Use your voice, "And trot." You can either post or ride the trot in a two-point position to free the horse's back. Many youngsters are most comfortable when you remain relatively still in a two-point position the first few times they trot under saddle; only post once they are a bit more balanced in trot. If you ride Western, you can still lighten your seat initially, and do a small rising trot once your horse is more secure with

10.18 When first trotting a green horse, he needs to go forward happily in a quiet, calm manner. Be careful about inadvertently giving mixed signals, and be sure to allow the horse to find his balance.

Lacking Forward Movement

When a horse is trained—as he should be—without intimidation and fear, he needs to learn to go forward from an understood signal rather than going forward out of instinct and anxiety as many horses do. Practice the *Dingo* leading position (p. 148) on the ground first so your horse learns to release the poll and step forward energetically. Be sure to use a clear verbal cue that can be transferred easily to under saddle work. Once your horse knows *Dingo* well, you can use the *Wand* on the croup when you are riding to give your horse a clear forward signal. Your horse should not be going forward because he is scared or expects discomfort; he should simply go forward because it is a recognizable signal he understands.

To give your horse more energy and impulsion, try riding with a *Body Rope* (p. 50). A *Body Rope* is attached the same way as a Body Wrap (p. 44) but with a rope as opposed to a bandage. A driving line works well for this and you simply tie the ends to the "D" rings of your saddle or the girth billets. The rope should sit on the gaskin—loose enough so that it does not restrict movement, but tight enough that it does not go below the hocks.

It can also be useful to go back to *Chest Line Driving* (p. 213) to help your horse understand the forward signal given by the leg and to listen to signals behind his head.

It is important that you keep your riding sessions interesting. Vary them by including new *Elements*, work with other horses, and go trail riding to encourage a more forward-thinking attitude.

If your horse suddenly becomes slow after being nicely forward, check for any physical issues, such as saddle fit, ulcers, tension in the back, or sore feet.

10.19 The *Balance Rein* (p. 275) is a great tool for helping a horse find his downward transitions in trot without negatively influencing his balance or posture. Using an "ask-and-release" upward motion on the *Balance Rein* with a light rein signal, in addition to your seat and voice, allows for a clear, smooth walk or halt.

your weight. While horses can manage it, sitting trot is not easy for youngsters or older horses that do not have a lot of weight-carrying strength.

If your horse raises his head, becomes nervous, or trots too fast, bring him back to a walk using the *Balance Rein* (fig. 10.19). Wait before trotting again, and keep working at the walk with a helper leading the horse. You can also use a *Body Wrap* (p. 44) to give the horse more security, and stroke him with the *Wand* while negotiating the *Playground for Higher Learning* (p. 175) for balance.

Troubleshooting

If your horse seems confused about going forward from only your signals from the saddle, it may be necessary to have the handler put the horse into a *Dolphins Flickering Through the Waves* (p. 162) leading position that allows you to have help at a distance. Sometimes it is useful to have the helper still walk beside the horse without actually leading him. It gives the horse an added sense of security and is a perfect transition to riding alone.

Another helpful step, if possible, is to ride the young horse with another, quiet older horse to follow. Horses gain a lot of confidence from other horses, and it can make the transition to going forward under saddle that much easier and clear from the horse's perspective.

Riding Through the Elements

Depending on how balanced and confident your individual horse is, you can incorporate the *Elements* from the *Playground for Higher Learning* early in your riding sessions (fig. 10.20). Practice your turns in the *Labyrinth* (p. 179), bending and surefootedness in the *Double Triangle* (p. 185), ride over *Ground Poles* (p. 187), and ask your horse for straight lines, slalom, circles, and ovals. In addition, change directions through the diagonal or on large loops, and praise your horse often to make sure he knows he is doing a good job. As he becomes more confident carrying you, don't hesitate to add in new aspects of the *Playground of Higher Learning*. Riding through the *Elements* provides you and your horse a great way to focus and communicate clearly and concisely. The familiarity of the *Elements* helps to maintain his

10.20 Incorporating the *Playground for Higher Learning Elements* (p. 175) keeps things engaging and interesting for you and your horse. In addition to developing confidence and trust, the *Elements* encourage a healthy posture and good overall use of the body.

confidence while creating interest, improving balance, and maintaining overall fun.

During the first two weeks of riding, you should keep your sessions short: 10 to 15 minutes under saddle are enough. In my experience, the horse benefits the most when he is ridden three to four times a week. Give him a few days to rest and assimilate what he has learned. This is the best way to teach him to trust you, find his balance under saddle, and build the necessary muscles.

During each ride, your horse should be physically, mentally, and emotionally in balance. If you notice that your horse is not well-balanced, repeat a few exercises and be mindful not to ask too much of the young horse. Do not worry about perfecting each exercise before moving on—coming back to a difficult exercise after doing other unrelated figures will create more progression than if you just use repetition.

Trail Riding

Hacking out is a fantastic way to encourage a forward way of going, increase confidence, and keep work interesting. Once you have ridden the horse in the ring for a few weeks at the walk and trot, he is probably ready for his first trail ride. Take a friend along on a calm, experienced trail horse, and pick a route that is suitable and without a lot of traffic. It can also be useful to walk your horse in hand once or twice so he has a good idea of what to expect. I am never afraid to hop off and lead a young horse on his first trail

10.21 A–C When working with horses remember the principle of chunking it down, even if you think the horse should be able to do it "by now." Chimera was not sure about being ridden over the *Bridge*, even though he had walked over it in hand. To help him be successful and understand that he could balance with a rider, I simply led him over. If this was still an issue for him, we would have made it easier by starting with the *Platform*—maybe even going back to it without a rider.

10.22 The *Balance Rein* and *Lindell Sidepull*, with a snaffle bit if you choose, are great tools for trail riding. The *Balance Rein* allows you to help your inexperienced horse find a steady rhythm along unpredictable footing and terrain without shortening the horse's neck or putting pressure on his head.

ride when the need arises. I reassure him often and like to avoid any escalations of stress or anxiety. There are no prizes for bravery and nothing gained from riding out a situation when you can calmly hop off and walk a few strides before it all becomes too much for the inexperienced horse.

First Canter

Once you have been on the trail a few times, your horse may be ready for his first canter. The timing depends on the individual. Some are ready to canter early on in their training, others need more time. It is best to canter up a slight hill, accompanied by a steady trail horse.

Allowing a horse to canter out of the natural forward propulsion found uphill (and outside of an arena) usually makes for a very easy, uneventful transition. The slight uphill helps the horse maintain his balance, and the natural energy of being outside of the arena means that the rider does not have to push the horse into the gait.

Rein-Back and Lateral Work

Note that many horses learn to back up by lifting the head and dropping the back. When teaching your horse under saddle, avoid this by teaching him to back quietly and in a good posture with the *Cha Cha* (p. 156) on the ground. Under saddle, you can teach a horse to back by using a combination of the *Lindell Sidepull* (p. 275) and the *Balance Rein* (p. 275). Using 60 percent or more of the pressure with the *Balance Rein* initially teaches the horse how to shift his weight through his entire body from the base up rather than by lifting his head. Always ask for slow, mindful steps when backing up a horse, on the ground or under saddle. Backing up should never be used when frustrated or as punishment. A horse that is backed out of fear and anxiety will often resort to backing up any time he is confused or anxious. This can be very unsafe and create other issues.

The *Cha Cha* is also an excellent way to introduce lateral work to your horse from the ground that can then be transferred to work under saddle. Slowly asking for one step at a time helps your horse understand how to shift his balance and reload weight right and left, up and down, and forward and back rather than just move away from pressure or a signal.

Rider Awareness

Being aware of your own mind and body while in the saddle is important for horses of all ages and training levels; however, it is perhaps doubly important during a horse's first few rides when being introduced or reintroduced to the idea of being ridden.

Most of us have unconscious habits that make us crooked in the saddle. This can be from past injury or simply our balance. Using a *Shrug Wrap for Riders* is a useful tool for becoming more aware of patterns of asymmetry. Using a simple 3- or 4-inch elastic bandage, make an "X" between the shoulder blades by wrapping the bandage on either side of your shoulders. This simple *Shrug Wrap* is a great one to try when you are constantly being told, "Shoulders back!" The bandages are done up without tension so you are not restricted in any way. The light pressure reminds your body that you are rolling your shoulders forward, without you having to think about it. For some riders, it also provides a sense of security and can boost confidence.

10.23 The *Shrug Wrap* is a great tool to use if you tend to hunch your shoulders forward or carry tension in the middle of your back.

As the rider, you need to take responsibility for your own patterns of posture and tension anytime that you sit on a horse. Good breathing, released joints, and dynamic balance are all important facets of being an effective, unobtrusive rider. These factors alone can easily comprise an extensive book. For more information on becoming a functional rider, I would recommend investigating *Centered Riding*®, *Connected Riding*®, or the *Murdoch Method*.

Mentally, it is up to the rider to stay grounded and present. Just as when working with your horse on the ground, it is not effective or useful to attempt a riding session with your horse if you are in a frazzled or muddled state of mind. We owe it our horses to be present any time we work with them, and this is very important when riding a horse that is learning to gain confidence under saddle.

Riding Equipment for Success

While not absolutely necessary, the pieces of equipment I describe in the pages that follow are incredibly helpful when riding youngsters or reeducating older horses. Each one helps encourage a functional, relaxed posture and provides the rider with additional ways to give the horse a clear signal without restricting his freedom of movement. All of these items can be found on my website www.ttouch.com.

10.24 The *Lindell Sidepull* is a wonderful tool for horses, young and old alike. The nosepiece molds to the shape of the nose and should not be adjusted too tightly. The jowl strap helps create lateral stability on the horse's head and the placement of the rings creates a clear signal left and right.

Shying

Shying is a common issue for horses of all disciplines and backgrounds. In most cases, changing the habitual posture will greatly reduce shying. Work with your horse through the entire *Playground for Higher Learning* (p. 175) exercises so he learns to walk, halt, and turn quietly in balance. Take the time to master walking under, over, and between plastic (p. 190). Chunk the exercise down into small steps, even when your horse seems "fine," checking in along the way that your horse is not shutting down or tense. A horse that learns to override his flight instinct, one that thinks and uses self-control, is a safe partner in every situation.

It often helps to simply loosen the noseband and girth because a horse that does not get enough air and feels trapped can be nervous. Sometimes poor saddle fit creates tension that causes a horse to be more reactive. Check your horse's body to see if he is in pain or is carrying excessive tension; observe his posture. A horse that shies or startles usually carries his head quite high and tightens the underside of his neck. Encourage him to *Lower the Head* (p. 65) and soften his neck or he will develop a very tight back. When a horse holds his breath, he will be tight through the entire body.

When in the saddle, you can remind your horse to *Lower the Head* and soften his neck by reaching forward and gently doing *TTouches* (p. 78) behind his ears and along his crest. Riding a horse with a *Promise Wrap* or *Head Wrap* (pp. 46 and 49) can also be a great way to help him feel more confident and self-aware.

Lindell Sidepull

The *Lindell Sidepull* is a key piece of equipment for starting horses under saddle (fig. 10.24). Using a bitless bridle that creates clear, concise signals helps a horse understand what the rider is asking and encourages cooperation. The *Lindell* has a noseband and jowl strap for stability. The reins are attached on the sides, which makes it easier for the horse to understand the rein signals right and left, because they are similar to those coming from the halter during groundwork. As I've mentioned, a young horse has an easier time finding his balance under the rider when he is not wearing a bit. The body's proprioception, which is the awareness of the body in space, is not inhibited by the *Lindell,* so the horse is able to carry the rider more easily.

Previously trained horses can benefit from the *Lindell's* clear lateral cues that encourage the horse to bend through the neck without tipping through the nose.

How to Use It

The *Lindell Sidepull* can be used on its own or with a snaffle bit. When riding with the *Lindell* on its own, it is important that you do not use a lot of heavy contact. Using it with a heavy hand can result in horses leaning against it and ignoring the signals, which is understandable when the pressure is constant and unyielding on the rider's part!

When transitioning to a snaffle bridle, you can experiment with how much you use the *Lindell Sidepull* reins versus the snaffle reins. As the horse becomes more familiar and comfortable with the snaffle, you can reduce the amount of *Lindell* rein used until you phase it out completely.

When fitting the *Lindell* it is important to leave the noseband relatively loose so that the horse is free to chew and yawn. The jowl strap is designed so that it can be fitted snugly to maintain laterally stability without inhibiting the horse.

Balance Rein

The *Balance Rein* is an amazingly useful piece of equipment for youngsters and seasoned horses alike (fig. 10.25). It lies around the horse's neck and is used as a second rein to help the horse find his balance. The *Balance Rein* assists in rounding the horse's back and lengthening and rounding the neck while it helps horses shift their weight off the forehand, release through

10.25 The *Balance Rein* works well with any bridle and is a great tool for helping horses that rush to rebalance and shift off the forehand. It also helps horses that duck behind the bit and get behind the vertical. The *Balance Rein* can help show them how to lift through their base and allow for an elongation of the neck.

10.26 Riding with the *Liberty Neck Ring* is a great deal of fun for horse and rider and helps develop new levels of trust, communication, and balance.

their topline, and maintain balance and rhythm under saddle. It is a very useful tool for teaching horses to halt without bracing through the back or neck, backing up in a good posture, and becoming more balanced on the trail or over fences.

How to Use It

The *Balance Rein* can be used with one or two hands, whichever makes you comfortable. Used in conjunction with the sidepull or bridle reins, the *Balance Rein* is a wonderful tool for teaching horses how to contain their speed without shortening through the neck. As you get comfortable with it, you can experiment with how much rein versus *Balance Rein* contact you use. It is a good rule to use 60 percent rein and 40 percent *Balance Rein*; however, it should be adjusted as needed.

When applying a signal with the *Balance Rein,* do not pull backward. The *Balance Rein* is most effective when used with an "up-and-back," ask-and-release rather than a steady signal.

Some scenarios where the *Balance Rein* is of great benefit include:

Steadying a rushing horse in transitions.
Encouraging balance down hills.
Reining back in a healthy posture.
Introducing lateral work.
Encouraging telescoping through the neck.
Establishing the *Half-Walk* (p. 266) and half-halts.

Liberty Neck Ring

The *Liberty Neck Ring* is a piece of equipment that builds your relationship with your horse, engages his mind and body, improves lateral flexibility, and encourages relaxation (fig. 10.26). If you have not ridden with a neck ring before or are not sure about how your horse will react to riding bridleless, it is best to go through the steps of safely riding bridleless as I outline in detail in my book *The Ultimate Horse Behavior and Training Book*.

Going Behind the Bit

Unfortunately, it has become very common to ride horses in a deep, overbent posture. Ideally, the poll is the highest point of the neck and the plane of the nose is just in front of the vertical to allow for an open throatlatch. Once a horse has been regularly ridden in a closed, compressed posture, it can be challenging to change it.

Riding with the *Lindell Sidepull* (p. 245) or a combination of the *Lindell* and snaffle bit can help change the relationship the horse has with the bit and allow for more relaxation and elongation. The *Balance Rein* (p. 275) is also very helpful, as is the *Liberty Neck Ring*. The *Balance Rein* helps to activate the seeking reflex and is a great tool for reestablishing a consistent, reaching, and soft contact. This *Liberty Neck Rein* helps the horse develop a new connection with his rider and balance freely without retracting and compressing through his neck.

Horses that avoid contact by going too deep are not engaging their hindquarters. Experiment by riding with a *Promise Wrap* (p. 49) and using a variety of *TTouches* (p. 78) around their hindquarters. You may also want to reexamine your own riding skills if this is an issue with a number of your horses.

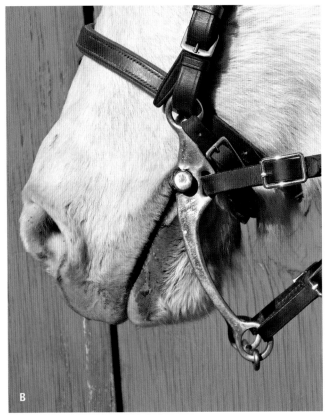

10.27 A & B When fitting the *Tellington Training Bit,* the curb chain or strap should not make contact with the horse's chin until the shank is at a 45-degree angle. During riding, the curb rein should remain soft and draped.

How to Use It

The *Liberty Neck Ring* can be used in conjunction with your regular bridle or a *Lindell Sidepull,* as well as on its own. When you find that your horse is stiff to turn in one direction, adding a *Liberty Neck Ring* to assist the aid can be very effective. It is also great to use when teaching a horse to neck rein.

Using the *Liberty Neck Ring* with the bridle is a safe first step. Even if you never take off the bridle, you and your horse will benefit from the added feeling of freedom and trust. Many horses find that this exercise helps release their neck laterally and allows for a wider, freer range of movement.

To Turn: Take the ring halfway up the horse's neck and use an ask-and-release signal. If you try to use a steady pressure you will likely end up with a braced horse or too much turn. Be sure to remain soft through your joints and released in your own back, swiveling your entire body to help ask for the turn.

To Halt: Make an "ask-and-release" signal at the base of the neck as you use your voice and seat aids. Watch that you do not pull straight back; instead, use a slight upward signal following the line of the horse's scapula. If your horse does not stop well with the ring at the base of the neck, try stopping with the ring higher up the neck, just below the jowl.

Tellington Training Bit

Don't judge a book by its cover! For many people, this bit looks intimidating or severe; however, when ridden with double reins it has amazing results without relying on curb-rein pressure. While not typically used on young or green horses, the *Tellington Training Bit* can make amazing changes for horses that are being restarted or reeducated (figs. 10.27 A & B).

Bits and their effects on horses fascinated me when I was a young girl showing horses. In the 1960s, I started to experiment with different bits. I used the Pelham with two sets of reins and double bridles in our nine-month program at the Pacific Coast School of Horsemanship. The results spoke for themselves. My students developed a softer hand and the horses happily accepted a variety of different types of bit.

In 1975, I had some new experiences when I was teaching pleasure riders with problem horses. I noticed that a lot of those horses had incredibly "hard" mouths and had become used to a strong contact from the rider's hands. That's when I discovered the roller bit, and it quickly became my favorite. This bit is made of stainless steel with a copper roller and lightly curved, moveable shanks. Although some people struggled with the use of the four reins in the beginning, they found the results so positive that it was worth learning how to use them. I had some improvements made on the bit and that is what became the *Tellington Training Bit* (fig. 10.28).

The *Tellington Training Bit* can do wonders when retraining a horse. The horse's coordination and balance is often improved in a single session as the bit encourages the horse to bring his hindquarters underneath him by softening the poll and releasing the pelvis. The port provides space for the tongue, and the roller encourages the tongue to move in the mouth, often releasing the TMJ and hyoid areas. Horses that shy, are resistant, or high-headed quickly change their behavior as their posture softens, and they are better able to quietly focus on their surroundings.

There are now thousands of people who regularly ride with the *Tellington Training Bit* or use it to reeducate horses. Very quickly, usually within half an hour, the horse's back will improve its swing, he will lengthen his stride, and he will activate his hindquarters. I recommend the bit for horses with a stiff back or that are ewe-necked, as well as those that are disconnected and too much on the forehand. The bit helps them to find their balance and happily cooperate. Horses that tend to rush are also easily regulated.

10.28 Use the *Tellington Training Bit* with a light, soft hand. The port and roller seem to encourage the tongue and TMJ to move and release in a quiet way. As the jaw releases, we have found that the horse's pelvis becomes freer, and the horse's whole way of going transforms.

10.29 Soft, releasing hands are key when riding with the *Training Bit*. Using Sally Swift's wonderful image of holding baby birds in your hands without dropping or crushing them is very helpful.

Fitting the Bit

Attach the headstall to the top ring of the bit, the same place as the curb chain. The rings have been bent out about one-quarter inch to make room for the horse's cheekbone.

Caution: Attach the curb chain only on the top ring of the bit, *not* the opening for the top rein, which is found on the top of the shank, right where the mouthpiece is attached. The bit should be placed in the horse's mouth so there is an obvious wrinkle in its corner. Check the fit to make sure the bar does not touch the canine incisors or back teeth.

The curb chain is fitted so it makes contact with the chin when you pull the bottom rein to a 45-degree angle between the shank and the horse's mouth. The curb chain should not be too loose or the port cannot push against the horse's palate when you take contact on the reins. If the curb chain is too tight, the bit becomes too severe and the horse will tighten and limit his freedom of movement.

The noseband should sit about two-to-three fingers-width below the horse's cheekbone. It cannot be tight because it is important that the horse is able to move his jaw. Only then can he release the poll. You should be able to easily place two fingers between the noseband and the bridge of the nose. The noseband should not restrict any motion in the jaw.

I recommend light narrow reins, about five-eighths of an inch for the top rein and a half-inch for the bottom rein.

How to Use It

Give your horse some time to get used to the bit. Some horses play a lot with the roller in the beginning. You can place a halter over the bit and lead the horse with the *Tellington Training Bit* at the walk and trot before riding with it. Use some of the obstacles of the *Playground for Higher Learning* or lunge him on an oval. Standing beside the horse on the ground, pick up the reins as you would when you are mounted to make the horse familiar with the bit so he learns to release though the poll.

When riding, a soft, releasing hand and loose rein are the keys to success. The *Tellington Training Bit* is used with a slightly opened hand and very soft contact (fig. 10.29). I let the top rein run along the outside of my little finger, which allows me to release easily. In the beginning, it is important to ride with a slightly longer rein so the horse trusts that he can stretch his neck down. The bottom rein runs between the little and ring fingers. There should always be some slack to the bottom rein, and you only use it lightly when you require the horse to bend more in the poll, but you never want steady pressure on the bottom rein.

Ride with your arms and shoulders relaxed and your wrists straight. The hands are slightly open, and the thumb has a soft curve to it and gently rests on the first joint of your index finger. Make sure to keep the joints of your fingers soft and flexible.

The *Tellington Training Bit* is especially effective for horses being restarted in combination with the *Balance Rein* (p. 275) and the *Body Wrap* (p. 44).

Parting Words

In the 1960s my first husband, Wentworth Tellington, and I wrote a monthly column entitled "Let's Go" for a major equestrian magazine. We wrote tips for a wide range of horse care topics, including feeding, breeding, and training. After several very successful years, "Let's Go" was cancelled because of an article we wrote describing how a horse owner could start a young horse under saddle without bucking. That concept did not fit the belief of the magazine's editor at that time.

We wrote the article in response to a piece published the previous month, showing how to "buck out" a young horse. Even today, in many equestrian circles it is still believed that a horse has to "get the bucks out," either on the lunge line or under saddle. The problem is that horses who have learned to buck too often resort to bucking when startled. In years past, landing on the hard ground was not such an issue. Today, the cost of recovery and time out of work is a much higher price to pay.

In the first article written about my method in *Equus* Magazine in 1983, then-publisher Ami Shinitzky dubbed the work I've described in this book *The Touch That Teaches*. In the decades since, tens of thousands of horse owners have discovered the value of this peaceful, safe, and inspiring approach to training and retraining. In the 1990s I added the second "T" to the name of my method, which stands for "Trust." It was then that *The TTouch That Teaches Trust* emerged.

It's been 72 years since I started my first young horse by ground driving her. Horse owners on five continents have learned the value of this peaceful approach to training, either from one of my 10 horse books published in 15 languages or by attending a training with me or with one of our Tellington Practitioners who share the method on five continents.

Now that you have this book in your hands it is my wish that you will recognize the many gifts you will receive as you find the cell-to-cell and soul-to-soul connection with your horse that is intrinsic to the Tellington Method.

Tellington Method

Checklist for Your Horse's Education

Use this checklist as a guide to the exercises and techniques described throughout this book. It will help you track progress and note changes as you improve your skills and expand your horse's education. Take the time to journal each session and you will be surprised at how much you and you horse have accomplished!

When practicing the *TTouches,* simply allow your hands to choose which *TTouch* you use. For some horses, beginning with *Leading Exercises* will be more appropriate. Do not feel confined to follow the order of the exercises as they are introduced; let your horse's response and level of acceptance guide the session. This checklist leads you on a journey, not a race! Enjoy each moment with your horse.

Use a scale of 1 to 5 to indicate your horse's level of acceptance of technique or activity on a specific date: **1 = no acceptance; 5 = optimum acceptance; 3 is average acceptance in first contact.**

	LIST LEVEL(S) AND DATE(S)

Observation & Trust Exercises

Body Exploration

    Accepts Over Body (Note Areas of Concern) _____

_____

The Wand

    Accepts Over Body   _____

Body Wrap

    Figure Eight & Bridged–At Walk   _____

Around Girth–Walk & Trot

    Promise Wrap   _____

    Promise Rope   _____

    Head Wrap   _____

	LIST LEVEL(S) AND DATE(S)

TTouch Bodywork

Clouded Leopard TTouch   _____

Lying Leopard TTouch   _____

Abalone TTouch   _____

Raccoon TTouch   _____

Lick of the Cow's Tongue TTouch   _____

Zebra TTouch   _____

Troika TTouch   _____

Tarantula Pulling the Plow TTouch _____

Jellyfish Jiggle TTouch _____

Python Lift TTouch _____

Coiled Python TTouch _____

Leg Circles

   Accepts Touch Down Legs _____

   Front: Circles with Hoofprint as Axis _____

   Levels: Knee; Mid-Cannon; _____

      Fetlock; Close to Ground _____

   Hind: Circles at Fetlock Level _____

   Circles under Belly _____

   Rest Toe _____

Belly Lift _____

Back Lift _____

Ear TTouch

   Accepts Touch _____

   Strokes/Slides _____

Mane Slides _____

Tail TTouch

   Accepts Touch _____

   Ability to Circle _____

   Tail Pull & Push _____

   "Pearling" Flex Vertebrae _____

Pelvis Tilt _____

Nostril TTouch _____

Mouth TTouch _____

Leading Exercises

Elegant Elephant

   Walk & Whoa—Both Sides _____

   Trot & Whoa–Both Sides _____

Grace of the Cheetah _____

Homing Pigeon _____

Dingo _____

Cueing the Camel _____

Boomer's Bound _____

   Walk & Whoa–Both Sides _____

Cha Cha _____

Trotting in Hand _____

Dolphins Flickering Through the Waves _____

Mindful Lungeing

    Short Line _____

    Oval–Walk Both Sides _____

    Oval–Trot Both Sides _____

Playground for Higher Learning

Labyrinth

    In Elegant Elephant _____

    In Dingo _____

Zebra _____

Fan _____

Pick-Up Sticks _____

Poles and Cavalletti

    Walk: Poles Set 4'–4.5' (Both Directions) _____

    Trot: Poles 4'–4.5' (Both Directions) _____

    Alternate Ends Elevated (Both Directions) _____

Platform & Bridge _____

Working with Plastic

    Walk Through "V" on Ground _____

    Walk Over Plastic _____

    Walk Under Plastic _____

Walk Between People and Under Objects

    Walk Under Wands _____

Ground Driving

Chest-Line Driving

    One Line _____

    Two Lines _____

Ground Driving from the Halter

    One Line _____

    Two Lines _____

    Trot _____

    With Surcingle or Saddle _____

    Walk & Whoa (Driver Only) _____

    Trot to Walk & Whoa (Driver Only) _____

Time to Saddle Up!

Belly Lifts with Towel or Elastic Bandage _____

Sliding the Saddle Pad Exercise

 Introduction to Pad _____

 Saddle Pad Falls _____

 Saddle Pad Under Surcingle _____

 Leader in Elegant Elephant (Walk & Halt) _____

Horse Comfortable Wearing Blanket or Sheet _____

Introduce Saddle

 Attach Breast Collar _____

 Belly Lifts with Girth _____

 Body Wrap _____

 Leader in Elegant Elephant (Walk & Halt) _____

 Leader in Elegant Elephant (Trot) _____

Prepare for Mounting

 *Horse Stands Quietly Between Mounting Blocks
  with TTouch, Wand, and Rocking Saddle* _____

 Horse Turns Head & Takes Treat _____

 Rider Adjusts Girth _____

 Rider Applies Pressure to Stirrup (Both Sides) _____

 Rider Lifts Quietly Over Saddle, Pauses, Steps Down _____

Mounting for the First Time

 Rider Eases Weight into Saddle from Both Sides _____

 Horse Accepts TTouch from Rider _____

 Horse Stands Quietly as Rider Dismounts _____

First Steps Under Saddle

 Leader Asks Horse to Walk & Halt _____

 Leader Reinforces Rider's Signals for Trot _____

 Rider Strokes Horse with Wand _____

 *Rider Signals Forward Movement
  with Wand on Croup (as in Dingo)* _____

 Rider Asks Horse to Turn His Head to Receive Treat _____

 Leader Removes Lead & Walks Beside Horse & Rider _____

 Horse & Rider Work without Leader (Walk & Trot) _____

Playground for Higher Learning Under Saddle

 Follow an Experienced Horse Through the Elements _____

Acknowledgments

There are many people to thank who are directly responsible for the completion of this book, and many who have contributed over the past 50 years to the development of the Tellington Training Method for training and re-schooling horses.

My heartfelt thanks to the team at my American publisher, Trafalgar Square Books, who has given phenomenal support for this book, and to me, for more than 20 years: Caroline Robbins, Rebecca Didier, and Martha Cook. Their patience, skill, and dedication to the Tellington Method makes this book shine and makes my heart sing.

It is such a joy to have my niece Mandy Pretty as my co-author for this book in English. Her experience with young horses began before birth when she was riding in the womb only days before she was delivered into the arms of my sister, Robyn Hood. Mandy has been responsible for the training of a herd of 80 Icelandic Horses belonging to her parents, Robyn Hood and Phil Pretty, for many years. And Mandy has been teaching the Tellington Method on multiple continents for more than a decade. It is such a joy to witness her skill and passion, working with people and their horses.

My deep thanks to my sister, Robyn, for our collaboration that continues to develop and spread this work worldwide, and for her dedication to and brilliance for teaching, training, and retraining with our Method for more than 45 years. The quarterly Tellington Newsletter she publishes has inspired countless people to explore and use the Tellington Method.

We couldn't have finished this book without the photographic skill of Lynne Glazer, who jumped in at the last minute and drove many hours on a holiday to finish the photos with Mandy and me under challenging weather conditions, with raging California fires filling the air with smoke. Thank you, Lynne.

And for the enticing cover photo, I thank photographer AnnaLena Kuhn—also a Tellington Practitioner for horses—and Lisa Sellmeyer for allowing us to feature her lovely mare Bonita.

For the photos of Big Surprise and Parytet I am grateful to our Italian photographers, Eugenia Mola di Larissa and DAREVets, as well as Massimo DaRe and Silvia Torresani, who organized the Italian sport horse trainings where these photos were shot and who co-teach the Italian horse trainings with me.

I am grateful to Christine Schwartz, who translated the German version of this book, and who provides countless translations for me at the drop of a hat. Christine attended her first Tellington Training with me in Germany in the 1970s, worked closely with Robyn and Mandy for almost 40 years, and holds an important place in the history of the young horse trainings.

It was a pleasure doing the primary photo shoot for this book at the beautiful Thoroughbred ranch of Barbara and Jack Owens in Modesto, California. Barbara is one of our most experienced Tellington Practitioners and provided the horses. She made it a fun and memorable experience.

Thank you, Barbara, for this, and for the many people and horses you have shared the Tellington Method with over many years.

I cannot imagine my life without the daily support of Kirsten Henry, who for more than two decades, working with the team of Judy Klein and Katie Nash, has been responsible for communication regarding the Tellington Method on five continents. My gratitude is unending. Thank you for making a difference in the world.

My boundless gratitude goes to Carol Lang, who ran my office for 20 years and organized our archives and videos, managed the website, and cared for the Pig-Tailed Macaques who lived at my office center for many years. Now she manages the website from her home in Michigan and keeps me informed about important inquiries and communications. Thank you, Carol!

The idea for this book was originally written and published in German with my co-author Andrea Pabel Dean. Andrea breeds Arabians on her ranch in New Mexico and trains young horses with the Tellington Method. Thank you, Andrea, for all the children and adults you have taught in your clinics and kids camp, and for the brilliant children's book we did with your father, legendary photographer Helmer Pabel, who came out of retirement to photograph *Let's Ride with Linda Tellington-Jones*.

Kate Riordan, Bobbie Lieberman, and Shannon Weil all bring an amazing amount of know-how from personal experience with the Tellington Method. Their books, written with me and about my riding school, as well as articles about the Tellington Method, have drawn countless fans to the work. It brings me such peace knowing I can pick up the phone and reach out to any of them for help and inspiration whenever I need it.

My thanks also to Anke Rechtenwald for the editing help and all she does for Facebook and our practitioner Zoom discussions.

In this English book we have used some of the photos that appeared in the German book that featured several young horses of varying breeds worked in a 10-day Tellington Training for starting young horses. The German book was photographed by Gabriele Metz. Thank you, Gabi, for all the work we have done together over several books and for the many years you have announced for me during demonstrations at Equitana in Essen, Germany.

I also acknowledge and thank Bibi Degn for her organization and co-teaching, and for all her work with the Tellington practitioner trainings and membership organization over more than two decades.

My gratitude to Margit and Bernd Löwenherz, who organized the venue and provided some of their young Arabians for the young horse training and photo shoot. Thank you for all you have done to promote my work in Germany over many years.

And of course, my deep thanks to the ongoing collaboration with my German publisher, Kosmos Verlag, and my co-author, Kosmos editor, and source of inspiration, Gudrun Braun, who continues to look for new ways to make the Tellington Method available to German-speaking readers.

The Tellington Method in its present form would not exist without the insistence and support of Ursula Bruns, publisher of *Freizeit im Sattel* and founder of the Reit-Zentrum Reken. Ursula was a major influence in the German horse world for many decades. She insisted I develop a method that anyone could use for starting young horses and re-schooling them, and she organized the five-week training that ultimately launched a new training method. Ursula Bruns was co-author of my first German book, which is still in print. My thanks to Jochen Schumacher, who has carried on the work of Ursula and the riding center she founded. Jochen attended one of the month-long Starting Young Horse Trainings, and is a Tellington Practitioner for horses and a major teacher and organizer in Germany. I thank Jochen for the many trainings he has organized for me at the center and for all the students he has pointed toward the Tellington Method.

These thanks could not be complete without acknowledging Dr. Moshe Feldenkrais and the training I was blessed to have with him from 1975 to 1978. He advised us to "develop our own fingerprints." His concept of enhanced learning from gentle non-habitual movements was the inspiration for the development of the *Labyrinth* in 1977 and inspired me to explore new ways of moving horses' bodies, beyond the "Gypsy massage" I had learned from my grandfather. During the training I was blessed to share a house with master Feldenkrais teacher Mia Segal. Mia accompanied me on numerous weekend outings where I worked with horses and gifted me with countless Functional Integration lessons outside of class. Thank you, Mia, for your friendship.

I would need a whole book to adequately thank Roger Russell for our time together when we were studying the Feldenkrais Method in San Francisco and teaching and learning from 1975 to 1980. Thank you, Roger, for the years of collaboration, deep discussions, and wonderful times.

My gratitude could not be complete without acknowledging all the gifts I receive from my husband, Roland Kleger. I could not have continued to travel and share this work without his patience and love and brilliance at finding the right word for an article or remembering the name of a person we have met or a place we have visited. I know he is sent by my guardian angel.

I want to thank Debby Potts and Edie Jane Eaton for their brilliant teaching and continued support and close collaboration with me over 35 years.

It would take another book to thank all our Tellington teachers, instructors, and organizers who have taken the work for training and retraining horses to more than 30 countries. Please feel my unspoken gratitude for all you do to Change the World, One TTouch At a Time.

For more information about the Tellington Method, visit ttouch.com and ttouch.ca.
For more information about the Bitterroot Ranch, visit bitterrootranch.com.

Index

in release of poll/jaw, 170, 179,
189, 196, 253, *260*, 280
Chimp TTouch, 89
"Chunking down"
benefits, 20, 22–23, 28, 192
of exercises, 184, *195, 201, 205,*
214, 265, *270*
Circles, in lungeing, 165
Circular TTouches, 82, 83–84, *85,*
89–94
Clouded Leopard TTouch, 90–91, *90*
Code of Authentic Living, The (King),
82
Coiled Python TTouch, 104, *104*
Cold-backed horses, 114, 247
Communication
by horse, 28, 59–60, 202, 250–
51, 255
by rider/handler, 25–26, 145,
146, 147, 255
Conditioning, 166
Confidence, of horse, 91, 116, 117,
141, 268
Confinement. *See* Containment
Connection
between horse and rider, 20, *263,*
281
in horse's body awareness, 118,
227, 258
of TTouch lines, 87, 92
Consciousness, casual, 247
Contact issues, 115, 277
Containment, 48, 69–71, *69–70,* 202
Coordination, 103, 183, 185
Coping mechanisms, 34
Crookedness
in horse, 136, 140, 143, 165
in rider/handler, 273
Cross-ties, 69
Croup, TTouches for, 92, 96, 109
Crowding, by horse, 143, 144
Cueing the Camel halt exercise,
153–54, *154,* 157
Cues
for forward movement, *191,*
193–94, 262–63
for halt, 264–65, *264*
learned vs. reflexive, 152–53
verbal, 135, 168, 263, *263,* 265
Curb chains, *278,* 280

Da Re, Massimo, 234

The Dance. *See* Cha Cha leading
exercise
Dance Steps
Leading Exercises, 132–164
Mindful Lungeing, 164–171
Desensitizing, vs. familiarizing, 192
Dingo
about, *134,* 148, 150–56, *150–52,*
154–56
in exercises, 148, 182, 188–89
as signal for forward movement,
191, 193–94, 262, 267
Dismounting, 261, *261*
Divine Spark, 82
Dolphins Flickering Through the
Waves, 162–64, *162–64,* 249, 268
Double Triangle, 185–86, *186*
Dressage with Mind, Body & Soul
(Tellington-Jones), 21
Driving. *See* Ground Driving

Ear shy horses, 47, 72–75, 85,
115–17, 129
Ear TTouch, 115–17, *115–16,* 236
Educating, vs. training, 281
Elegant Elephant
about, *134,* 138–141, *139*
uses of, 147, 148
Emotions. *See also* Positivity
in horse, 18–20, 125, 129, *176,*
180, 251, 252
in rider/handler, 8–9, 21, 23, 270
Engagement, 49–50, 118, 159, 227,
258, 277
Equipment
familiarizing horses with, 218,
218, 226–29, *229, 244, 253*
for ground work, 40–51, 213
for riding, 274–281
Experiential learning, 33. *See also*
Thinking, by horse
Extremity TTouches, 82–84, *84,*
105–28, *105*

Face, TTouches for, 92, 126
"Facing up" (turning around), 216
Faint response, 34
Familiarization
vs. desensitizing, 192
of horse, with equipment, 218,
218, 226–29, *229, 244, 253*
as training approach, 269–270
Fan obstacles, *183,* 183–85

Fearful horses, 60, 63–64. *See also*
Stress
Feedback, 89. *See also observation*
entries
Feet, TTouches for, 94
Feldenkrais Method, 11, 251
Fidget response, 34, 94
Fight response, 34
Flanks, TTouches for, 92, 101
Flexibility
of horse, 136
of Tellington Training Method,
32–33, *32–33, 35, 36,* 135
Flight response, 18, *19,* 34, 65–66,
274
Foals
leading exercises for, 48–49,
48–49, 135
observation and trust exercises,
54
training guidelines for, 177–78,
212, 242, 252
TTouch for, 78–79
Food rewards. *See* Treats
Forehand, falling onto, 166, 183–84,
279
Forward movement
cues for, *191,* 193–94, 262–63,
267
exercises for developing, 153, 228
Fox, Mel and Bayard, 198
Freeze response
case studies, 206
as coping mechanism, 34
exercises for, 96, 192, 203, 223
posture and, 18
Front Leg Circles, 106–8, *106–7*

Girth area
sensitivity around, 92, 166
TTouches for, 95–96, 101, 111
Girths, 227, 243, 247–48, *248,* 274
Grace of the Cheetah
about, *134,* 141–43, *141*
in exercises, 147, *147,* 148
Graciet, Jean, 82
Grooming, observation during,
59–60
Ground Driving
benefits, 8, 24, 211, 233, 256
in case studies, 74–75, *74*
from the halter, 226–233, *226,*
229–233

Teeth, issues with, 40–41, 126–27
Tellington, Wentworth, 9, *10*
Tellington Training Bits, 170, 237, 278–281, *278–79*
Tellington Training Method. *See also* TTouch bodywork
  benefits, 5
  components overview, 23–24
  flexibility of, 32–33, *32–33*, 35, 36, 135
  getting started, 33
  keys to success, 24–28
Tellington Wands. *See* Wands
Tellington-Jones, Linda
  background, 4–15
  publications of, 11, 13, 21, 281
Tempo, in TTouch, 86
Temporomandibular joint. *See* TMJ
Tension. *See also* Stress
  patterns of, 80
  TTouches for, 101, 105
Terrain, variety of, 172–73
Thighs, TTouches for, 92
Thinking, by horse
  bodywork for, 64, 86, 91
  chunking down for, 20
  exercises for developing, 143–44, 176–77, 179, 192–95, 274
  self-confidence from, 206
Thoracic sling, TTouches for, 106
TMJ (temporomandibular joint), *61*, 94, 115, 279, *279*
Topline, 106, 115
Torresani, Silvia, 234
Touch, generally, 56, *57*, 63. *See also* TTouch bodywork
Trail riding, 270–72, *271*
Trailering, 187, 189, 191, 202
Training. *See also* Backing; Tellington Training Method
  approaches to, 6–7, 281
  vs. educating, 281
  innovation in, 13, 24
  mindset for, 18, 26–27

session duration, 26, 270
  variety in, 267
Transitions, 160, 266
Treats
  in familiarizing horse to objects, 196, *197*, 203, *222–23*, 246
  as reward, 260, *260*
  tips regarding, 179
Tripping, 183–84
Troika TTouch, 97–99, *98*
Trot, 231, 266–68, *266*
Trotting in Hand
  about, 160–62, *160–62*
  uses of, 187, 227, 229, *229*, 246
Trust
  in horse/handler relationships, 5, 27, 60, *61*, 112
  TTouches for, 105, 126
TTouch bodywork
  about, 13–15, 23, 81
  benefits, 9, 64, 78, 252, 256
  Circular TTouches, 82, 89–94
  components of, 83–89
  connection of lines in, 87, 92
  with exercises, 67–68, 203
  Extremity TTouches, 82, 83, 105–28
  flexibility of, 83
  for foals, 48–49
  hand position in, 83–86, 89
  horse's stage of training and, 78–81
  Slide and Lift TTouches, 81–82, 95–105
Turn-on-the-forehand, *158*
Turns and turning, 140–41, 148, 224, 278
Tying, exercises for, 68–71

Ultimate Horse Behavior and Training Book (Tellington-Jones), 281
Uncooperative horses, 26. *See also* Resistance
Unloading. *See* Trailering

Verbal cues, 135, 168, 263, *263*, 265
Visualization, 89, 256

Walk
  in first rides, 262–65
  in ground driving, 200–205, *200–201*, *203–5*, 216, 221, 223
  lowering head in, 66, 67
  over plastic, 194–97, *195–96*, *200*
Wands, 43, *44*, 62–64, *63*
Water crossings, preparation for, 190–91
Weanlings. *See* Foals
Weight, shifting of, 183
Weil, Shannon Yewell, 9
Whips. *See* Wands
Wise, Anna, 179
Words, importance of, 22–23, 43

Young horses
  back of, 262–63
  bits for, 275
  bucking in, 6–7, 166–67
  familiarizing with equipment, 226–29
  leading exercises for, 136–37, 144
  lungeing, 164–65
  ridden work, introduction to, 242–272
  training guidelines for, 6–7, 35, 54–55, 178, 212, 252
  TTouch for, 79–80, 89–90, 95, 96, 103, 115, 118
  verbal cues for, 135
  Wyoming clinic for, *14*, *15*, 26, 198, *198–99*

Zebra obstacles, 183, *183*
Zebra TTouch, 96–97, *97*, 244
Zephyr leads, 40–41, *41–43*, 43
Zimmer, Mandy, 206, *207*